To
Ellen & Dave   96'

Merry Christmas

Our love,

Kathy & Dick

GREAT COOKING
WITH
Country Inn Chefs

GREAT COOKING

❦ WITH ❦

Country Inn Chefs

GAIL GRECO

A CULINARY JOURNEY

ACROSS AMERICA

RUTLEDGE HILL PRESS

Nashville, Tennessee

Published in Nashville, Tennessee by Rutledge Hill Press, Inc., 513 Third Avenue South, Nashville, TN 37210. Distributed in Canada by H. B. Fenn & Company Ltd., Mississauga, Ontario.

All of the chef portraits and food photos were created specifically for this book and styled or directed by author Gail Greco, except for those on pages 39, 227, 229, and 230.

Photographs on pages 8, 14–15, 16, 17, 18, 19, 20 (both), 21, 22, 24, 34, 37, 40, 41, 42, 45, 47, 48, 49, 68, 69, 70, 71, 72, 73, 74, 75, 76–77, 92, 93, 95, 97, 112, 114, 115, 116, 118–19, 120, 122, 123 (both), 124, 125, 126, 127, 128, 130, 132, 144, 145, 146, 149, 150, 152, 153, 154, 155, 156, 158, 159, 168–69, 180, 185, 189, 190, 191, 216, 217, 220, 223, 224, and 225 by Tom Bagley.

Photographs on pages 25 and 27 (left) © 1990 by Michael S. Thompson. Photographs on pages 27 (right), 28, 29, 31, and 32 © 1992 by Michael S. Thompson.

Photograph on page 39 courtesy of *Midwest Living*.

Photographs on pages 50–51, 52, 53, 56, 57, 59, and 61 by Nancy Campiche.

Photographs on pages 62, 65 (both), 66, and 67 by Alec Marshall.

Photographs on pages 78, 80, 81, 82, 83, 232, 233, 234, 235, and 237 by Bruce Muncy.

Photographs on pages 84, 85, 86, 87, 89, 90, and 91 by Charles E. Walton IV.

Photographs on pages 99, 100 (both), 101 (both), 103 (both), and 104 by Robert Leahy.

Photographs on pages 105, 107, 108, and 110 by Jerry Ruotolo.

Photograph on page 106 by Joachim Heer.

Photographs on pages 133, 135, and 137 by Robert McClintock.

Photograph on page 136 by W. Allan Gill.

Photographs on pages 138, 140, 142, and 143 by Doug Mindell.

Photographs on pages 160, 161, 163, 164 (all), 165, 166, and 167 by John Warner.

Photographs on pages 170, 171, 173, 175, and 177 by Chel Beeson.

Photographs on pages 179, 182, 183, and 184 by Brad Davis.

Photograph on page 187 by Gerald Liebert.

Photographs on pages 193, 195, 196 (both), 197, and 198 by Chip Simone.

Photographs on pages 199, 200, 201 (both), 202, and 203 by Robert Nash.

Photographs on pages 204–05, 206, 207, 208, 210, and 213 by Michael Cardacino.

Photograph on page 211 by Lawrence M. Stone.

Photographs on pages 214, 215, and 219 by James Papa.

Photograph on page 221 by Stuart Lorenz.

Photographs on pages 227, 229, and 230 by Randy O'Rorke.

Photographs on pages 238, 240 (all), 241, 242, and 243 by Steven Underwood.

Jacket and text design by Bruce Gore, Gore Studios.

Typography by D&T/Bailey Typography, Nashville, Tennessee.

Color separations made in Singapore through Palace Press, International.

Printed in the United States of America by R. R. Donnelley & Sons.

Library of Congress Cataloging-in-Publication Data

Greco, Gail
    Great Cooking with country inn chefs / a culinary journey across America / Gail Greco.
       p.   cm.
    Includes index.
    ISBN 1-55853-157-2
    1. Cookery, American.   2. Hotels, taverns, etc. — United States.
    I. Title
TX715.G81147   1992
641.5973—dc20   92-28147
                                   CIP

1 2 3 4 5 6 7 8 9 — 98 97 96 95 94 93 92

Contents

From Mobcaps to Toque Hats
The Country Inn
Cooking Story

*P*reparing recipes from great country inn chefs means much more than just cooking up another dish. It means re-creating a feeling—the feeling and the spirit of America's country inns—right in your own home.

Enticing descriptions and sumptuous pictures of the food are enough of an allure. But couple them with thoughts of each recipe's unique origin with a talented country inn chef, and that get-away-from-it-all ambience and attraction of the inns begins to envelop you. Read about the person and the place behind a country inn recipe, and suddenly the regimen of preparing the food is no chore at all. As you julienne the vegetables, bring the consommé to a gentle boil, and fashion the stiffened peaks of whipped cream into the regal crown of a noble cake, you can almost hear the birchwood snapping in the centuries-old hearth, envision the pastoral hillsides painting a canvas of impressionistic color, and sense the rush of calm as memories of your last visit to a country inn zoom into focus.

Memories—that's what country inns are all about. And that's what you're re-living for yourself and providing to your own family and dinner guests when you serve inn

recipes. Cooking up these tried-and-true dishes bridges your fantasies with reality when you simply cannot get out to the inns themselves.

To help you recapture the spirit of the country inns at home, I've been visiting and writing about these delightfully unique lodging and dining places for more than a decade, collecting tips from today's home lifestyle experts—the keepers of small inns. Now, in *Great Cooking with Country Inn Chefs*, I'm trumpeting those who cook up all that fine food so that you can share the gastronomic keepsakes of my most recent sojourns.

Pacific Northwest chef David Campiche of The Shelburne Inn tames a salmon from local waters for breakfast fare. Peter Zimmer fashions exotic tastes with organic ingredients from small Santa Fe farms for the Inn of the Anasazi. And Claudia Ryan of Windflower enriches her New England table every summer with unusual and heritage fruits and vegetables from her private garden. Their menus offer you the option to cook sublimely or dramatically, depending on your mood and the occasion.

Using the recipes from the inns instigates conversation among friends or strangers

at a dinner party. When I prepare a buffet, I like to put out labels, identifying the inn that inspired each dish. For smaller gatherings, I write the inns and their contributions on an artist's easel in the dining room or inside a small picture frame on the table. This never fails to initiate talk about inns, then travel and where this person or that person has been. I like offering my guests a common ground, and it also allows me to run into the kitchen when necessary while they chatter along.

Each chef, like each inn, is as individual as a fingerprint, but there is a common denominator. Whether they cook over a Colonial hearth in a frilly mobcap, at the latest stove-top in a tall, starched and pleated toque, or with no hat at all, they are all driven to make their meals memorable events. This means they offer up true gifts from the kitchen, the most significant of which is freshness. Whether from the garden

or the winter pantry, the local farms, or nearby waters, fresh ingredients are one of the hallmarks of country inn dining.

Another is special attention to guests. Chef Doug Morgan of The Checkerberry Inn in Goshen, Indiana: "As a country inn chef, you get more involved with the diners who are often overnight guests. You don't just plan a menu; you plan events with more than the right dishes in mind."

In choosing the chefs for this book, I did not confine myself with rigid gourmet guidelines. A statement by a renowned food critic, the late James Beard, tells you why: "I don't like gourmet cooking, or 'this' or 'that' cooking. I like good cooking." And that's what I have brought you: a variety of styles and recipes—everyday, gourmet, and everything in between—for all manner of entertaining possibilities and adventures. But lest you think otherwise, let me assure you that the country inn chefs hold their own in the world of sophisticated cuisine, often setting trends.

Most of the chefs I chose are also innkeepers. As such, they have added challenges that go far beyond the boundaries of the dining room and kitchen. We cannot forget their courageous preservation of historic properties and the price they pay in time and money to pull off these admirable feats. Peter Sushka of High Meadows in Scottsville, Virginia, knows the trials of the innkeeper/chefs that guests don't even think about while enjoying the benefits of their talents. Regarding the restoration of his inn, Peter writes:

It was indeed a gem in fine disguise. With no indoor plumbing or working electricity, restoration soon became a weekend struggle in the organization and stretching of time, money, and energy. Clean fingernails we seldom had; and new and fashionable clothing or a night out, we saw other folks wear or do. Pulled muscles and lean wallets were companion to nighttime reading of paint-can labels and instructions of The National Trust for Historic Preservation. We pushed on, however, continuing from the top of the Victorian house to the bottom of the Federalist portion—all holidays and weekends, as well. Along with the swirling plaster dust, bruised bodies, and late hours of planning, paperwork, and even sewing,

came the restored High Meadows for future guests.
—Innkeeper's Diary

The hard work of innkeepers is not in vain. The Professional Association of Innkeepers International reports that some 22 million people traveled to small inns in 1990. One of the main reasons they went was the food. Country inn cooking is some of the finest this nation has to offer. As a result, history is in the making as this book reaches your hands. Country inn dining rooms are becoming formidable and unique alternatives for the going-out-to-dinner crowd. As you will see, there are many reasons why they are such sought-after places to dine. In many cases, they've actually become destinations in and of themselves.

There are far more great country inn chefs than space permits me to feature in this book. But the many recipes that follow will help you re-create the fine food and gracious spirit found at bed and breakfast inns, country inns, and country house hotels all across America. So I wish you bon appétit and hope that I have helped you turn your country inn reveries into at-home realities through *Great Cooking with Country Inn Chefs*.
—*Gail Greco*

About the Chapters

I have divided the book into easy sections you can turn to when you need to host a special occasion or plan for an everyday meal. The menus were coordinated solely for this book.

Although the recipes are in menu form, I urge you to have fun putting together your own bill-of-fare. And do add salads to any menu. The recipes were selected with a reverence to healthier eating (desserts notwithstanding). There are many seafood and poultry dishes, plus a L'Auberge Country Inn recipe for rabbit, a meat that is actually lower in cholesterol and higher in protein than chicken. The gourmet-light menu from The Inn at Twin Linden, even allows you to be weight-conscious in style. And check the index under Low-fat for a complete listing of recipes in the book that are low in fat content.

The Hosting History chapter features inns that are housed in historic properties and cater to their heritage with the food. Chef Cindy Clark at Randall's Ordinary is a classic example of a chef who isn't cooking nouvelle cuisine, but nonetheless has guests in awe of her tasty dinners. Cooking up the victuals of former centuries just adds to your experience at an inn, and it provides an interesting theme at home while making your entertaining easier. There is no reason you cannot serve up an old-fashioned meal—setting the table with antiques and old linens to create an aura of the past—even if you have a modern dining room.

Some inns serve lunch, and all serve breakfast in one form or another. In Daytime Pleasures you'll find the recipes of The Shelburne's David Campiche, who cooks up one of the most ambitious and unusual country inn breakfasts in America. This chapter also offers you a scrumptious lunch from chef Kevin Schmitz. It was tough deciding whether to put The White Hart into this section or into Enchanted Evenings, as Kevin's dinners are also superb. Finally, tea-time is another wonderful gastronomic feature that sets inns apart. And The Mansion at Elfindale, with its authentic English pastry chef, has a bevy of Old World tea treats for you to bake.

Romantic dining is a cornerstone of country inn-going. The menus presented in Enchanted Evenings are designed to result in dishes that are rapturous and ideas that set that special tone for just two or a large party.

Cooking Inn Season contains recipes you can turn to when celebrating changes in weather or special holidays.

Since inn cooking styles are often dictated by region, you'll journey from the exotic to the traditional in Regional Classics.

Foreign O' Fares is a chapter with recipes that invite exploration of ingredients that may be new to you but are nonetheless fun to use and serve. Ethnic cooking is becoming increasingly popular in the United States. In fact, the National Restaurant Association reports that the number of ethnic entrées appearing on non-ethnic menus has risen from 242 to 360 items—49 percent—from 1986 to 1991. Country inns have followed right along with this trend, expanding their culinary horizons in the process. In cooking up these dishes, you'll find that the ethnic ingredients give the recipes terrific dispositions.

As you make your everyday meals and your special occasions as memorable as the country inn chefs make theirs, these chapters—oriented toward theme entertaining—will guide you every step of the way. I enjoy entertaining inn style. I know you will, too.

In Appreciation

To best illustrate their real story and ambience, I gathered the hundreds of props you see in the photos from the inns themselves, except for a few items provided by: my dear cousin, Michael Sabatino of New York, for lending me his fragile new china without flinching; friend, Cindy Manarin along with Bill and Mimi Cooper, of Washington, D.C., who supplied me with cherished collectibles from Europe with no questions asked; Gail Rudder Kent and her *Country Inns* magazine for being at the James Beard House as usual, this time with exquisite fabrics; and Crate and Barrel stores for allowing me the generous use of kitchen and table wares for the Italian menu.

My thanks also goes to Brenda Boelts Chapin, a colleague and the author of *Recommended Country Inns of the Mid-Atlantic and Chesapeake Region,* for her valuable "innsight"; Jeff Smith for asking me, "What are tobacco onions?"; and Julia Child for setting the record straight for me on James Beard and his house.

In addition, photography professor Doug Gleason, of Montgomery College in Rockville, Maryland, was a great source of expertise and encouragement to both me and my husband during our photography work for this project. A big thanks also goes to Rockville photographer Sam Stamoulis for sharing his enthusiasm and ideas.

Once again, my greatest respect and praise goes to *all* the folks at Rutledge Hill Press who value their authors. Thank you Ron and Julie Pitkin, and especially Larry Stone for his long hours and for making me a part of the process every step of the way. There aren't very many publishers who care so directly about each and every book and who would take time out on their vacation—as Larry did—to stop by an inn just to get a better photo! (See page 211).

I'd also like to thank the chefs (and innkeepers) for bearing with my constant communications—their patience during the long hours of photography, interviewing, cooking, and repeated recipe checking and testing. Putting together a collection of recipes from such a wide variety of cooks took a great deal of time, study, and persistence on everyone's part for consistency and accuracy. But it was all part of producing a high-quality cookbook, and I hope they had as much fun as I had, despite the hard work. They are truly great country inn chefs in every way.

For my grandmother, Sarah Composto, who loved to cook
and who—more than anyone else I know—seemed
to live just to share her generous table
with others.

GREAT COOKING
WITH
Country Inn Chefs

Hosting History

"About four o'clock we were called to dinner.
Turtle and every other thing, flummer, jellies,
sweetmeats of twenty sorts, trifles, whipped
syllabubs, floating islands, fools, etc., with a
dessert of fruits, raisins, almonds, pears, peaches.
A most sinful feast again . . ."
John Adams, 1787

Randall's Ordinary, North Stonington, Connecticut
Sandy Chiangi and Dave Miguel

Dinner from the Hearth

Randall's Ordinary
North Stonington, Connecticut

INNKEEPER/CHEF CINDY CLARK

Recipes for an Old or New Kitchen

Early American Peach Sangaree

◆

Old-Fashioned Soft Pretzels

◆

Coriander and Ginger Loaf

◆

Onion-Plumped Goose with Wild Rice and Grape Stuffing

◆

Nantucket Scallops

◆

Squash and Cheddar Pudding

◆

Red Cabbage and Apple Sauté

◆

Chocolate Cordial Truffles

◆

Thomas Jefferson's Favorite Bread Pudding with Chocolate Sauce

*T*owering hardwoods embrace the drive up the lantern-lit roadway to Randall's Ordinary. Two leathery oxen are often crunching on their own evening meal, offering you nary a glance from behind a hewn post-and-rail fence as the inn of mocha-tinted clapboard comes into view. When you set foot onto this land—grazed since our forefathers reached these once-so-foreign shores—be prepared to experience an adventure in Americana as wonderfully primitive as you can find in these United States. Randall's Ordinary, which takes its name from the farm's original owner plus the old British term for an eatery providing fixed price meals on a regular basis, is probably the only country inn anywhere that cooks breakfast, lunch, and dinner over an open hearth every day of the year.

Bill and Cindy Clark are the modern-day

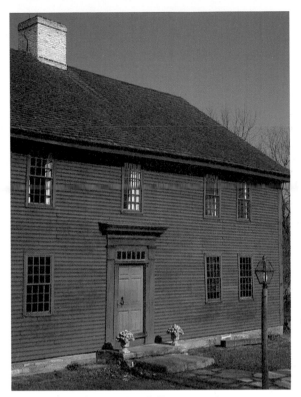

The 1685 Farmhouse at Randall's

with antiques and four-poster beds covered in cheerful, jacquard-style quilts handwoven on original looms. Some rooms have televisions and whirlpool tubs. Yet, the blend of the ages is most harmonious.

Three even more primitive rooms are found upstairs in the main house. Downstairs, the inn's three dining rooms are footed with wide-board floors, brightened by twelve-over-twelve paned windows and accented with a couple of eighteenth-century settle benches. Each dining room has a fireplace, and the constant cookery consumes roughly a cord of scrap tiger maple and other hardwoods each week.

I found a brandy snifter filled with Randall's homemade apple cider/rum concoction to be the perfect preamble to my dining experience at the inn. A Colonial flip, much like an eggnog with rum, is another libation offered along with historic sherries, Madeira, and an extensive list of other fine domestic and imported wines. You'll find an authentic bar-and-grill at Randall's from an old Connecticut tavern. Such wooden rails kept the public out of the liquor supply in Colonial days, thus the term for a tavern as we know it today—bar-and-grill—developed.

Dinner begins with guests gathered around each hearth, learning about early American cooking techniques from Cindy and her staff of costumed practitioners while anxiously eyeing an array of simmering traditional and gourmet comestibles. There is no limit to what Cindy can cook on her hearths. Cindy maneuvers Colonial spider bread under a bed of hot coals and monitors a whirling broiler to make sure her salmon cooks evenly. She twirls a long spit, sealing in juices for a luscious loin of pork from the inn's own butchering and smokehouse. Soups, vegetables, and some entrées that are also cooked in cast-iron kettles and pans have added flavor because the vintage pots are seasoned from years of use.

Executive chef Dave Miguel fusses over a lamb in a reflector oven and checks on freshly baking bread in the beehive oven.

proprietors of the twenty-seven-acre farm and rustic inn that started life as a 1685 farmhouse. The couple spent a good bit of time looking at old buildings in need of restoration before they purchased Randall's in 1987. Peeling paint, lack of plumbing and heating, shutters half-closed like sleepy eyelids, and even sunken roofs—while not desired—were problems Bill and Cindy felt they could manage. However, if a structure lacked adequate fireplace flues to withstand continuous cooking, it was rejected on the spot. Although they were three centuries old, the hearths at Randall's were in perfect condition. So Bill and Cindy fired them up and opened their inn.

Today, Randall's includes an imposing nineteenth-century barn moved from upstate New York by the Clarks and converted into eleven rooms, plus a suite in the silo. Decor here is "early farmhouse" as it would have been, simple and unadorned but accented

Innkeeper Bill Clark at the beehive oven

"We fire up the oven [with wood] and when I stick my arm in and feel it's at 350 degrees, in goes the bread," Dave told me, making the hair on my arm stand up as he thrust his own arm into the brick oven. Dave, a graduate of the New England Culinary School, never imagined he would put his skills to the test by cooking in the style of an earlier century!

As innkeeper and chef, Cindy's goal is to offer an adventure in addition to great food. She and Bill are serious about hosting history. This is not make-believe or mere demonstration. They live in the past. During the writing of this book, they were building a log home for themselves next to the inn and had the floors distressed to look old. Bill installed a crane in the family room fireplace for hearth cooking for family and friends. Bill dresses in Colonial preacher's garb to perform marriage ceremonies at the inn, and he's always worn his hair in a patriot ponytail tied with a ribbon.

Everyone dresses the part at Randall's. Cindy wears a dainty mobcap, petticoat, and chemise with a reproduction pinner apron. Her skirts tend to be ankle-length or even higher as death by fire was the number two killer of her culinary forbears, who wore floor-length frocks. When Cindy bends over the hearth, stirring a heavy skillet of scallops, her skirt barely dusts the ashes.

Although Cindy's recipes are for us to cook with modern-day appliances, the chef encourages us to try at least the non-oven recipes over the hearth at home. The only difference in method would be in cooking times and temperatures, which—as you now know—are all determined by feel and eye. She suggests purchasing hearth cooking utensils that are in good condition or buying reproduction pieces, which you can usually order through restored historic villages. To add a crane to your hearth, it is best to mount an antique one, says Cindy.

"Hearth cooking is really no different than contemporary cooking," she notes. So what is there to learn in the cooking classes Cindy gives at the inn? "History, cookware, and the mechanics that build the confidence to cook this way," the chef answers.

A self-taught cook, Cindy learned by poring through old receipt books and by having friends over for dinner. Those efforts were so successful that Cindy and Bill realized they had to open an inn where guests could wine, dine, and then just fall into bed only a few steps away.

Now she offers a full schedule of cooking classes throughout the year at Randall's. They are part of the experience. So are frequent nights with an Early American entertainment group on hand in full costume to perform their tavern ballads and antics. All these delights make Randall's extraordinary. There is just no other way to say it.

Lunch is also served at the inn.

Early American Peach Sangaree

❖

Flips, shrubs, and sangarees were among the many Colonial libations offered in Early American taverns, which often doubled as meeting houses. Randall's serves an assortment of these beverages, usually as guests wander about the hearths, watching their dinner being cooked.

➤ ½ cup sliced peaches
➤ 2 tablespoons lemon juice
➤ ⅛ teaspoon salt
➤ 3 tablespoons sugar
➤ 1 whole allspice
➤ ½ cup red wine
➤ Sparkling water

1. Mix the above ingredients well and chill for 1 hour.
2. Strain into a 6- or 8-ounce glass with ice, and add sparkling water to fill the glass.
   Yield: 1 serving

Old-Fashioned Soft Pretzels

❖

The cooking method of these pretzels differs from most homemade pretzels in that you boil them first and then bake them. The sugar adds just a hint of sweetness to the salty appetizers. They are superb!

➤ 4 to 4½ cups all-purpose flour
➤ 1 package active dry yeast
➤ 1½ cups milk
➤ ¼ cup sugar
➤ 2 tablespoons cooking oil
➤ 1½ teaspoons salt
➤ 3 tablespoons salt
➤ 2 quarts boiling water
➤ 1 egg white
➤ Coarse salt

1. In a large mixing bowl combine 2 cups of the flour with the yeast. Set aside. In a saucepan heat the milk, sugar, oil, and 1½ teaspoons of salt until warm (115°), stirring constantly. Pour the warm liquid into the flour mixture. Beat with an electric mixer for 3 minutes. Stir in as much of the remaining flour as possible with a spoon. Turn the dough onto a floured board and knead in the remaining flour to make a stiff dough that is smooth and elastic, about 6 to 8 minutes. Place the dough in a greased bowl. Cover the bowl with a kitchen towel and let the dough rise until doubled in size, about 1½ hours. Punch the dough down. Cover it again and let it rest for 10 minutes.
2. On a floured board roll the dough out into a 12 x 8-inch rectangle. Cut into 16 strips 12 x ½-inch wide. Roll each strip into a 16-inch rope and shape it into a pretzel. (See the photos at left.) Let the pretzels rise uncovered for 20 minutes.
3. Preheat the oven to 350°. In a large stock pot dissolve the 3 tablespoons of salt in the boiling water. Boil the pretzels for 2 minutes, turning once. Remove them with a slotted

Form pretzels as though hands at prayer.

Coriander and Ginger Loaf

Coriander and Ginger Loaf
❖

➤ 1 package active dry yeast
➤ ¼ cup warm water (115°)
➤ ¼ cup sugar
➤ 1 cup warm milk (115°)
➤ ¾ teaspoon coriander
➤ ½ teaspoon salt
➤ ½ teaspoon cinnamon
➤ ¼ teaspoon ginger
➤ ¼ teaspoon cloves
➤ ¼ cup vegetable oil
➤ ¼ cup peeled orange, roughly puréed
➤ 1 egg, lightly beaten
➤ 3½ cups or more all-purpose flour

1. In a small bowl dissolve the yeast in the warm water. Add the sugar and let bubble to activate the yeast. Set aside.
2. In a large mixing bowl combine the remaining ingredients. Add the yeast mixture and stir to form a dough. Turn the dough onto a floured board and knead slowly, adding more flour until the dough is manageable and not sticky. Place the dough in a greased bowl. Cover the bowl with a kitchen towel and let the dough rise until doubled in size.
3. Preheat the oven to 375°. Punch the dough down. Shape it into a loaf and place it in a greased 9 x 5-inch loaf pan. Bake the bread for 50 minutes or until golden brown. Remove the bread from the pan and let it cool on a wire rack.
Yield: 1 loaf

spoon. Drain well. Place the pretzels on a greased baking sheet ½ inch apart. Brush them with the egg white. Sprinkle with the coarse salt. Bake the pretzels for 25 to 30 minutes or until golden brown. Or, grill on the hearth using a whirling broiler set over a bed of hardwood embers. Grill for 2 to 3 minutes per side.
Yield: 16 pretzels

Onion-Plumped Goose with Wild Rice and Grape Stuffing

❖

➤ 1 8-pound goose
➤ 1 large onion
➤ 8 whole cloves
➤ Dried sage
➤ Salt and pepper
  Stuffing
➤ 4 ounces wild rice
➤ 1¼ cups chicken stock
➤ 1 tablespoon butter
➤ 1 medium onion, diced
➤ 4 ounces mushrooms, sliced
➤ 4 stalks celery, diced
➤ ¾ cup whole seedless grapes
➤ 3 ounces dry sherry
➤ ½ teaspoon salt
➤ ¼ teaspoon pepper

1. Preheat the oven to 450°. Stuff the goose with the onion. Stud the goose with the cloves. Sprinkle the goose generously with sage, salt, and pepper. Place the goose in a large roasting pan. Bake the goose for 30 minutes. Reduce the oven temperature to 300° and cook for another 2 hours or until crisp and golden brown.
2. In a small saucepan combine the rice and stock. Cover and cook until tender, about 30 minutes. Set aside.
3. In a small skillet melt the butter and sauté the onion, mushrooms, and celery just until softened. Do not brown. In a serving dish combine the vegetables, rice, grapes, sherry, salt, and pepper. Serve warm with the goose.
Yield: 8 to 12 servings

Nantucket Scallops

❖

To cook scallops over the open hearth, use a large iron skillet and hang it over a hot fire from the crane. Follow the same method as below, making sure to heat the skillet well before sautéing. Cooking time will be longer.

➤ 1 cup (2 sticks) butter
➤ 2 cloves garlic, minced
➤ 2 bunches scallions, chopped
➤ ½ teaspoon paprika
➤ ¼ teaspoon pepper
➤ 2 pounds sea scallops
➤ ¼ cup seasoned dry bread crumbs

1. In a large skillet melt the butter and sauté the garlic and scallions until soft but not browned. Toss in the paprika and pepper, and leave the mixture in the skillet.
2. In a mixing bowl toss the scallops with the bread crumbs until lightly coated, and then add them to the skillet. Cook over low heat, stirring occasionally, until the scallops are cooked through, about 6 to 8 minutes.
Yield: 8 servings

Squash and Cheddar Pudding

❖

➤ *2 pounds winter squash, cooked and puréed*

➤ *½ pound sharp Cheddar cheese, diced*

➤ *1 tablespoon butter*

➤ *½ cup chopped onion*

➤ *Salt and pepper to taste*

➤ *2 eggs, beaten*

➤ *¾ cup milk*

➤ *2 tablespoons dry bread crumbs*

➤ *1 teaspoon nutmeg*

---

1. Preheat the oven to 350°. In a large mixing bowl combine the squash and cheese, reserving about 2 tablespoons of the cheese.
2. In a small skillet melt the butter and sauté the onion until tender. Mix the onions into the squash. Sprinkle the mixture with salt and pepper.
3. In a separate bowl beat together the eggs and milk. Spoon the squash into a lightly greased 2-quart baking dish. Pour the egg-and-milk mixture over the squash. Sprinkle with the bread crumbs and nutmeg. Bake the pudding for 30 minutes or until the squash is golden brown.
Yield: 8 servings

Red Cabbage and Apple Sauté

❖

➤ *1 large head red cabbage*

➤ *½ cup (1 stick) butter*

➤ *½ cup chopped onions*

➤ *6 small red baking apples, peeled, cored, and diced*

➤ *½ cup or more water*

➤ *¾ cup packed brown sugar*

➤ *¾ cup cider vinegar*

---

1. Core and quarter the cabbage. Cut it into large chunks.
2. In a large skillet melt the butter and sauté the onions and apples until soft. Add the cabbage and enough water to steam the vegetables and apples for 10 to 15 minutes or until softened.
3. In a small bowl mix together the brown sugar and vinegar. Add the brown sugar mixture to the cabbage-apple mixture, stirring well. Serve warm.
Yield: 8 servings

Chocolate Cordial Truffles

❖

Sweet truffles have long been a popular dessert, and at Randall's they serve a medley of them, using a basic recipe with three different liqueurs and spices. These are a cinch to make.

➤ *6 ounces semisweet chocolate*

➤ *¼ cup confectioners' sugar, sifted*

➤ *3 tablespoons butter*

➤ *3 egg yolks, lightly beaten*

➤ *1 tablespoon brandy, hazelnut, or Irish cream liqueur*

➤ *2 ounces finely grated semisweet chocolate, ground cinnamon, or finely chopped hazelnuts or walnuts*

---

1. In the top of a double boiler over hot (not boiling) water melt the chocolate with the sugar and butter. Remove the pan from the heat. Stir a small amount of the mixture into the egg yolks. Return the yolk mixture to the hot mixture, stirring well. Blend in one of the liqueurs. Chill 1 to 2 hours.
2. Shape the mixture into 1-inch balls. Roll each ball in either chocolate, cinnamon, or nuts, or some of all three.
Yield: 12 truffles

Thomas Jefferson's Favorite Bread Pudding with Chocolate Sauce

The great president, statesman, writer, and architect, was also a good cook. After I tasted and then made this dish, it quickly became one of my favorite puddings, too.

Jefferson pudding cooks over hot coals.

Pudding

➤ 2 *cups scalded milk, kept warm*

➤ ½ *cup (1 stick) butter, melted and kept warm*

➤ ½ *cup brandy*

➤ 1 *tablespoon vanilla extract*

➤ 1½ *cups sugar*

➤ 4 *eggs*

➤ 1 *teaspoon nutmeg*

➤ ¾ *cup cubed crusty bread*

Chocolate Sauce

➤ ¾ *cup sugar*

➤ 1 *tablespoon all-purpose flour*

➤ 1 *1-ounce square milk or dark chocolate, melted*

➤ ½ *cup water*

1. Preheat the oven to 350°. In a mixing bowl combine the milk, butter, brandy, and vanilla extract.
2. Beat in the sugar, eggs, and nutmeg. Add the bread cubes, submerging until thoroughly moistened. Transfer the pudding mixture into a 3-quart buttered baking dish gently, so that the bread doesn't break up. Bake the pudding for 30 to 45 minutes or until set.
3. In a small saucepan blend the sugar with the flour. Stir in the melted chocolate and the water. Place the pan on a burner and bring the sauce to a boil over medium high heat, stirring constantly for 5 minutes. Pour the sauce over individual servings of the pudding.
Yield: 6 servings

A Table Set for Victoria

The John Palmer House
Portland, Oregon

INNKEEPER/CHEF DAVID SAUTER

Dinner for Eight

Consommé Colbert

◆

Sherried Melon

◆

*Halibut en Papillote with Rosemary and
Caper Sauce*

◆

*Cotelettes d'Agneau with
Apple Horseradish Sauce*

◆

Asparagus Provençale

◆

Charlotte Royal

"**I** stopped driving when I was 90. They tried to take my license away a few years earlier, but that would have been like taking wings off a butterfly," reminisces Maybelle Emerick. As she finishes hand-washing and drying an evening's cache of lipstick-stained and thumb-smudged antique cut crystal from her grandson's gourmet kitchen, feisty, 94-year-old "Granny" is certainly at home in the early 1900s mansion and inn called The John Palmer House. Born on Valentine's Day 1898, she has a memory at her age that most of us would relish in our prime. I mention Granny first here, as she is an integral element of the inn, a large part of what makes this inn's chef tick.

David Sauter is indeed a chip off the old, old block. He and Granny are soulmates, even though David is barely a third his grandmother's age. They interact playfully in the kitchen, this dubious pair, whenever Granny is home. (She lives beside the inn in a house she keeps spick-and-span and has a very busy social schedule of her own.) Granny is perhaps David's best asset in the kitchen. She displays great initiative, reaching for a linen towel or setting to some chore from the moment she enters. If there is a job to be done, her sense of duty and responsibility kicks in along with great physical agility. David's energy level is renewed through osmosis.

When it comes to cooking, David keeps filling the plates with almost no kitchen linemen, a tiny countertop, and a meager four-burner stove. Most of his days are spent in the kitchen, juggling the telephone and wire whisk. Nothing stops him from putting out the meals he creates—as many as twenty-eight in an evening single-handedly. He is addicted to cooking. When David was seven, he was flipping pancakes. At eight, he was making dough rise and rolling his first apple strudels from scratch. By the time he was ten, the family was not too surprised when he wrote out a shopping list of ingredients for his first Châteaubriand.

"That's when we knew he was serious about cooking," notes his father, Richard. David went on to formal training as the youngest student of the California Culinary Academy in San Francisco and was an executive chef for a fancy Portland restaurant by the time he was twenty-three. But what else would you expect from the offspring of a model granny and a pair of great-great-grandparents who made their way from Germany and—against all odds—later braved the open land in a wagon train from Iowa to Oregon.

In modern times, David's own parents, Richard and Mary, took a gamble of their own, buying the John Palmer House in an older, unrestored section of the city. Would anyone come when they opened their gentrified inn in 1985? In a short while—

thanks to the remodeling, the decorating of every room in Bradbury & Bradbury hand-screened wallpapers, the lush high teas served by Granny, and David's exquisite dinners—they came in droves. Now, celebrities, such as singer/musician Kenny Loggins, seek out the inn when they are in Portland for the night. The inn was also awarded a place on the National Register of Historic Places.

The John Palmer House is an escape from the rigors of the city. Once you close the original stained-glass doors, the sense of another time prevails. Richard and Mary have an incredible collection of antique furniture and housewares. You may even book a ride in one of Richard's antique carriages or join him in singing at the piano while Mary plays. It is just like a Victorian holiday, and it made me think it most appropriate to share a Victorian menu of David's so you can bring home a little bit of that spirit, too.

David researched the culinary history of his city's most famous hotel, the Hotel Portland, built in 1890. With the help of a Portland historian, he found old menus from the hotel, which had been used to serve visiting presidents dining on Haviland china. Specialties such as Shoalwater oysters, consommé Louisiana, pig's feet plain or breaded, lyonnaise, lamb, mush, halibut, huckleberry pie, and charlotte russe were among the choices in 1890. Old menus also listed dining times for ladies and gentlemen and "nurses and children."

The menu David has presented here is a creation of his own, based on some of these and other items he discovered during his attic-rummaging. David presents many theme dinners at the inn. Even teas have a carefully planned motif, such as the inn's Japanese Tea Ceremony. To serve your own unique historical dinner party, David suggests researching landmark eateries in your own area and devising a fitting menu.

Besides his Victorian dishes, David cooks up such notables as sautéed veal in an apple-with-brandy cream sauce, salmon in puff pastry, homemade ravioli, and venison

medallions with juniper-gin sauce. No matter what style of cuisine he has prepared, visitors feel happily out of time and place with the globe lamps glowing softly, the rare black-and-white lithograph of Queen Victoria presiding over the dining room, and the respite of the upstairs rooms awaiting overnight diners.

This is an invigorating and happy little urban country inn that makes you feel like giving something back, but a card in your room reminds that you've already done that. David, Richard, Mary, and Granny want you to know: "If you have enjoyed the attempt we have made to preserve this house, you must also take credit for its continuation. By staying here, you have helped to provide the income necessary to keep the house alive."

There, I thought, you've won me over again, and I'll take that rewarding thought back with me to the twentieth century.

The John Palmer House at dinner time

Consommé Colbert, Cotelettes d'Agneau, and sherbet in orange shells

Consommé Colbert

❖

David has adapted an old soup. In Queen Victoria's day, cooks used hen eggs instead of quail.

- ➤ 1 dozen eggs, shells rinsed clean
- ➤ 1 gallon plus 1 pint chicken stock (not bouillon)
- ➤ 4 medium carrots, julienned (2-inch long strips)
- ➤ 4 turnips, julienned (2-inch long strips)
- ➤ 16 quail eggs (available from Oriental markets)
- ➤ ¼ cup chopped fresh parsley
- ➤ ½ cup dry sherry

1. Separate the eggs, and reserve the egg shells. Save the yolks for the Charlotte Royal or another recipe. In a mixing bowl beat the whites until just combined.
2. In a large saucepan bring the stock to a rolling boil. Add the egg whites and shells. Cover and reduce the heat to simmer. Simmer 30 minutes then remove from the heat and allow to cool. Gently ladle the broth through a fine cheesecloth and into another saucepan. (Be careful not to break up the egg white mixture.) Set the broth aside. Discard the egg whites and shells.
3. In a saucepan blanch the carrots and turnips in boiling water for about 3 minutes. Remove the vegetables and cool them under cold water. Set aside.
4. In a small saucepan place the quail eggs into cold water and bring the water to a boil. Cook for 3 minutes, and then remove the eggs from the heat. Run the eggs under cold water and peel.
5. Heat the strained broth to a simmer. Add the carrots, turnips, and eggs, and heat for 4 minutes. Remove the vegetables and eggs from the soup. Arrange the vegetables in serving bowls to form a nest. Position 2 quail eggs in the center of each nest. Ladle the warm broth over the vegetables and garnish with chopped parsley and 1 tablespoon of the sherry for each bowl.
Yield: 8 servings

Sherried Melon and Sauter family antiques

Sherried Melon

❖

- ➤ 1 ripe melon (honeydew, cantaloupe, or casaba)
- ➤ 1 bottle cream sherry (750 milliliters)
- ➤ 6 cups chopped ice
- ➤ Salt

1. Cut a 3-inch wide hole out of the top of the melon. Save the cut out rind for the top. With a tablespoon remove the seeds and membrane. Fill the melon to about 1 inch from the top with the sherry. Replace the cut-out rind and chill the melon for at least 2 hours.
2. Fill a large bowl with crushed ice and set the melon into the ice. Sprinkle salt around the base of the melon.
3. Remove the cut rind. With a long-handled spoon scoop out the marinated flesh of the fruit. Serve on chilled plates with 1 or 2 tablespoons of sherry over the top.
Yield: 8 servings

Halibut en Papillote with Rosemary and Caper Sauce

❖

This dish is as interestingly woven as a piece of Victorian Battenberg lace.

- ➤ 8 4-ounce halibut fillets
- ➤ 1 cup fish broth or clam juice
- ➤ 1 cup white wine
- ➤ 1 tablespoon fresh rosemary leaves
- ➤ Juice of 1½ lemons
- ➤ ¼ cup (½ stick) plus 1 tablespoon butter
- ➤ 2 tablespoons capers, drained and 1 tablespoon of the juice reserved
- ➤ ¼ cup roasted pine nuts
- ➤ 8 sheets baking parchment (12½ x 8 inches each)
- ➤ Fresh rosemary sprigs and lemon slices for garnish

---

1. In a medium saucepan combine the broth and wine, and bring the mixture to a boil. Continue boiling until the liquid is reduced by half. Add the rosemary and lemon juice, and return to a boil for 2 to 3 minutes. Add the butter and continue to boil until the sauce is pale yellow. Stir in the capers and reserved juice, and remove the pan from the heat. Set the sauce aside.
2. Fold a piece of parchment in half at the longer end. With a pair of scissors start at the folded edge and cut as if making half of a heart shape almost out to the edge of the paper.
3. Preheat the oven to 400°. Unfold the heart and place a piece of fish on half of the paper. Spoon 1 tablespoon of sauce over the fish and sprinkle with ½ tablespoon of pine nuts. Fold the paper over the fish and starting at the point end of the heart, fold the paper over to seal the edge. Repeat for all 8 pieces of fish.
4. Place the wrapped fish on a baking sheet. Bake the fish for 15 minutes or until the

parchment browns and the fish is tender. Garnish with sprigs of rosemary and lemon slices. Serve with the remaining sauce.
Yield: 8 servings

Cotelettes d'Agneau with Apple Horseradish Sauce

❖

- ➤ 24 lamb loin chops
- ➤ Juice of 3 lemons
- ➤ 6 shallots, finely chopped
- ➤ 1 medium onion, diced
- ➤ 1 teaspoon dried thyme
- ➤ 3 bay leaves
- ➤ ½ cup (1 stick) butter, melted
- ➤ 3 cups dry bread crumbs
- ➤ 6 medium Rome apples, peeled, cored, and diced
- ➤ 2 tablespoons butter
- ➤ ½ cup white wine
- ➤ 2 teaspoons horseradish
- ➤ Salt and pepper

---

1. Clean the lamb chop bones. In a mixing bowl combine the lemon juice, shallots, onion, thyme, and bay leaves. Place the lamb chops in a non-reactive dish and spoon the lemon mixture over all. Allow the chops to marinate in the refrigerator for at least 1 hour, turning once.
2. Preheat the oven to 400°. Remove the chops from the marinade and dip each into the melted butter and then into the bread crumbs. Place the coated chops on a baking sheet. Bake the lamb chops for 20 minutes or until lightly browned.
3. Place the apples in a medium saucepan. Add 2 tablespoons of butter. Cook the apples over medium high heat until very soft. Pass the apples through a sieve. Add the wine and horseradish to the applesauce. Return the sauce to the stove and simmer until thickened. Season to taste with salt and pepper. Serve with the lamb chops.
Yield: 8 servings

Halibut en Papillote with old china and glass

Charlotte Royal over Battenburg lace

Asparagus Provençale

❖

This has quickly become one of my most frequently served side dishes for everyday family meals.

➤ *2 pounds thin fresh asparagus, woody ends snapped*

➤ *4 small ripe tomatoes*

➤ *3 tablespoons olive oil*

➤ *6 cloves garlic, minced*

➤ *1 teaspoon dried basil*

➤ *2 tablespoons white wine vinegar*

➤ *Salt and pepper to taste*

---

1. Steam the asparagus just until tender, but not limp. Keep warm.
2. Cut the tomatoes into quarters. Remove the seeds and meat, leaving a flattened exterior wall. Julienne the tomatoes and then dice.
3. In a medium skillet heat the olive oil over medium high heat. Add the diced tomatoes, garlic, basil, and vinegar, and cook just until the garlic and tomatoes are lightly glazed. Add seasonings to taste. Portion the asparagus evenly among 8 plates. Pour some of the tomato mixture evenly over each plate.
Yield: 8 servings

Charlotte Royal

✦

Charlotte Royal is a classic Victorian dessert prepared by first making a jelly roll and cutting it up to form a shell for a filling of pudding. The result is an attractive dish that's easy to make and extremely light in taste. Begin preparations a day ahead.

Jelly Roll
- ➤ 5 *eggs, separated*
- ➤ 1 *cup sugar*
- ➤ 3 *ounces soft almond paste*
- ➤ 1 *cup cake flour*
- ➤ ⅔ *cup raspberry preserves*

Pudding Filling
- ➤ 12 *egg yolks*
- ➤ 1 *cup sugar*
- ➤ 2 *cups milk*
- ➤ 2 *pints heavy cream*
- ➤ 2 *envelopes unflavored gelatin, dissolved in ⅓ cup water*
- ➤ 2½ *cups broken pieces vanilla wafers*
- ➤ 1½ *cups fresh or frozen raspberries*

Topping
- ➤ ½ *cup apricot preserves*
- ➤ 3 *tablespoons water*
- ➤ *Unsweetened whipped cream to form rosettes for garnish, if desired*

1. Preheat the oven to 500°. In a mixing bowl beat the egg yolks, ¼ cup of the sugar, and the almond paste until ribbons form. Set aside.
2. Beat the egg whites and remaining sugar until soft peaks form. Don't over-whip the whites or the cake will become crumbly. Fold ⅓ of the whites into the yolk mixture. Add the flour, and fold in the remaining egg whites.
3. Grease an 11 x 13-inch jelly roll pan and cut a piece of parchment or waxed paper to fit the pan. Grease the parchment. Spread the cake batter evenly over the bottom. Bake for 3 to 5 minutes or until the cake is golden and shows a dent when touched with a fingertip. Remove the cake from the oven and cool slightly.
4. Remove the cake from pan, inverting it onto another piece of parchment. Peel the paper from the back and spread the cake with raspberry preserves. Using the parchment as a guide, roll the cake up tightly from the wider side. Refrigerate the cake for 1 hour.
5. Slice the chilled roll into ¼-inch thick slices. In a 3-quart stainless steel mixing bowl arrange slices of the jelly roll, starting with slices on the bottom and then in circles around the sides as close together as possible (see photo on page 32). Refrigerate while assembling the pudding.
6. In a large bowl combine the egg yolks and sugar, and beat until ribbons form. Set aside.
7. In a medium saucepan bring the milk to a boil. Pour half of it into the yolk mixture, stirring constantly. Return the pan to heat. Add the egg mixture to the remaining milk and cook until the first bubbles appear. Keep stirring constantly, but remove the pan from the heat and quickly place the saucepan in an ice bath (or the eggs will scramble).
8. Whip the cream to a stiff consistency and fold it into the cooled egg mixture. Whisk in the dissolved gelatin. Pour half of the mixture into the lined bowl and sprinkle with crushed wafers and then berries. Repeat the layers until the bowl is filled. Refrigerate overnight.
9. To make the glaze, in a saucepan heat the apricot preserves and water until boiling. Remove the pan from the heat.
10. Just before serving place the bowl containing the Charlotte in a pan of hot water to loosen it. Place a plate on top of the bowl and invert. Remove the bowl. Glaze the Charlotte with the apricot glaze, using a pastry brush. Garnish with unsweetened whipped cream piped through a large rosette tip around the base of the cake.

Yield: 8 to 10 servings

Recipes from a Stagecoach Stop

The Buxton Inn
Granville, Ohio

CHEF EDDIE BIHN

Dinner for Ten

*Coquille of Seafood and Mushrooms in
Mornay Sauce*

◆

*Cherry Pine-Nut Salad with
Raspberry Vinaigrette*

◆

*Apple-and-Nut-Stuffed Pork Loin with
Raspberry-Brandy Sauce*

◆

Daisy Hunter's 1900s Walnut Fudge Cake

◆

*Old-Fashioned Ginger Cake with
Lemon Sauce*

When Audrey and Orville Orr bought The Buxton Inn in 1972, folks thought they were mad. The dilapidated former stagecoach stop, dating from 1812, was about to be torn down, but the ensuing story of the Buxton Inn is one of courage and vision.

Audrey and Orville felt a calling, so to speak, to save the Ohio landmark, said to be the oldest continually operating inn in the state. The Orrs were elementary school teachers (Orville even served several years as principal) before they decided to trade in their golden rule for a renovator's tape measure. They gutted the old building right down to its studs, refurbished it, and then reopened the Buxton with five guest rooms after two years of hard labor.

As country inns go, the Buxton is a large one and it's still growing. Despite its size and accommodations for far more diners (250 patrons in 7 dining rooms) than overnight guests, Audrey and Orville have maintained much of the spirit found at smaller inns, so much so, in fact, that they are regular recipients of awards for gracious service and fine dining on the country inn scene.

After finishing the Buxton, the Orrs began buying other houses on the same block, adding ten more guest rooms. Like many of the rooms in the Buxton and the surrounding homes, mine had delightfully uneven old floors and was filled with antiques. Even more guest rooms may be available when the Orrs complete their dream of owning the entire block. There is only one more house left to buy before they will have accomplished that goal.

The secret to the Orr's success is their hands-on ownership philosophy, most unusual for a property this size. Many days you will find Orville behind the bar and Audrey assisting in the kitchen. As a result, they are able to hang on to a faithful staff. A prime example is Buxton general manager Cecil Snow, a seventeen-year veteran who came shortly after the inn opened and never left. "I feel like family," says Cecil. "I grew up with the Orrs in this business, and as they learned it, so did I."

Key kitchen personnel have been around the Buxton for awhile as well. Chef Wayne Neal, who ironically scaled back his hours so he could teach, recently passed the head chef's hat over to Eddie Bihn after nearly eight years. Now Eddie, who has been at the inn for seven years, is at the helm, having come a long way to get there.

It may seem an inauspicious beginning to some, but for Eddie, winning a blue ribbon from the 4-H program for an outstanding casserole dish as a sixth-grader inspired him toward a career at an age when most kids are thinking only of junior high. His first jobs in the industry were anything but glamorous, but as a teenager working his way through school, Eddie began to learn his trade in the kitchens of local family-style restaurants. He soon advanced to more upscale dining rooms. The progression allowed Eddie to determine the kind of

The Buxton Inn, a travelers stop since 1812

cooking and type of establishment he would prefer. Eventually, Eddie Bihn marched his way up to chef's apprentice at the Bryn Mawr restaurant in Ohio. From there he attended advanced culinary and food management classes put on by the National Restaurant Association.

Eddie found what he was looking for at the Buxton Inn in 1985, when he was hired as a chef's assistant to Wayne Neal. The Orrs were impressed by the skills and the spirit of teamwork Eddie displayed in the kitchen.

The menu he prepares at the Buxton is an exhaustive one. Breakfast, lunch, and dinner are served here. In addition to daily specials, Eddie prepares a long list of historic dishes that are always on the Buxton menu.

"Holding onto old recipes goes with the history of the inn," explains Audrey. Oese Robinson's chicken supreme, for instance, is an adapted recipe from a prominent Granville citizen whose house has been turned into a museum. The coquille of seafood is a traditional dish that might have been served during the Buxton's earlier heydays.

Countless other traditional items are on the inn's menu, such as a Buxton bean soup, a traditional cobb salad, and chicken Victoria. You will also find new American dishes, including a turkey kebab wrapped in bacon and a veal sauté paprikache with snow crab and sweet red pepper sauce. And all the food is scrumptious, another indication that size is not a negative here.

No doubt the food was a big drawing card back in 1812, but ballroom dancing also brought in the patrons. The ballroom is now a dining room, and where feet once glided and shuffled, visitors dine today under chandeliers and candles. The inn was also a stagecoach stop between Worthington and Zanesville in its early days. Back then, many travelers couldn't read. But they knew that a sign with a symbol stood for food and lodging. To this day, the Buxton Inn displays the sign of the cat, carrying on the tradition that signals centuries of fine food and hospitality.

Coquille of Seafood and Mushrooms in Mornay Sauce

❖

Large scallop shells are available in most kitchen supply shops. You may also serve this traditional dish in small ramekins or in clam shells. The Buxton Inn serves this as an entrée with two shells per person. For this menu I suggest one each as an appetizer.

Seafood/Mushroom Preparation

➤ 2 tablespoons butter
➤ 2 cups sliced fresh mushrooms
➤ 1 pound bay scallops
➤ 1 pound popcorn shrimp
➤ ¾ cup sherry
➤ ½ teaspoon salt
➤ ¼ teaspoon white pepper
➤ 1 bay leaf
➤ 2 tablespoons minced scallions
➤ ½ pound cooked crabmeat, separated with a fork
➤ ¼ cup chopped pimiento
➤ Parmesan cheese
➤ Paprika

Sauce

➤ ¼ cup cooking sherry
➤ 1 pint half-and-half
➤ 1 pint heavy cream
➤ ¼ cup reserved liquid from seafood/mushroom preparation
➤ ⅛ cup chicken stock or broth
➤ ½ teaspoon onion powder
➤ ½ teaspoon garlic powder
➤ ⅛ teaspoon white pepper
➤ ⅛ teaspoon thyme
➤ ½ teaspoon fresh lemon juice
➤ ½ cup (1 stick) butter
➤ ¼ cup all-purpose flour

Timeless Coquille and Ginger Cake with Lemon Sauce

1. In a medium skillet melt 2 tablespoons of butter and sauté the mushrooms until tender and the liquid disappears. Set the mushrooms aside.
2. In a medium saucepan simmer the scallops, shrimp, sherry, salt, pepper, bay leaf, and scallions for 5 minutes in enough water to cover. Drain the liquid into a separate saucepan and cook it over higher heat, reducing it to 1 cup. Set it aside for making the sauce.
3. Add the crabmeat, pimiento, and mushrooms to the scallops and shrimp. Spoon about 3 ounces of the mixture into each shell. Place the shells in a shallow baking pan. Pour a little water in the pan to create a moisturizing steam around the shells.
4. In the top of a double boiler combine all of the sauce ingredients except the butter and flour. Bring the mixture just to a boil. Remove the pan from the heat and set it aside.
5. Preheat the oven to 400°. In a small saucepan make a roux by cooking the butter and flour over medium heat for about 20 minutes, stirring with a wooden spoon.
6. Add the sauce to the roux, stirring constantly until the sauce thickens. Pour the sauce evenly over the seafood, but don't allow the sauce to spill over the shell. Sprinkle with cheese and paprika. Bake the shells for 10 minutes or until the top is brown and bubbly.
Yield: 12 to 16 shells

Cherry Pine-Nut Salad with Raspberry Vinaigrette

❖

Immersing oranges in boiling water for one minute makes them easier to peel. If you don't have raspberry juice, buy frozen berries, boil them, and strain. The vinaigrette is appropriate for just about any green salad you serve.

Raspberry Vinaigrette

- ➤ ¾ tablespoon unflavored gelatin
- ➤ 3 cups raspberry juice, strained and sweetened to taste
- ➤ 3 tablespoons fresh lemon juice
- ➤ 2 tablespoons raspberry vinegar
- ➤ 1 tablespoon fresh parsley, minced
- ➤ ⅛ teaspoon salt
- ➤ ¼ teaspoon dry mustard
- ➤ ¾ cup oil

Salad

- ➤ 2 small heads Bibb or romaine lettuce, cleaned
- ➤ 2 oranges, peeled and sliced
- ➤ 3 ounces dried Michigan or other dried red cherries
- ➤ 2 ounces toasted pine nuts
- ➤ 1 small red onion, sliced in rings

1. To prepare the vinaigrette dressing, in a large bowl dissolve the gelatin in the juice and cool until nearly set. Add the lemon juice, raspberry vinegar, parsley, salt, dry mustard, and oil, and whip or blend until emulsified. Set aside.
2. Break off individual leaves from the lettuce and divide them evenly among the plates. Layer the orange slices and onion slices, and top with pine nuts and cherries. Serve with Raspberry Vinaigrette.
Yield: 8 to 10 servings

Apple-and-Nut-Stuffed Pork Loin with Raspberry-Brandy Sauce

❖

An everyday meal will get a lift from this succulent pork loin rendition. And what a splendid dish for company!

Pork Preparation

- ➤ ½ cup (1 stick) butter
- ➤ 1 cup coarsely chopped onion
- ➤ 2 stalks celery, coarsely chopped
- ➤ 2 medium tart red apples, peeled, cored, and chopped
- ➤ ½ teaspoon allspice
- ➤ ¼ teaspoon cardamom
- ➤ 4 to 5 cups plain dry bread cubes
- ➤ ½ cup pecans, coarsely chopped
- ➤ 1 4-pound boneless pork loin roast
- ➤ ¼ teaspoon each salt, pepper, and garlic powder

Raspberry-Brandy Sauce

- ➤ 2 cups fresh or frozen thawed raspberries
- ➤ ½ cup red currant jelly
- ➤ ½ cup apricot nectar
- ➤ 2 tablespoons brandy
- ➤ 1 tablespoon honey
- ➤ ¼ cup cornstarch
- ➤ 1 tablespoon water

1. In a large skillet melt the butter and sauté the onion and celery until tender but not brown. Stir in the apples, allspice, and cardamom. Cook, uncovered, for 5 minutes or until the apples are tender, stirring occasionally. Transfer the cooked apple mixture to a large bowl and add the bread cubes and pecans. Toss gently and set aside.
2. Preheat oven to 325°. Trim the excess fat from the roast. Split the roast lengthwise almost

through and lay it flat. Spoon about half of the stuffing over the meat. Spoon the remaining stuffing into an ungreased 1-quart casserole and set the dish aside.

3. Fold the roast with the stuffing inside. Place it in a baking pan and insert a meat thermometer. Sprinkle with salt, pepper, and garlic powder.

4. Roast the meat, uncovered, for 60 to 70 minutes, or until the internal temperature reaches 160°. Cover and bake the stuffing in the casserole during the last 40 minutes of roasting.

5. Prepare the raspberry sauce while the meat is cooking. In a medium saucepan combine all of the sauce ingredients except the cornstarch and water. Cook over medium heat until the mixture comes just to a boil, stirring frequently. Strain the sauce into a bowl to remove the seeds. In the same saucepan combine the cornstarch and water. Stir in the raspberry mixture and cook, stirring constantly, until thick and bubbly. Continue to cook for 2 minutes, stirring constantly. Serve the sauce with the roast and extra stuffing.
Yield: 8 to 10 servings

Daisy Hunter's 1900s Walnut Fudge Cake

❖

Daisy Hunter was known as one of Granville's best bakers. This carefully preserved brownie-like cake recipe was given to The Buxton Inn several years ago by Daisy's son.

➤ 1¼ cups (2½ sticks) butter

➤ 5 1-ounce squares semisweet chocolate, cut up

➤ 6 eggs

➤ 3 cups all-purpose flour

➤ 2½ cups sugar

➤ 1 cup chopped walnuts

➤ Ice cream with chocolate sauce, if desired

➤ Walnut halves dipped in melted semisweet chocolate

1. In a small saucepan melt the butter and chocolate over low heat, stirring frequently. Remove the pan from the heat, and let the chocolate cool for about 30 minutes.

2. Preheat the oven to 350°. In a large mixing bowl whisk the eggs.

3. In another bowl stir together the flour and sugar. Fold the mixture into the eggs, stirring until moist. Stir in the chocolate mixture. Pour the batter into a 15 x 10-inch baking pan. Sprinkle the chopped nuts over the batter. Bake the cake for 25 minutes or until the top springs back when lightly touched. Serve with ice cream and chocolate sauce, if desired. Garnish with chocolate-dipped walnuts.
Yield: 20 servings

Walnut Fudge cake

Old-Fashioned Ginger Cake with Lemon Sauce

❖

The melding of the sweet ginger cake with the tart lemon sauce lingers endearingly.

➤ 1½ cups shortening
➤ 1½ cups firmly packed brown sugar
➤ 4 eggs
➤ 2 cups light molasses
➤ 5 cups all-purpose flour
➤ 4 teaspoons baking powder
➤ 4 teaspoons ginger
➤ 3 teaspoons cinnamon
➤ 1 teaspoon cloves
➤ 1 teaspoon salt
➤ 2 cups boiling water

   Lemon Sauce

➤ 2 cups sugar
➤ ¼ cup cornstarch
➤ 4 cups water
➤ ¾ cup fresh lemon juice
➤ 1 cup (2 sticks) butter
➤ 1 teaspoon each grated lemon and orange rind
➤ Lemon or orange rinds for garnish

1. In a large bowl cream together the shortening and sugar until light and fluffy. Add the eggs one at a time, beating well after each addition. Add the molasses and mix well.
2. Preheat the oven to 350°. In another bowl sift

Amy Stephens, the innkeepers' daughter, in a nineteenth-century hostess hat

together the dry ingredients, and add them to the egg mixture alternately with the water. Pour the batter into a greased and floured 16 x 11-inch baking pan. Bake the cake for 45 to 55 minutes or until the center springs back when lightly touched. Cool on racks and cut into 12 squares.
3. To make the lemon sauce, in a medium sauce-pan combine the sugar and cornstarch. Stir in the water and cook over medium heat until thickened. Remove the pan from the heat. Stir in the lemon juice, butter, lemon rind, and orange rind, and keep warm. Place a square of ginger cake on each dessert dish and drape with lemon sauce. Garnish with a twist of lemon or orange rind, if desired.
Yield: 10 to 12 servings

Old Yankee Boiled New England Supper

Rowell's 1820 Inn
Simonsville, Vermont

INNKEEPER/CHEF BETH DAVIS

Dinner for Eight

Old-Fashioned Wassail

♦

Homemade Butter Braid Bread

♦

Maple Bacon Dressing for
Garden Salad

♦

Vintage Fiddlehead Fern Soup

♦

Corned Beef in Cabbage Nests with
Herbed Mustard Sauce

♦

Vermont Cheddar Cheese Pie

♦

Old Vermont Cocoa Layer Cake with
Maple and Nut Frosting

Rowell's 1820 Inn
is one of Vermont's best-kept secrets. During ten years as a country inn, Rowell's has somehow missed the spotlight. Yet this former stop on a stagecoach trail with its treasury of family keepsakes, sophisticated country dining, and wonderland of amusement rooms, deserves center stage.

Innkeepers Beth and Lee Davis, former Ohio residents, found Rowell's while searching New England for an inn during vacations from their retail clothing store. Their dream was specific. "We wanted a place with a few guest rooms that had the tradition of always being an inn," says Lee. In fact, they were inspired by just such a

place: the Buxton Inn (see page 34), where they often dined before moving from Ohio. So when they discovered Rowell's, a former lodging house rich in history, they soon realized it was time to sell one business and pack up their two daughters to launch a new venture in Vermont.

To seal the deal, Beth and Lee tracked down the real estate agent, who was "sugaring off" in his wooden maple sugar shack. The Midwesterners adapted quickly to this springtime New England ritual, each pulling up a barrel as a seat to hammer out the purchasing details. "We never imagined how much sugar can fall on you while sitting around a boiling bin of sap," recalls Beth of the unorthodox, eventful meeting.

Before long, the restoration process began, and today Rowell's is one of the most meticulously preserved historic inns in America and yet one of the most comfortable. You can sip a Vermont-brewed ale or stout by a wood stove in the intimate English tavern, catch rays with a good book and a cup of tea in the sunroom, or shell a few fresh peanuts at the old-fashioned ice cream soda bar. Or you may challenge a fellow guest to backgammon on an authentic game table Beth restored, while sipping wassail or a stem glass of wine from the innkeeper's modest but discerning wine list. And all this under one roof.

The best is yet to come when dinner is served by candlelight in the dining room that seats only twelve. Windsor chairs welcome diners beside Early American hutches in a room with most unusual accoutrements, including a contrasting floor of maple-and-cherry boards and a painted tin-panel ceiling.

Dinner is always five generous courses prepared in Beth's most inviting kitchen, which features an old black-iron stove and decorated countertops. There is little or no stainless steel here. It is truly a cook's room, accented by Beth's collection of cookery books, antique tins, and wooden utensils.

Here, the self-trained chef dishes out what her husband calls "comfort food." One of Beth's most requested menus is the New England boiled dinner, which harkens back to the early days of the inn. She brings her own interpretations to old and new receipts from the Rowell family and her own. As a result, her dinners are much more decorous than those prepared by her predecessors. In fact, the meal here is a melt-in-your-mouth one, from the Cheddar pie through the buttery cocoa cake. Note in the recipe how Beth embellishes the entrée of corned beef with a cabbage she has flavored with balsamic vinegar. The contents of this menu change frequently and are announced on a flier that shows a dated knickers-clad proprietor ringing a dinner bell beside a marquee touting the evening fare.

The innkeeper/chef cooks with a gourmet flair—integrating the old with the nouvelle and always serving the results on a historically inspired spatterware set of Bennington (Vermont) pottery. When not cooking up her boiled dinners, she serves a variety of beef, poultry, and seafood fashionably, but with a nod to the past. For instance, traditional new potatoes might earn a draping of her herbed dill sauce. A mushroom strudel might be graced with a sprinkling of white wine.

Beth's applesauce, served at breakfast, is a piquant blend of puréed apples and fruit chunks—you wonder how you can ever go back to eating the relish any other way. Her morning oatmeal pie is famous among repeat visitors, who savor this unusual blend of nuts and oats congealed with maple syrup into a pâté brisée. With the return to so-called comfort foods nationwide, Beth's style is right up to date.

Otherwise, the Davises are refreshingly old-fashioned in the way they run their inn. "We set out to live the dream of owning a quiet country inn," recalls Lee. Thus, they have resisted many changes. As you enter the

Authentic tin ceiling above a supper table at Rowell's

inn, the first sign of another time is the vintage apparel hanging from an iron peg rail. At the registration desk the sense of the past is reinforced with their day and month calendar—antique, but always showing the current date.

The reception area is a spacious front room with a fireplace and a large innkeeper's desk covered with wainscoting. Innkeeping consultants have suggested the Davises turn this welcoming room into another profit-making guest room. "We just can't do that," confides Beth. "It would spoil the integrity of the inn." So would whirlpool tubs, the Davises believe, but their facilities are none-theless most comfortable and inviting.

Each guest room gives the illusion that an important traveler is about to arrive. In one room you can read about some who did by finding their signatures on a framed page from an old guest ledger. I was intrigued by one nameless nineteenth-century entry that merely stated: "chauffeur." Two bedrooms on the third floor are the inn's showcases. These rooms once formed a grand ballroom where locals and travelers danced the night away. You can just imagine them waltzing merrily and effortlessly about the wooden floors high above the town of Simonsville.

Pleasant images from the past are ever present at this inn. You don't feel like a stranger looking in on history; you feel a part of it. Ever since that first taste of Vermont in the real estate agent's sugarhouse, Beth and Lee have been providing guests with sweet memories, one of which is from the wonderful cocoa cake you simply must bake in your own kitchen.

Old-Fashioned Wassail

Wassail is often thought of as a Christmas holi-day drink. Actually, it is a welcoming punch and can be served any time of year. Rowell's recipe is done in a crock pot, which allows an entire home to be scented with a delicious fragrance as prepa-rations are being made for the party.

➤ 2 quarts apple juice
➤ 1 pint cranberry juice
➤ 2 cinnamon sticks
➤ 1 teaspoon whole allspice
➤ 1 orange, unpeeled and cut into quarters
➤ 8 whole cloves
➤ 1 cup rum
➤ Thin orange slices for garnish

1. In a crock pot combine all of the ingredients and simmer on high for 1 hour.
2. Turn the crock pot setting to low and brew for 4 to 8 hours. Strain the wassail through a sieve and into a punch bowl. Float the orange slices in the wassail for garnish.
Yield: 10 punch-cup servings

Homemade Butter Braid Bread

➤ 2 packages active dry yeast
➤ ½ cup warm water (115°)
➤ 1 cup scalded milk
➤ ⅔ cup sugar
➤ ½ cup (1 stick) butter
➤ 1 teaspoon salt
➤ 5½ to 6 cups all-purpose flour
➤ 2 eggs
➤ 1 egg, beaten well with 1 tablespoon water for egg wash

Warm fire and wassail on the chef's family quilt in the parlor

1. In a small bowl combine the yeast and the water. Set aside until the yeast starts foaming, 5 to 10 minutes.
2. In a large bowl combine the milk, sugar, butter, and salt; let cool. Add 1 cup of the flour, and mix well. Stir in the yeast mixture and eggs, beating well. Add the remaining flour to make a soft dough. Turn the dough out onto a floured surface. Cover the dough with a kitchen towel and let it rest for 10 minutes.
3. Knead the dough until smooth and elastic. Place the dough in a lightly greased bowl, turning once to grease the surface. Cover the bowl with a kitchen towel and let the dough rise in a warm place until doubled in size. Punch the dough down. Cover and let it rise again until almost doubled in size.
4. Turn the dough out onto a lightly floured surface, and divide it into 6 even portions. Form each into a ball. Cover and let the dough rest for 10 minutes.
5. Roll out each portion to form a 16-inch strand with tapering ends. Line up the strands 1 inch apart on greased baking sheet. Form 2 bread braids, each using 3 strands. Braid them loosely without stretching the dough. Pinch the ends together. Cover and let the braids rise until almost doubled.

6. Preheat the oven to 375°. Brush the egg wash over the braids. Bake the bread for 25 minutes or until golden brown.
Yield: 2 loaves

Maple Bacon Dressing for Garden Salad

❖

Rowell's serves this dressing over a salad of spinach, Bibb lettuce, halved grapes, and Cheddar cheese.

➤ 2 cups oil
➤ ¾ cup cider vinegar
➤ ½ cup lightly packed brown sugar
➤ ½ cup maple syrup
➤ 5 strips bacon, crisply cooked
➤ 1 small onion
➤ 1 teaspoon dried mustard

Process all of the ingredients together in a food processor until well blended. Pour the dressing into a container with an airtight lid and refrigerate until serving.
Yield: 3½ cups

Vintage Fiddlehead Fern Soup

❖

Fiddlehead ferns are young tender fronds shaped like the head and neck of a violin. They grow alongside streams and other soggy, woodsy places in springtime. They may be frozen or canned for use year-round.

- ➤ ½ cup (1 stick) butter
- ➤ 2 leeks, cleaned and cut, including ⅓ of the tender green leaves from each stalk
- ➤ 1 large onion, diced
- ➤ 1 clove garlic, minced
- ➤ 2 medium potatoes, peeled and cut into chunks
- ➤ 4 dozen fiddleheads, cleaned
- ➤ 6 cups chicken broth
- ➤ Salt and freshly ground pepper to taste
- ➤ ½ cup heavy cream

1. In a large saucepan melt the butter. Add the leeks, onion, garlic, potatoes, and fiddleheads, and sauté for 5 minutes. Add the broth and bring it to a boil. Skim the surface if necessary. Add the salt and pepper. Cover and simmer for 40 to 60 minutes or until the vegetables are very tender.
2. Purée the mixture in the blender, and return it to the saucepan. Stir in the cream and heat through.
   Yield: 8 to 10 servings

Corned Beef in Cabbage Nests with Herbed Mustard Sauce

❖

Corned beef never had it as good as this preparation of Beth's.

Meat Preparation

- ➤ 1 5-6 pound round of beef
- ➤ 2 tablespoons pickling spice
- ➤ 2 bay leaves
- ➤ 2 cloves garlic, unpeeled
- ➤ 6 fresh whole beets, peeled, roots and ends trimmed
- ➤ ¼ cup (½ stick) butter
- ➤ 3 pounds small red potatoes, skins washed
- ➤ 1 pound parsnips, peeled and cut into 2-inch sticks
- ➤ 1 pound carrots, peeled and cut into 1-inch thick slices
- ➤ 1 pound small turnips, peeled and cut in quarters
- ➤ 1 cup (2 sticks) butter
- ➤ ¼ cup drained horseradish
- ➤ ⅓ cup minced fresh dill
- ➤ Salt and freshly ground pepper to taste

Cabbage and Mustard Sauce

- ➤ 2 tablespoons bacon drippings
- ➤ 1 small head cabbage, finely shredded (4 cups)
- ➤ ¼ cup balsamic vinegar
- ➤ 2 tablespoons sugar
- ➤ 1 teaspoon caraway seed
- ➤ 1 cup corned beef liquid (see step 2)
- ➤ 1½ cups heavy cream
- ➤ ¼ cup tarragon mustard
- ➤ ¼ cup Dijon mustard
- ➤ Fresh parsley and dill for garnish

1. In a large Dutch oven combine the beef and enough water to cover 1 inch above the beef. Add the pickling spice, bay leaves, and garlic and bring the water to a boil uncovered. Lower the heat and simmer gently for 4 to 5 hours or until a fork inserted in the center of the meat penetrates easily but the meat doesn't shred.

2. Remove the meat from the pot and wrap it in foil. Reserve 1 cup of the corned beef liquid for later use. Allow the beef to sit for 30 minutes before slicing.

3. Meanwhile, prepare the vegetables. In a saucepan combine the beets and enough water to cover them. Bring the water to a boil, cover, and simmer until the beets are tender. Drain and peel the beets. In a saucepan melt ¼ cup of butter and add the beets, tossing gently. Keep the beets warm.

4. In a separate saucepan steam the potatoes, parsnips, carrots, and turnips together in a small amount of water for 8 to 12 minutes or until tender.

5. In another small saucepan melt 1 cup of butter. Stir in the horseradish, dill, salt, and pepper. Cook until heated through and pour the mixture over the steamed vegetables. Place all of the vegetables in a covered container and keep warm in a 200° oven.

6. In a large skillet heat the bacon drippings and add the cabbage, cooking over low heat until tender. Add the vinegar, sugar, and caraway, and keep warm. In a small saucepan over medium heat cook 1 cup of the reserved corned beef liquid to a syrupy consistency. Stir in the heavy cream and reduce the mixture to a sauce-like consistency. Reduce the heat to low and add the mustards, blending well. Remove the bay leaves.

7. To serve, place a nest of cabbage on each plate. Top each nest with sliced beef, and drizzle with mustard sauce. Sprinkle with freshly chopped parsley and flank with the vegetables. Garnish with sprigs of dill.
Yield: 6 to 8 servings

The chef's great-grandparents oversee the corned beef, fern soup, and butter braid bread.

Vermont Cheddar Pie on an antique billiard table in the tap room

Vermont Cheddar Cheese Pie

✣

 ⅓ cup fine, plain, dry bread crumbs

➤ ¼ cup Parmesan cheese

➤ 4 8-ounce packages cream cheese

➤ 5 eggs

➤ 3 egg yolks

➤ ⅓ cup heavy cream

➤ ¼ cup all-purpose flour

➤ 2 cloves garlic, minced

➤ 1 yellow onion, grated

➤ 2 to 3 cups grated Cheddar cheese

➤ 1 tablespoon minced parsley

➤ 1 teaspoon chopped fresh basil leaves or ½ teaspoon dried

➤ ½ teaspoon chopped fresh tarragon or ¼ teaspoon dried

➤ 1 teaspoon chopped fresh dill or 1 teaspoon dried

➤ ⅓ cup beer

1. Preheat the oven to 250°. Wrap the outside of a 10-inch springform pan in aluminum foil. Butter the bottom and sides of the pan, and sprinkle with bread crumbs and Parmesan cheese.
2. In a large bowl beat together the cream cheese, eggs, yolks, cream, and flour until well mixed. Fold in the garlic, onion, Cheddar cheese, and herbs. Add the beer, mixing just until blended. Pour the filling into the spring-form pan.
3. Prepare a bain marie by placing the spring-form pan in a larger pan. Add enough boiling water to come halfway up the sides of the springform pan. Bake the pie for 1 hour and 40 minutes. Turn the oven off and leave the pie for 1 hour. The pie is done when the top is light brown and the center is firm, deter-mined by shaking it from side to side. Remove the pie from the oven and let it cool for 2 hours.
4. Remove the foil from the pan and discard it. Cut the pie into wedges to serve.
   Yield: 12 pieces

Old Vermont Cocoa Layer Cake with Maple and Nut Frosting

- ½ cup unsweetened cocoa
- ½ cup boiling water
- ¼ cup (½ stick) butter
- ¼ cup shortening
- 2 cups sugar
- ⅛ teaspoon salt
- 1 teaspoon vanilla extract
- 2 eggs
- 1½ teaspoons baking soda
- 1 cup buttermilk
- 1¾ cups all-purpose flour
- 2 tablespoons sour cream
- 1 tablespoon maple syrup
- ⅓ cup chopped walnuts

Frosting

- ¼ cup (½ stick) butter
- ¼ cup cocoa
- 1 tablespoon corn syrup
- ½ teaspoon maple syrup
- 1½ cups confectioners' sugar
- 3 tablespoons milk

Old Vermont Cocoa Layer Cake

1. Preheat the oven to 350°. Grease 3 9-inch round cake pans and line the bottoms with waxed paper.
2. In a small bowl combine the cocoa and boiling water. Set the mixture aside.
3. In a large bowl cream the butter, shortening, sugar, salt, and vanilla until fluffy. Add the eggs, beating until combined.
4. In a medium bowl combine the baking soda and buttermilk. Add the buttermilk mixture to the creamed mixture alternately with the flour. Measure 1⅔ cups of batter into a small bowl. Stir in the sour cream, maple syrup, and nuts. Pour the batter into one of the prepared pans.
5. Blend the cocoa mixture into the remaining batter and pour it evenly into the other 2 pans. Bake the cake for 25 to 30 minutes or until a tester comes out clean. Cool for 5 minutes before removing the cake from the pans.
6. To make the frosting, in a medium bowl combine the butter, cocoa, and syrups. Add the sugar alternately with the milk, and beat to a spreading consistency. Frost the top and sides of cooled cake.

Yield: 8 to 10 servings

Daytime Pleasures

To invite someone to your house means devoting yourself to ensuring his happiness the whole time he is under your roof.
Jean-Anthelme Brillat-Savarin

Breakfast with a Northern Exposure

The Shelburne Inn
Seaview, Washington

INNKEEPER/CHEF DAVID CAMPICHE

Recipes for Four to Twenty

❖

Brandied Cranberry-Ricotta
French Toast with
Cinnamon-Orange Syrup

◆

Flaming Sherried Eggs with
Shrimp, Apple, and Spinach

◆

Smoked Salmon Soufflé Roll with
Tomato-Cheese Béchamel Sauce

◆

Fruit-and-Nut-Filled Apple en Croûte with
Spiced Whipped Cream

◆

Hot Cross Buns

◆

Tarragon and Wine Turkey Sausage

◆

Basil Chicken Frittatas with
Fennel and Mint Salsa

◆

Pesto Potatoes

*I*n his tidy culinary studio at the Shelburne Inn, David Campiche works as a gastronomic artist. In minutes he turns out commissioned works, based on orders inn guests have placed from Early American oak tables where morning guests dine. The menu is designed daily with a nod to what is in season locally: wetland grasses, ferns, mushrooms, goose tongue, sea bean, and cranberries. Such edi-

bles are picked by David's three sons or by a Seaview resident who makes a regular routine of foraging for several area restaurants. David himself often digs for clams or retrieves ripened fruits and herbs from the inn's impressive garden.

As David's artistry is brought to the table, guests stare in silence at the unexpectedly picturesque breakfast fare. It is not unusual for breakfasters to run upstairs for their cameras to photograph the plate before they eat up the artwork.

David works on canvases of Dijon, deep pink, turquoise, and snow-white reproduction fiestaware. They are an ideal backdrop for the still lifes he paints with nature, his only artist's supplies. A few brush strokes of white sauce, dabbed with a little berry color, followed by swirls of green pesto or tomato béchamel, a Pointillist composition of khaki and hunter chives, surrounded by a Monet garden of edible flowers, and voilà: another masterpiece hits the table, but not before David lets it sit a minute to make adjustments. There are so many artful garnishes on the plate, it's a bit hard to count them.

But it's fun to watch the chef step back with a focused eye and thumb to apply just a touch of ochre rose or purple pansy to complete the picture.

And there's more artistry of another kind during breakfast. While he's cracking eggs and shelling oysters, the raconteur-chef theorizes about life, people, places, the universe, and nature, and he may even quote poetry from his self-published book, *The Bear River Poems.* As he takes the salmon out of the oven, you might hear a line from "Salmon Swim at You." The ode to fish caught in nearby waters describes salmon as huge, with heads that "spangle like sequins through a black labyrinth of night . . . they swim into your dreams."

You can spot David's manner and outlook in many of the fictitious characters in the hit television series, "Northern Exposure," especially in the city of Cicely's radio announcer, Chris. It must be indigenous. After all, Seaview isn't all that far from Alaska, the setting of the series, which is filmed only a few hundred miles north of The Shelburne in Roslyn, Washington.

David's soft-spoken musings, always delivered with a characteristic wry smile and polite gesture, are in contrast to an underlying adventuresome spirit. A case in point is the tale of how he met his wife and fellow innkeeper Laurie Anderson. He spotted a beautiful damsel in distress when her car got stuck in the sand. The hero-of-the-moment offered a conditional helping hand: she would have to share candlelight and wine (another of his passions) with him that night. You can hear the violins singing, but it's a true story. And it is backed up by his mother Val who, by the way, David credits for his culinary training. ("Val is a great cook and should write her own book," he says.)

David is an art history major whose background and creative bent may qualify him as a Michelangelo of breakfasts in America. But do not take just my word for it. The Shelburne offers some of the best of Pacific Northwest cuisine, according to *Bon Appétit, Gourmet,* and other magazines, and they were also referring to The Shoalwater lunch and dinner restaurant at the inn. I wanted to include breakfast recipes in the book to offer readers another entertaining alternative—one I find refreshing and easy to do in my own home. I thought of David Campiche and immediately flew out to the Shelburne. What I brought back are the recipes here, which you may also serve for brunch. Even though this is just breakfast, David is a noteworthy chef who could turn dinner meals into artistic compositions that taste wonderful as well, but he enjoys putting all that energy into the morning meal instead.

"I'm a morning person, and I think taking time out to enjoy a special meal first thing is a great way to start the day. And I feel as if I'm carving a niche. There aren't too many people who have pursued gourmet breakfast cuisine," explains David.

In 1791 President George Washington unexpectedly paid a visit to the home of Colonel John Allen. In a little over an hour Mrs. Allen had breakfast of young pig, turkey, country ham, fried chicken, sausage, waffles, batter cakes, various-style eggs, and hot soda biscuits. The President sat down, looked at all the food, and asked whether it would be possible to have only one hard-boiled egg and a cup of coffee with a little rum in it.

The Seasonal Hearth

The bonus of eating David's food is enjoying it in the atmosphere of the Shelburne and its environs. The inn is in one of several Victorian seaside towns that dot the twenty-eight-mile Long Beach peninsula, a hooked finger of land that begins at the mouth of the Columbia River and divides the waters of the Pacific Ocean and Willapa Bay.

David and Laurie, formerly antiques dealers, bought the rundown Shelburne in 1977 and performed extensive renovations. Guest rooms sport a variety of American and European antiques, handmade quilts, and claw foot tubs. They are a part of Laurie's personality at the inn, which also comes through in the delicate baking she does. (The recipe here for hot cross buns is hers.)

When not enjoying hearty conversation in the inn's parlor area, guests meander about the peninsula's bird sanctuaries, lighthouses, shops, and other panoramic vistas. There is plenty to explore, and the energy needed to do it is provided in bountiful supply by this wise and talented coastal chef.

Brandied Cranberry-Ricotta French Toast with Cinnamon-Orange Syrup

❖

David wonders why we do not adopt the term American Toast instead of French Toast: "Americans are passionate about French Toast, but have you ever seen French Toast on a menu in France?" Garam masala is a spice of India that David encourages you to use. If you do not have it on hand, substitute with cinnamon, but it will make a difference in the flavor.

Cinnamon-Orange Syrup

➤ 1½ cups water
➤ 2 cups sugar
➤ 24 ounces (3 cups) fresh cranberries
➤ ½ cup dry white wine
➤ Juice and zest of 1 orange
➤ 1 cinnamon stick

Filling

➤ 2 tablespoons butter
➤ ½ cup fresh cranberries, chopped
➤ ½ cup walnuts, chopped
➤ 3 tablespoons brandy
➤ 1 teaspoon garam masala
➤ 2 tablespoons honey
➤ 2 cups ricotta cheese

Bread Preparation

➤ 1 loaf French bread (not baguettes)
➤ 6 eggs, beaten
➤ ½ cup heavy cream
➤ ½ cup orange juice
➤ ¼ teaspoon cinnamon
➤ 1 tablespoon grated orange rind
➤ 1 teaspoon or more Grand Marnier
➤ ⅛ teaspoon grated nutmeg

---

1. In a small saucepan bring the water and sugar to a boil. Add the cranberries, wine, orange juice, orange zest, and cinnamon stick, and bring the mixture to a boil. Reduce the heat and simmer for 15 minutes or until the cranberries are tender. Remove and reserve the cinnamon stick. Strain the mixture, reserving the liquid and placing the solids in a food processor. Process for 1 minute and transfer to a saucepan with the reserved liquid and cinnamon stick. Simmer for 15 minutes or until thickened. Discard the cinnamon stick. Keep the syrup warm.

2. In a non-stick skillet melt the butter and sauté ½ cup of cranberries and the nuts until the nuts brown. Add the brandy and flambé in the pan. Add the garam masala and honey. Stir in the ricotta. Remove the pan from heat and set the filling aside.

3. Slice the bread diagonally every 2 inches. Make a cut in the center top of each piece to create a pocket. Fill each pocket with cheese mixture, then firmly press the pockets closed.

4. In a large bowl mix together the eggs, cream, orange juice, cinnamon, orange rind, Grand Marnier, and nutmeg. Submerge each stuffed bread slice in the mixture for 20 to 30 seconds, until a good amount of the mixture is absorbed. Sauté the bread on a hot griddle, turning to cook each side until golden brown. Serve with warm cranberry-orange syrup.

Yield: 6 servings

Flaming Sherried Eggs

2. In a medium skillet heat the butter and sauté the apples, shrimp, and chives for 1 minute. Add the spinach. Pour the sherry into the skillet and flambé. Add the eggs, turning frequently until the eggs begin to harden. (Don't let them turn brown.) Add the cheese, folding it into the eggs. Serve immediately.
Yield: 8 to 10 servings

Flaming Sherried Eggs with Shrimp, Apple, and Spinach

- ➤ 12 eggs
- ➤ ¼ cup heavy cream
- ➤ 1 tablespoon cilantro, finely chopped
- ➤ Salt and pepper to taste
- ➤ 2 tablespoons clarified butter
- ➤ ½ Granny Smith apple, unpeeled, diced medium fine
- ➤ ¼ cup chopped fresh shrimp
- ➤ 2 tablespoons minced chives
- ➤ ¼ cup fresh spinach, shredded into narrow strips
- ➤ 3 tablespoons sherry
- ➤ ¼ cup crumbled blue cheese

1. In a large bowl beat the eggs with the cream, cilantro, salt, and pepper until well mixed. Set the mixture aside.

Smoked Salmon Soufflé Roll with Tomato-Cheese Béchamel Sauce

Prepare this recipe the night before you serve it.

Sauce
- ➤ ¼ cup (½ stick) butter
- ➤ ¼ cup all-purpose flour
- ➤ ¼ cup dry white wine
- ➤ 1½ cups heavy cream
- ➤ 1 cup spaghetti sauce or plain tomato sauce
- ➤ ½ cup grated Gruyère cheese
- ➤ 2 tablespoons chopped fresh chives
- ➤ ¼ teaspoon salt
- ➤ Freshly ground pepper and nutmeg to taste
  Filling
- ➤ 1 cup less 2 tablespoons sour cream
- ➤ 8 finely sliced green onions
- ➤ ½ pound smoked salmon, chopped
- ➤ 1 cup ricotta cheese
- ➤ Juice of ½ lemon
  Soufflé Roll
- ➤ ¾ cup (1½ sticks) butter
- ➤ 1½ cups all-purpose flour
- ➤ 4 cups hot milk
- ➤ 6 eggs, separated
- ➤ 1 teaspoon salt
- ➤ 1 teaspoon Tabasco
- ➤ 1 teaspoon vermouth
- ➤ 2 tablespoons sour cream

Salmon Soufflé Roll and Pesto Potatoes

1. In a medium skillet melt the butter over medium heat. Blend in the flour, stirring constantly for 2 or 3 minutes until the mixture bubbles. Remove the pan from the heat and add the wine and cream, beating vigorously to remove lumps. Return the mixture to high heat and bring it to a slow boil. Reduce the heat and continue whisking until the sauce thickens. Stir in the tomato sauce, cheese, chives, salt, pepper, and nutmeg. Cool, cover, and refrigerate until morning.

2. In a large bowl mix together the ingredients for the filling. Set the filling aside.

3. Preheat the oven to 350°. In a large skillet melt the butter over medium heat. Add the flour, stirring until golden. Add the hot milk, stirring vigorously to remove the lumps. Remove the pan from the heat. Beat the egg yolks lightly and add them to the skillet, incorporating them a little at a time. Add the salt, Tabasco, vermouth, and sour cream. Beat the egg whites until stiff. Fold half of the whites into the yolk mixture, then gently fold in the other half. Spread this batter evenly onto a buttered 15 x 10-inch jelly roll pan lined with parchment. Bake the soufflé roll for 30 minutes or until it turns golden and is firm to the touch. Allow it to cool.

4. Spread the salmon filling evenly over the roll. Carefully, starting at a narrow edge, roll up from one end to the other, peeling the parchment back. Wrap the roll in aluminum foil and refrigerate it until morning. To serve, reheat the roll in a moderate oven. Slice it into 2-inch widths and serve with the tomato-béchamel sauce.

Yield: 8 slices

Fruit-and-Nut-Filled Apple en Croûte with Spiced Whipped Cream

✤

Crust

➤ *2 cups unsifted, unbleached flour*
➤ *1 teaspoon salt*
➤ *1 tablespoon sugar*
➤ *⅓ cup cold sweet butter*
➤ *⅓ cup cold margarine*
➤ *Zest of 1 lemon (reserve the juice)*
➤ *⅓ cup ice-cold water*

Filling

➤ *6 Pippin or Rome baking apples*
➤ *Juice of 1 lemon*
➤ *¾ cup dried apricots, finely chopped*
➤ *½ cup walnuts, chopped*
➤ *½ cup orange marmalade*
➤ *1 egg, slightly beaten for egg wash*

Spicy Whipped Cream

➤ *1 cup chilled heavy cream*
➤ *2 tablespoons honey*
➤ *1 teaspoon vanilla extract*
➤ *¼ teaspoon each cinnamon, freshly grated nutmeg, and ginger*

1. In a large bowl mix together the flour, salt, and sugar. Cut in the butter and margarine until the mixture resembles coarse crumbs. Add the lemon zest. Sprinkle in the water a few drops at a time until the mixture can be gathered into a ball. Wrap it in plastic and refrigerate it while making the filling.
2. Peel and core the apples. Sprinkle with the lemon juice. In a bowl mix together the apricots, walnuts, and marmalade. Stuff each apple cavity tightly with this mixture.
3. Preheat the oven to 375°. Grease and flour a 13 x 9-inch baking dish. Cut the dough into 6 equal pieces and roll each out into a circle, about 6 inches or larger, to enclose the apples. Center a circle over each apple and pinch the bottom to seal. Cut away the excess dough, saving it to make decorative shapes such as leaves, which may be attached to the apple with milk or water. Place the apples in the prepared pan. Brush the dough with the egg. Bake the apples for 40 to 45 minutes or until an apple is pierced easily with a cake tester. Allow the apples to cool for a few minutes.
4. Beat the cream with the honey. Add the vanilla and spices and beat until stiff peaks form. Top the apples with cream and serve.
Yield: 6 servings

Hot Cross Buns

Glaze

➤ *¼ cup sugar*
➤ *5 tablespoons milk*

Buns

➤ *8 cups all-purpose flour*
➤ *½ cup plus 2 teaspoons sugar*
➤ *2 tablespoons active dry yeast*
➤ *1½ cups warm milk (115°)*
➤ *1 cup warm water (115°)*
➤ *2 teaspoons salt*
➤ *1 teaspoon allspice*
➤ *1 teaspoon cinnamon*
➤ *1 teaspoon nutmeg*
➤ *½ cup (1 stick) butter, softened*
➤ *2 eggs, lightly beaten*
➤ *⅔ cup currants*
➤ *⅔ cup each dark and golden raisins*

Paste for Cross

➤ *½ cup all-purpose flour*
➤ *3 to 4 tablespoons water*

1. In a small saucepan over low heat dissolve the sugar in the milk. Stir and set the glaze aside.
2. In a large bowl mix together 2 cups of the flour, 2 teaspoons of the sugar, the yeast, milk, and water. Cover the bowl with a kitchen towel and set it in a warm place for 20 minutes.
3. In a separate bowl mix the remaining flour with the salt, spices, and remaining sugar. Add the dry ingredients, butter, eggs, currants, and raisins to the yeast mixture. Mix well to form a soft dough, adding extra flour if the dough is too sticky to handle.
4. Turn the dough onto a lightly floured surface and knead until smooth, or use a mixer and dough hook. Shape the dough into a ball and place it in a greased bowl. Cover the bowl with a kitchen towel and let the dough rise until doubled in size.
5. Turn the dough onto a lightly floured surface. Punch it down and knead for 2 minutes. Divide the dough into 24 even pieces and shape them into round buns. Place the buns 2 inches apart on greased baking pans. Cover and let the buns rise in a warm place for 30 minutes, until doubled.
6. Preheat the oven to 375°. Just before putting the buns into the oven, make the crosses by mixing the remaining flour and water into a paste. Place the mixture in a pastry tube with a small flat opening, and make a cross on the top of each bun. Bake the buns for 15 to 20 minutes or until the tops are browned except for the white crosses. Transfer to a rack and brush immediately with sugar glaze.

Yield: 24 buns

Hot Cross Buns served in a guest suite

Tarragon and Wine Turkey Sausage

✤

Making sausage combinations is one of David's fortes. Here, he offers a lean white sausage that may also be cold-smoked with a sweet wood such as apple or cherry.

- ➤ 2½ pounds boneless turkey breast cut into 1-inch cubes
- ➤ 2½ pounds boneless pork loin cut into 1-inch cubes
- ➤ 10 cloves garlic, minced
- ➤ ½ cup each fresh Italian parsley and tarragon, chopped
- ➤ Freshly ground pepper to taste
- ➤ 3 tablespoons salt
- ➤ 2 tablespoons Cajun dust or 1 teaspoon cayenne pepper
- ➤ ½ cup freshly chopped chives
- ➤ 1 cup white wine
- ➤ ½ cup nonfat dry milk powder
- ➤ Sausage casing

1. In a large bowl mix all the ingredients together except the casing. Marinate the sausage in the refrigerator for 6 hours.
2. Push the mixture through a sausage grinder with ¼-inch diameter holes, stuffing the meat directly into the casing. Cook the same as any other sausage. Freeze any unused portion.
   Yield: 20 servings

Basil Chicken Frittatas with Fennel and Mint Salsa

Salsa
- ➤ 3 large tomatoes, chopped medium fine
- ➤ 1 small red onion, finely chopped
- ➤ ½ each yellow, red, and green bell pepper, chopped medium fine
- ➤ 2 tablespoons finely chopped fresh fennel or dill
- ➤ 3 tablespoons finely chopped fresh mint
- ➤ 3 tablespoons tomato sauce
- ➤ ¼ cup red wine
- ➤ ¼ cup red wine vinegar
- ➤ ¼ cup olive oil
- ➤ 1 teaspoon sugar
- ➤ 1½ teaspoons Tabasco sauce
- ➤ ½ teaspoon cayenne pepper

Frittata
- ➤ 12 eggs
- ➤ ¼ cup whipping cream
- ➤ ½ cup fresh mint, chopped
- ➤ ½ cup fresh basil, chopped
- ➤ ½ cup pine nuts
- ➤ ¼ cup olive oil
- ➤ ½ teaspoon or more cayenne pepper
- ➤ ¾ cup chopped chicken breast
- ➤ ½ cup fresh corn, cooked and cut from the cob
- ➤ ½ cup shredded Cheddar cheese

1. In a large bowl mix together the salsa ingredients. Set the salsa aside.
2. In a separate bowl beat the eggs with the cream to incorporate. Set the eggs aside.
3. In a small bowl mix together the chopped herbs, pine nuts, olive oil, and cayenne. Place ¼ of this mixture in a heated 8-inch non-stick skillet. When the nuts are browned, add ¼ of the chicken and ¼ of the corn. Reduce the heat to medium. Pour in ¼ of the eggs and ¼ of the cheese.

4. As the egg mixture firms up, pull in the edges. When the bottom of the frittata is golden, flip and continue cooking until the other side is golden. Turn the frittata onto a warmed plate. Keep it warm in the oven while making the others. Repeat the process 3 times. Serve with salsa and crème fraîche.

Yield: 4 servings

Pesto Potatoes

❖

➤ ¼ cup olive oil

➤ 3 cloves garlic, minced

➤ 1 tablespoon cumin seed

➤ ¼ cup pesto

➤ ½ teaspoon turmeric

➤ ¼ teaspoon cayenne pepper

➤ Salt and freshly ground pepper to taste

➤ 3 cups red potatoes, skins washed, and boiled and cut into bite-size pieces

Basil Chicken Frittata

In a large skillet heat the olive oil over medium high heat and sauté the garlic until golden brown. Add the cumin and sauté for 30 seconds. Combine the pesto and spices and add the mixture to the skillet, mixing with the oil. Add the potatoes. Cook, stirring constantly, until the pesto has completely coated the potatoes. Reduce the heat to low and sauté until the potatoes are lightly browned around the edges.

Yield: 6 servings

Gourmet Luncheon in the Country

The White Hart Inn
Salisbury, Connecticut

CHEF KEVIN SCHMITZ

Lunch for Eight

Roasted Red Pepper and
Fennel Soup

•

Vegetable Napoleons with Roasted
Garlic Vinaigrette

•

Maryland Crab Cakes with
Basil Aïoli

•

Almond Trifles with Mascarpone
and Berry Port

White Hart food connoisseur Kevin Schmitz is a chef's chef. Working away in his enormous kitchen with miles of counter space and skilled assistants, he embodies the characteristics one typically envisions in an American chef: young but not too young, trained but not jaded, proud but not boastful, articulate but not always with the last word, businesslike but not unfriendly, creative but not so much so that you cannot pronounce what you're eating much less swallow it, and talented without any "buts" about it.

The White Hart, a twenty-six-room, small hotel-style country inn in a centuries-old building, certainly has an exemplary chef in Kevin Schmitz. His menu is filled with exciting nouvelle concoctions that are also edible and inviting, thanks to perennial ingredients applied in inventive ways. Kevin's lamb, for instance, has been served grilled on the outside and pink on the inside with a garlic flan and emerald green snow peas; and he has done salmon fillets in poppy seed crusts or jazzed up ordinary tomato soup by using roasted tomatoes, shallots, cream, and goat cheese. Kevin believes that too many gourmet chefs tend to overdo the food. "They will send out a combination just because they think it's unique, even if it doesn't have any appeal," he says.

Kevin suggests we all cook "as Picasso painted—giving familiar things just a little different look." His own repertoire of mixed-and-matched dishes is virtually endless. "It's all because of teamwork," he explains modestly. "Five people might be back here creating one recipe," he says, choosing not to mention that it is all under his supervision and usually his idea whether for breakfast, lunch, or dinner. Kevin is in charge of all three meals at the inn.

Food service was never the route Kevin intended to pursue. He earned his college degree in biology on his way to veterinary school. Needing funds to continue schooling, he ended up in restaurant kitchens and found he had a natural flourish for the field. The chef went to work for five years at Chillingsworth, a fine restaurant on Cape Cod, where he trained under visiting European and American chefs, and watched Julia Child in action. It was there that he picked up his classical skills before going to New York City, where he worked in a variety of restaurants and finally in the prestigious executive dining room of Shearson, Lehman, Hutton.

He came to The White Hart when he heard it was being restored by Terry and Juliet Moore, "two people who are committed to what they do and are in it for the right reasons," says Kevin. "I had no desire to leave New York City until Juliet and Terry came along." The couple, also owners of two non-inn restaurants, bought the sagging White Hart at a foreclosure auction in 1989. Since then, the Moores have created a designer showcase of floral fabrics, canopied beds, and dressing tables in the guest rooms.

Lunch is served in the Garden Room, colored with African violets on every table, tall green plants, and floors of flagstone, reminiscent of an outdoor courtyard. You are encouraged to linger here for a leisurely afternoon with friends or for a special occasion.

The menu in this book is for your own special luncheon with friends. You may serve all of the items or just a salad with the soup and napoleon. But always serve the White Hart's incredible trifle.

Everyday midday meals at The White Hart usually consist of light soups, grilled salads, and fancy foccacia. The items in this menu have been served at the inn for special luncheons as well as parties and dinners.

For dinner in Julie's New American Sea Grill or in the Tap Room, Kevin is likely to turn out one of his signature dishes of charbroiled tuna with a rare inside and an outside styled with papaya and mango salsa. He enjoys cooking seafood more than anything else and tells me that tuna should be served rare or medium-rare, "otherwise the flavor gets too strong and tastes as though it were out of a can." In fact, nothing is canned here—not the food, the decor, the people, and certainly not the laughter or enjoyment you receive from stopping here for a respite with Kevin's inventive but familiar offerings.

Roasted Red Pepper and Fennel Soup

❖

I love any excuse to use fresh fennel. Kevin's use of it in this soup came as a new idea to me, and I have not stopped making it since.

- ➤ 4 *red bell peppers, cut in half, seeded, tops and bottoms removed*
- ➤ *Olive oil*
- ➤ *Salt and pepper*
- ➤ 4 *fennel bulbs, roots removed and bulbs cut into ¼-inch slices*
- ➤ 2 *medium Spanish onions, chopped*
- ➤ 2 *cloves garlic, minced*
- ➤ 2 *ripe tomatoes, chopped*
- ➤ 8 *cups heavy chicken stock*
- ➤ 4 *ounces Pernod or slightly sweet white wine*

1. In a large bowl mix the bell peppers with the olive oil, salt, and pepper. Lay the peppers on a hot indoor grill (or use a barbecue grill), skin-side down. Place a baking sheet on top of the peppers. Roast until the peppers are charred. Remove them to a bowl of ice water. Peel off the charred skin and set them aside.
2. In a separate bowl toss the fennel with the oil, salt, and pepper. Place the fennel slices on a grill (or baking sheet) and cook until tender. Remove and let the fennel cool.
3. In a medium saucepan heat ½ cup of olive oil. Add the onions and garlic, and sauté until the onions are translucent. Add the tomatoes, fennel, and peppers, and sauté for 10 minutes. Add the stock and bring the mixture to a boil. Reduce the heat and simmer for 30 minutes. Remove the pan from the heat. Purée the mixture in a food processor and then pass it through a coarse strainer. Discard the solids. Return the soup to the stove and heat through. Stir in the Pernod just before serving.

Yield: 8 servings

Vegetable Napoleons with Roasted Garlic Vinaigrette

❖

Cut into bite-size pieces, the napoleons may also be served as an hors d'oeuvre.

Roasted Garlic Vinaigrette
- ➤ *Kosher salt*
- ➤ 1 *bulb plus 1 clove garlic*
- ➤ ¾ *cup olive oil*
- ➤ 1 *shallot*
- ➤ ¾ *cup balsamic vinegar*
- ➤ ¾ *cup plus 2 tablespoons extra virgin olive oil*
- ➤ *Salt and pepper*
Napoleons
- ➤ 2½ 10 x 15-inch puff pastry sheets (¼-inch thick)
- ➤ 1½ *pounds eggplant*
- ➤ ¾ *cup olive oil*
- ➤ 2 *tablespoons fresh lemon juice*
- ➤ 1 *clove garlic, minced*
- ➤ 2 *tablespoons sesame tahini (from gourmet food aisles of grocery store)*
- ➤ *Salt and pepper*
- ➤ 4 *ounces shiitake mushrooms, stemmed and julienned*
- ➤ 3 *tablespoons finely chopped shallots*
- ➤ 12 *ounces fresh spinach, stemmed, washed, and dried*
- ➤ 3 *ounces white wine*
- ➤ *Red colored crème fraîche for garnish, if desired*
- ➤ *Diced red and yellow bell peppers for garnish, if desired*
- ➤ *Dried parsley or chives for garnish, if desired*

1. Preheat the oven to 350°. Spread kosher salt ¼-inch thick in a 6-inch square or smaller baking pan. Place the bulb of garlic in the

Red Pepper and Fennel Soup

center, root-side down. Drizzle 2 tablespoons of the olive oil over the garlic. Bake the garlic for 35 to 45 minutes, until bulb is soft. Remove it and let it cool. Cut the root end off the bulb and squeeze out the roasted garlic. Discard the skin.

2. In a food processor combine the shallots, garlic, and roasted garlic pulp. Process the mixture for 1 minute. While the machine is running, slowly add the vinegar and then the oil to emulsify. Season with salt and pepper. Set the vinaigrette aside. Prepare napoleons.

3. Turn oven up to 400°. Place each pastry sheet onto a baking pan to fit. Place a second baking pan of the same size over the top. Put an oven-proof weight on top. Bake the pastry for 15 minutes or until the sheets have a light golden color. (If your oven isn't large enough or you don't have enough pans, bake the sheets one at a time.) Reduce the oven temperature to 350°. Place the warm sheets on a cutting surface. Cut each in half lengthwise. Divide each half again into 5 3 x 4-inch rectangles. This should make 25 rectangles. Set the pastry aside.

4. Slice the eggplants in half. Score their surfaces with a knife and brush lightly with olive oil. Season with salt and pepper. Place the eggplant halves on a baking pan, scored side up. Bake for 30 minutes or until soft. Let the

eggplant cool. When the eggplant reaches room temperature, scoop out the pulp and place it in a cheesecloth. Squeeze out the excess liquid and discard it. In a large bowl combine the pulp, ¼ cup of olive oil, the lemon juice, minced garlic, and sesame tahini. Whisk until a smooth paste forms. Season with salt and pepper.

5. In a large skillet heat the remaining olive oil over medium heat. Add the mushrooms and sauté for 20 seconds. Add the shallots and cook for 1 minute. Add the spinach and cook for 30 seconds. Deglaze the pan with the wine, and cook for 30 seconds. Remove the pan from heat. Season with salt and pepper.

6. Spoon the mushroom mixture evenly over 8 pastry rectangles. Over another 8 rectangles spread each with 2 tablespoons of the eggplant mixture. Place these rectangles on top of the mushroom mixture, eggplant-side up. Place another rectangle over the eggplant on top of each napoleon. Drizzle ¼ cup of the vinaigrette around each serving plate. Garnish the bottom layer of the napoleons if desired with slightly blanched squares of red and yellow peppers. Pipe the crème fraîche onto the napoleons using a thin pastry tip, and finish with a sprinkle of parsley or chives.
Yield: 8 napoleons

Vegetable Napoleon

Maryland Crab Cakes with Basil Aïoli

Basil Aïoli

➤ 2 ounces (¼ cup) each fresh basil, parsley, and chives, chopped
➤ ¼ cup extra virgin olive oil
➤ 1 egg yolk
➤ 1 teaspoon finely chopped garlic
➤ 2 tablespoons lemon juice
➤ ½ cup olive oil
➤ Salt and pepper

Crab Cakes

➤ 3 pounds Maryland lump crab meat, cleaned
➤ 1 each red, green, yellow bell peppers, finely diced
➤ 6 eggs
➤ 3 ounces (6 tablespoons) chopped shallots
➤ 3 tablespoons mixed freshly chopped chives, parsley, tarragon, thyme
➤ 12 slices white bread, crusts removed and ground into crumbs
➤ ¼ cup heavy cream
➤ 3 teaspoons Tabasco sauce
➤ Salt and pepper
➤ ¼ cup olive oil

1. Blanch the herbs in boiling water for 15 seconds. Remove and plunge them into cold water for 30 seconds. Drain the herbs and pat them dry. In a blender purée the herbs with ¼ cup of the olive oil. Set the mixture aside. In a food processor combine the egg yolk and garlic, and process for 1 minute. Add the fresh lemon juice while the machine is running. Slowly add the herb purée. Add the remaining ½ cup of oil in a thin stream while the machine is running. Season with salt and pepper. Set the aïoli aside.
2. Squeeze out any excess liquid from the crab meat. In a large bowl combine the crab meat and the peppers. Add the eggs and mix well. Add the shallots and herbs. Gradually mix in the bread crumbs. Add the heavy cream, Tabasco, salt, and pepper; mix well. Form the mixture into 16 cakes.
3. Preheat the oven to 350°. In a large skillet heat the olive oil over medium heat and sauté the crab cakes until golden brown on both sides. Place them on a baking sheet. Bake the crab cakes for 10 minutes or until heated through. Garnish with aïoli.
Yield: 8 servings

A table set for lunch at the White Hart

Almond Trifles with Mascarpone and Berry Port

✥

As trifles go, this recipe is probably one of the most unusual and equally delicious. The mascarpone offers a change from heavier, custard-style trifles. Chef Schmitz credits his associate chef, Ted Wagner, with this recipe. When Kevin was interviewing chefs for the inn, Ted made this for his tryout and Kevin hired him on the spot. If you can't get fresh berries, buy the frozen ones that are not packed in juice.

A designer guest room at the inn

Almond Cake

➤ 12 ounces almond paste
➤ ¾ cup (1½ sticks) butter
➤ 2 cups sugar
➤ 5 eggs
➤ 1½ tablespoons rum
➤ 1 teaspoon almond extract
➤ ¾ cup all-purpose flour
➤ 3 ounces ground almonds
➤ ½ teaspoon baking powder

Mascarpone Cream

➤ 8 egg yolks
➤ ½ cup sugar
➤ 1 pound Mascarpone cheese

Port and Fruit

➤ 3 cups port
➤ ¾ cup sugar
➤ 1 cinnamon stick
➤ 7 black peppercorns
➤ 1 tablespoon allspice
➤ 1 pint fresh or frozen strawberries, hulled and sliced
➤ ½ pint fresh or frozen raspberries
➤ ½ pint fresh or frozen blackberries, halved
➤ Chocolate shavings for garnish

1. Preheat the oven to 350°. Cream together the almond paste, butter, and sugar. Add eggs 1 at a time, beating after each addition. Add the rum and extract. Add the flour, almonds, and baking powder, blending until smooth. Pour the batter into a parchment-lined 12 x 18-inch sheet pan. Bake the cake for 15 to 20 minutes, or until the cake is light golden brown and springs back to the touch. Allow the cake to cool on a rack.

2. In the top of a double boiler over hot water combine the egg yolks and sugar, and whisk constantly until thick and ribbony. Add the cheese and whisk until smooth. Refrigerate the mixture until cooled.

3. In a skillet combine the port, sugar, cinnamon stick, peppercorns, and allspice and bring the mixture to a boil. Reduce the heat and simmer until the liquid is reduced by half. Strain and set aside to cool. When cooled, add the fruit and let the mixture stand for at least 15 minutes.

4. Cut the almond cake into rounds to fit into the shape of a 10-ounce white-wine goblet (or other stemmed glass). Begin building the trifle by spooning about 1½ ounces of cream into the bottom of each glass. Add the same amount of fruit mixture and then an almond cake round. Add more fruit and cream and finally, chocolate shavings for garnish, if desired.

Yield: 8 trifles

An English Tea from the Heartland

The Mansion at Elfindale
Springfield, Missouri

PASTRY CHEF DOROTHY ROUTH

Recipes for a Baker's Dozen

*Cinnamon Scones with
Strawberry Butter*

◆

*Walnut Viennese White Chocolate
Cookie Whirls*

◆

Apricot Yorkshire Tartlets

◆

*Strawberry-Almond
Battenberg Cake*

◆

*Caramel Apple and Walnut
No-Bake Cheesecake*

◆

Raspberry Pavlova

*F*rom the research for my previous book, *Tea-Time at the Inn*, I know that The Mansion at Elfindale is one of the only American bed and breakfast inns where an honest-to-goodness English pastry chef bakes up all of the afternoon tea treats every Wednesday through Saturday. Formerly a chef at four-star hotels in London, Dorothy came to this country after meeting her American husband, Bill.

Dot came to be the mansion's tea-time specialist in a roundabout fashion. She and Bill, an airplane mechanic, were doing some side jobs for the mansion in 1990 when the former convent was being refurbished as an inn. She overheard someone mention they would like to serve tea at the inn, and the rest is history. Now Dot is the pastry chef and also the banquet cook for special occasions.

Tea is served at tables in the spacious tea room, which is dressed in bold Waverly print fabrics and wallpaper. Dot designed the menu to include cream teas, English teas, or à la carte teas. Teapots clad in homemade cozies are brought to each table with a choice of more than ten kinds of tea. A full tea includes sandwiches, cookies, scones, fresh fruit, a pastry, and a piece of cake.

It seems fitting to take tea in a place such as The Mansion at Elfindale. The mansion, with its wonderfully high-ceilinged rooms, is rich in history and graciousness. Built by real estate tycoon John O'Day in 1888, the

Tea table in the drawing room with Raspberry Pavlova on the pedestal plate

A former convent and school is now a bed and breakfast.

Elfindale. She said that early morning mist rising from a lake on the property made it appear as though tiny elves were playing in the dale: thus elf-in-dale. The name has also stuck with the area surrounding the mansion to this day.

Eventually, Mrs. O'Day sold the property, guided by what she felt was divine intervention. She was offered several bids for the house as high as $259,000 in the early 1900s but sold it instead to an order of Catholic nuns for $30,000. In 1906 the sisters turned the mansion into an academy for girls, housing both students and nuns, as it had thirty-five bedrooms back then. The school closed in 1964, and the building was left unoccupied until 1989 when religious connections came into play once again. An independent ministry, The Cornerstone World Outreach Church, bought the mansion and the surrounding property.

Pastor and president Jess Gibson came up with the idea to renovate the mansion and turn it into an inn, where inspirational books once again reside. Thirteen suites, plus a parlor, the tea room, and sitting areas on all three floors, now make up the bed and breakfast. Each room is a brilliant study in theme decorating, from the art deco suite to the tower room complete with two-story turret and top-floor telescope.

In what spare time she has, Dot finds that creating porcelain dolls—much sought after by collectors—is both a relaxing and rewarding hobby. But as would be expected, I found her busy in the inn's kitchen, molding sugar and dough into delectable artwork. Her pavlova is just one of the many sculptural pastries she makes up for teatime. The inn serves tea in delightfully mismatched china cups. This English tea from America's heartland is truly traditional and can be a most relaxing way for you to entertain at home, even if you've never been to England.

mansion comprises 27,000 square feet and was put together over three years by the skilled hands of fifty stone masons from Germany.

Adding to the historical intrigue, John O'Day and his wife, Slymena Alice, were divorced after the home was built, with the mansion going to Mrs. O'Day. She changed the name of the property from Park Place to

A sunny guest room at the mansion

Cinnamon Scones with Strawberry Butter

❖

Scones

➤ 1 cup self-rising flour
➤ 1 tablespoon cinnamon
➤ ½ teaspoon salt
➤ 6 tablespoons butter
➤ 1 egg
➤ ¼ cup milk
➤ 3 tablespoons sugar

Strawberry Butter

➤ 1 cup (2 sticks) butter
➤ 1 cup strawberry jam
➤ 2 tablespoons fresh lemon juice

1. Preheat the oven to 400°. Into a large bowl sift together the flour, cinnamon, and salt. Cut in the butter. In a separate bowl beat together the egg and milk, and add the sugar. Add the milk mixture to the dry ingredients and mix until a soft but not sticky dough forms.

2. Turn the dough onto a lightly floured surface and knead quickly until smooth. Roll out the dough to ½-inch thickness. Cut into 12 rounds with a 1-inch biscuit cutter. Place the scones on a greased baking sheet. Bake the scones for 10 to 15 minutes, or until golden. Cool on a wire rack.

3. In a medium bowl beat together the butter, jam, and lemon juice with an electric mixer until very light and fluffy, about 15 to 20 minutes. Serve the butter at room temperature with the scones.

Yield: 12 scones

Viennese Cookie Whirls

to 15 minutes, or until golden brown. Cool on a wire rack.
3. In a small saucepan melt the white chocolate chips. Dip half of each cooled cookie into the chocolate and then into the nuts. Let the chocolate harden before serving.
Yield: 12 cookies

Apricot Yorkshire Tartlets
✣

Use 3-inch wide by ½-inch deep tart shells.

Tartlet Shells
➤ *1 cup all-purpose flour*
➤ *⅛ teaspoon salt*
➤ *2 tablespoons butter*
➤ *Cold water to mix*
Filling
➤ *¼ cup butter*
➤ *¼ cup sugar*
➤ *1 egg*
➤ *2 tablespoons finely ground almonds*
➤ *2 tablespoons self-rising flour, sifted*
➤ *2 drops almond extract*
➤ *2 drops vanilla extract*
➤ *2 tablespoons apricot jam*

1. In a medium bowl sift together the flour and salt. Cut in the butter until the mixture resembles fine bread crumbs. Add water as needed by the tablespoonful until a soft but not sticky dough forms. Turn the dough out onto a lightly floured surface and knead until smooth. Roll out the pastry to ⅛-inch thickness. Cut 5-inch circles to fit tart cups. Line each of 10 cups with a pastry circle.
2. Preheat the oven to 350°. In a small bowl cream together the butter and sugar. Add the egg and beat well. Add the almonds, flour, and extracts, and mix to a soft consistency. Place a small amount of the jam into each tartlet crust and top each with a teaspoon of filling. Bake the tartlets for 30 minutes. Cool them on a wire rack.
Yield: 10 tartlets

Walnut Viennese White Chocolate Cookie Whirls
✣

➤ *½ cup (1 stick) butter*
➤ *2 tablespoons confectioners' sugar, sifted*
➤ *½ cup plus 2 tablespoons all-purpose flour, sifted*
➤ *¾ cup white chocolate chips*
➤ *½ cup chopped walnuts*

1. In a small bowl cream the butter and sugar until very soft and white. Stir in the flour and mix well. (If the mixture seems too stiff, a few drops of milk may be added. The mixture is too stiff if it's too hard to pipe.) Put the mixture into a pastry tube fitted with a large star tip. Pipe the cookies onto a greased baking sheet in 1½-inch rosettes. Place the sheet in the refrigerator for 15 minutes.
2. Preheat the oven to 375°. Bake the cookies 10

Strawberry-Almond Battenberg Cake

❖

Battenberg cake was a popular English cake of the Victorian era. It is a colorful addition to any tea table.

Strawberry-Almond Battenburg Cake

Cake

- ➤ ¾ cup (1½ sticks) butter
- ➤ ¾ cup sugar
- ➤ 3 eggs, lightly beaten
- ➤ 2 cups self-rising flour
- ➤ 1 teaspoon vanilla extract
- ➤ 1 teaspoon strawberry extract
- ➤ 1 tablespoon strawberry jam
- ➤ Strawberries and kiwi slices for garnish

Paste

- ➤ 1½ cups finely ground almonds
- ➤ ¾ cup sugar
- ➤ ¾ cup confectioners' sugar
- ➤ 2 egg whites
- ➤ 1 teaspoon almond extract
- ➤ 3 tablespoons strawberry jelly, warmed

1. Grease and line a 7-inch square cake pan. Divide the pan by placing a piece of folded greaseproof paper down the center. (The pan sides should hold the paper up).
2. Preheat the oven to 350°. In a mixing bowl cream the butter and sugar until light and fluffy. Add the eggs and flour, and mix well. Divide the mixture in half. Add vanilla extract into one half and the strawberry extract and jam into the other.
3. Pour each mixture into half of the pan. Bake for about 50 minutes or until a tester inserted in both sides comes clean. Turn the cake out and cool it on a wire rack (discarding the paper divider. Trim the cake on all sides and cut each half into 2 even-sized sections. Sandwich them together with jam, alternating the colors white and pink, like a checkerboard. (See the finished cake.) Set it aside.
4. In a medium bowl combine the almonds, sugar, and confectioners' sugar. Blend in the egg whites and almond extract to make a soft dough. Knead until smooth. Set the dough aside.
5. Brush the warm jelly onto the outside edges of the cake. Dust the entire cake with confectioners' sugar.
6. Roll the almond paste into a square large enough to cover the top and sides of the cake. Place it over the cake, sealing well. Dust with confectioners' sugar. Decorate with strawberries and kiwi fruit slices.

Yield: 8 to 10 servings

Cheesecake in an art-deco room

Caramel Apple and Walnut No-Bake Cheesecake

❖

Cake

➤ 6 *tablespoons unflavored gelatin*
➤ 1 *cup boiling water*
➤ 2 *pounds cream cheese, room temperature*
➤ 2 *cups confectioners' sugar*
➤ 1 *cup heavy cream, lightly whipped*

Crumb Base

➤ 2 *cups graham cracker crumbs*
➤ 2 *tablespoons sugar*
➤ *½ cup (1 stick) butter*

Topping

➤ 2 *large red apples, cored, sliced, and chopped (peel left on for color)*
➤ *½ cup chopped walnuts*
➤ *Quality caramel topping*

1. Grease a 12-inch springform pan and line the bottom with waxed paper. In a small bowl dissolve the gelatin in water and let it cool.
2. In a mixing bowl combine the cream cheese and confectioners' sugar, and beat until light and fluffy. Add the gelatin and beat until thoroughly mixed. Fold in the whipped cream. Turn the mixture into the prepared pan and chill.
3. Blend together the crumb base ingredients. Sprinkle the mixture over the chilled cheese cake, pressing the crumbs into the surface lightly. Turn the cheese cake over, crumb-side down, and remove it from the pan. Top with the chopped apples and walnuts, and generously pour the caramel sauce over the top. Serve.

Yield: 10 to 12 servings

Raspberry Pavlova

❖

Ballerina Anna Pavlova was so well liked that a dessert was designed in her honor by an Austrian baker who was enamored with the dancer's talents. This soft meringue nest of vanilla custard with a fruit topping is as delicate as a pirouette frozen in time.

➤ *4 eggs, separated*
➤ *½ cup plus 2 tablespoons sugar*
➤ *1 tablespoon cornstarch*
➤ *1 cup evaporated milk*
➤ *½ teaspoon vanilla extract*
➤ *2 16-ounce packages frozen raspberries, thawed and drained*
➤ *Whipped cream for garnish*

Making the foundation for the Pavlova

1. Preheat the oven to 300°. In a large bowl beat the egg whites until stiff peaks form. Add ¼ cup of the sugar and beat again until thick. Fold in ¼ cup more of the sugar.
2. Using a metal spoon transfer the mixture into a large pastry bag fitted with a star tip. Pipe a 12-inch circle of meringue mixture onto a baking sheet, filling the center of the circle to make a base. Pipe around the edge of the circle to build up the sides. Bake the meringue on the lowest shelf of the oven for 2 to 3 hours, or until it is completely dried out. (**Note:** If you line the baking sheet with waxed paper or tin foil before piping out the meringue base, you will know the meringue is done when it releases freely from the foil.)
3. In a separate bowl mix the cornstarch and remaining sugar with a teaspoon or so of the milk to make a smooth paste. Set the paste aside.
4. In a small saucepan bring the remaining milk to a boil. Pour the hot milk over the cornstarch mixture and return it to the pan. Bring the mixture back to a boil and stir constantly until thick. Cook for 2 to 3 minutes more, stirring constantly. Add the egg yolks and vanilla. Beat well and heat through gently. Do not boil. Remove the pan from the heat and let it sit until cooled.
5. Spread cold vanilla cream into the Pavlova base. Arrange the raspberry mixture over the vanilla cream and decorate with whipped cream, if desired.

Yield. 10 to 12 servings

Enchanted Evenings

The soft, extractive note of an aged cork being
withdrawn has the true sound of a man
opening his heart.

William Samuel Benwell

Antrim 1844, Taneytown, Maryland

Twilight Dining in the Vineyard

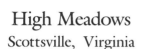

High Meadows
Scottsville, Virginia

INNKEEPER/CHEF PETER SUSHKA

Dinner for Two

Baked Smoked Salmon and Feta Cheese en Croûte

•

Tenderloin Tips of Roast Venison au Vin Rouge

•

Poached Stuffed Chicken in Tomato-Wine Sauce

•

Baked Plum Tomato au Gratin

•

Cinnamon Cappucino Torte

I had just returned from scouting the twenty-three acres surrounding the inn, including the five that host the inn's grapes, now clipped and dormant for the season. With my feet propped gingerly on a dainty antique footstool and a cup of hot herbal tea in hand, I warmed my fingers by a wood stove in one of the inn's parlors and imagined the sight of the grapes in full bloom at harvest time.

When the temperature is just right and the grapes are robust and hearty, inn guests help pluck the white and red jewels, which get pressed and bottled at Simeon Vineyards in nearby Charlottesville. The inn's special vin gris grapes have been praised by wine aficionados, including *The Wine Spectator* magazine.

High Meadows is the rare country inn

that grows and harvests grapes for production and bottling, and Peter Sushka likes to use the results of the harvest in his cooking, as you can see in the recipes here. He strongly advises using only quality wine. "The cheaper wines are made from remainder grapes and you need a quality grape to hold the robust and hearty flavor in cooking," he says.

The Sushkas want everyone to celebrate the pleasure of fine wines; so most weekends include a wine-tasting where Peter and his wife and fellow innkeeper, Jae Abbitt, mix with their guests, pouring the wine and serving Peter's hors d'oeuvres. As the Sushkas' dinner party progresses, everyone is escorted to the two small dining rooms with fireplaces, next to Peter's kitchen in the basement of the house.

This is a most appropriate spot for the fruits of Peter's labors. The chef, who dons a Thomas Jefferson shirt and knickers in keeping with the inn's location not far from Thomas Jefferson's Monticello, is accustomed to cooking down below. It was not that long ago that he wore the uniform of the U.S. Navy and spent many of his days underwater in a submarine, managing food supplies and other day-to-day operations.

As a chief officer aboard submarines during his thirty-year naval career, Peter had to ensure that the cooking on board helped ease the mundane routine of sea life for those who could be underwater for as many as ninety days at a stretch. "Pleasant meals would keep their morale up," says Peter. He applies that same thinking at the inn, reinforcing the old maxim about the way to one's heart being through the stomach.

Peter's underground food galley at High Meadows is a cheerful place. Light streams through a window at ground-level, spreading onto a terra-cotta tile island where Peter is maestro over the pots and pans. It is a homey kitchen, open to guests who might amble in for a chat with the chef about cooking and wine.

"We planted the grapes before we put in the plumbing and heating," Peter says, still amazed at his and Jae's renovations at High Meadows. Originally, Peter, Jae, and the family had to live in one room where they had a constant fire going to keep warm. "Had to do it that way," notes Peter. "We knew it would take several years before we saw a harvest."

They actually had to renovate two houses—an 1832 Federal and a late Victorian—that were uniquely built only a few feet away from each other because the original owners both wanted to take advantage of the views. An airy hallway now connects the two buildings and serves as the inn's check-in post. And the Sushkas' restoration of the property has earned High Meadows a place on the National Register of Historic Places.

There is often a choice of milieu for dinner at High Meadows. Guests may eat in either of the two intimate dining rooms underground, of course. But they also have the choice of taking a European-style supper basket to their quiet room in winter or anywhere on the grounds in warm weather.

"In America we have our tailgate parties. In Europe they have their supper baskets," quips the chef. Each basket is filled with china, crystal, linens, and, of course, a meal for two. That's why I asked Peter to provide this romantic menu for two at home. Why not pack it into your own supper basket and steal away one night?

High Meadows is fully dedicated to pampering guests and lavishing them with just enough attention, yet leaving them to their own romantic interludes.

With this dedication to guests and grapes, there are twice as many reasons for a visit. There's double everything to be found here in these two historic houses—twice the number of common rooms and antique-laden guest rooms and double the warmth and cheer from Peter and Jae. A nice place indeed for a dinner for two.

Baked Smoked Salmon and Feta Cheese en Croûte

1. Preheat the oven to 375°. In a medium bowl hand mix the salmon, cream cheese, Feta cheese, egg, capers, parsley, and scallions.
2. Roll out the pastry sheet to double its size. Liberally brush it with the melted butter. Spread the salmon mixture over the sheet.
3. Roll up jelly roll-style, folding the ends in to seal. Brush the top of the roll with melted butter and sprinkle with poppy seeds. Make ½-inch deep diagonal slashes across the roll to allow steam to escape. Place the roll on a small baking sheet. Bake the roll for 20 to 30 minutes or until golden. Serve warm.
Yield: 2 servings

Baked Smoked Salmon and Feta Cheese en Croûte
❖

You may also serve this dish as a light meal for one person, accompanied by a green salad.

➤ *3 ounces quality smoked salmon, diced*
➤ *6 ounces cream cheese, softened*
➤ *3 ounces Feta cheese*
➤ *1 egg, slightly beaten*
➤ *1 teaspoon capers*
➤ *2 tablespoons finely chopped parsley*
➤ *4 scallions (green tops only), finely diced*
➤ *1 frozen pastry sheet, cut into a 3 x 8-inch rectangle*
➤ *Melted butter*
➤ *1 tablespoon or more poppy seeds*

Tenderloin Tips of Roast Venison au Vin Rouge
❖

Marinade
➤ *1 pound venison roast, cut into 1-inch cubes*
➤ *2 cups red wine*
➤ *1 cup red wine vinegar*
➤ *¼ cup olive oil*
Preparation
➤ *3 ounces (3 strips) bacon cut into 3 pieces each*
➤ *2 tablespoons all-purpose flour*
➤ *1 teaspoon black pepper*
➤ *2 cloves garlic, chopped and mashed*
➤ *1 cup red wine*
➤ *1 tablespoon tomato paste*
➤ *1 teaspoon dried thyme*
➤ *1 bay leaf*
➤ *1 to 2 tablespoons butter*
➤ *½ pound button mushrooms, sliced*
➤ *¼ pound shiitake mushrooms, sliced*
➤ *10 pearl onions, sliced*

1. In a medium glass bowl marinate the venison in the red wine, vinegar, and oil for at least 24 hours. Drain and reserve the marinade. Pat the venison dry with a paper towel.

2. Preheat the oven to 350°. In a large skillet cook the bacon, adding the venison when the fat from the bacon begins to render. (Do not remove the bacon.) Cook the venison cubes on one side. Sprinkle with 1 tablespoon of the flour and ½ teaspoon of the pepper. Stir and cook over medium heat until browned on both sides. Add the garlic and remaining flour and pepper.
3. Pour the contents into a 2-quart casserole. Add the reserved marinade, the additional cup of red wine, tomato paste, thyme, and bay leaf. Bake for 2 hours or until the venison is tender.
4. In a medium skillet heat the butter and sauté the mushrooms and onions until tender and lightly browned. Add the mixture to the casserole, tossing gently to incorporate. Bake for another 30 minutes. Remove the bay leaf and serve.

Yield: 2 servings

The atmosphere of a European bistro at High Meadows

Poached Stuffed Chicken in Tomato-Wine Sauce

ture in the center of each breast. Reserve any remaining filling for the sauce. Roll each breast up around the filling. Place each breast at one end of a 5-inch-square piece of plastic wrap. Roll the wrap tightly around the breast and twist at each end. Repeat with the same size square of aluminum foil.

2. Bring a 3-quart pot of water to a boil. Drop the foil-covered breasts into the water and boil them for 20 minutes at a moderate boil.

3. In a medium skillet heat the oil over medium heat and sauté the leek, mushrooms, and tomatoes until tender, about 10 minutes. Add the flour, mix thoroughly, and cook for an additional 5 minutes. Add the wine and remaining pepper-and-cheese mixture. Simmer over low heat until ready to use.

4. Remove the breasts from the water. Unwrap each carefully and slice into 1-inch thick diagonal pieces. Place the slices on a platter and spoon the tomato-wine sauce over them just before serving.
Yield: 2 servings

Poached Stuffed Chicken in Tomato-Wine Sauce

❖

➤ *½ each red, green, and yellow bell peppers, diced*

➤ *8 ounces Feta cheese, crumbled*

➤ *2 boneless chicken breasts, pounded to ¼-inch thickness*

   Tomato-Wine Sauce

➤ *1 tablespoon olive oil*

➤ *1 leek (white end only) finely chopped*

➤ *¼ pound mushrooms, chopped*

➤ *2 medium tomatoes, chopped*

➤ *1½ tablespoons all-purpose flour*

➤ *½ cup white wine*

1. In a medium bowl combine the peppers and cheese. Place 2 to 3 tablespoons of the mix-

Baked Plum Tomato au Gratin

❖

➤ *1 ripe plum or Italian tomato*

➤ *1 tablespoon butter*

➤ *¼ cup seasoned dry bread crumbs*

➤ *⅛ cup freshly grated Parmesan cheese*

➤ *⅛ teaspoon each sage, basil, and oregano*

1. Preheat the oven to 350°. Cut the tomato in half lengthwise.

2. In a small bowl combine the butter, bread crumbs, cheese, and herbs. Spoon a tablespoon of the mixture onto each tomato half. Place the tomato halves on a baking sheet. Bake for 30 minutes. Serve.
Yield: 2 servings

A ripe harvest bursts forth in the inn's vineyard.

Cinnamon Cappucino Torte

❖

A marriage of chocolate and coffee flavors kisses a crunchy chocolate wafer and gingersnap cookie center. Surprisingly easy to prepare!

➤ *1 pint quality coffee ice cream*
➤ *4 chocolate wafer cookies, coarsely crushed*
➤ *1 pint chocolate ice cream*
➤ *4 gingersnap cookies, coarsely crushed*
➤ *¼ cup heavy cream, whipped stiffly with ¾ tablespoon sugar*
➤ *Cinnamon*

1. Evenly cover the bottom of 2 8-ounce ramekins with a layer of coffee ice cream. Sprinkle a layer of chocolate wafer crumbs over the ice cream. Spoon a layer of chocolate ice cream over the crumbs and press down with the back of a spoon. Sprinkle ginger-snap crumbs on top and add a second layer of coffee ice cream, pressing down with the back of the spoon. Cover ramekins with aluminum foil and freeze for 5 hours or overnight.
2. Whip the cream with the sugar. To serve the tortes run a knife dipped in hot water around the inside of the ramekins. Invert the tortes onto a plate. Spoon whipped cream on top, and sprinkle with cinnamon.
Yield: 2 tortes

An Evening of Wine and Roses

The Inn at Blackberry Farm
Walland, Tennessee

CHEF GREGG REITER

Dinner for Eight

Warm Asparagus Salad with
Mountain Trout Cakes

•

Roasted Quail-Rosemary with
Citrus Marinade

•

Mushroom Duxelle with
White Wine

•

Creamy Saffron Risotto

•

Hearts-A-Bustin' Blackberry Tarts with
Caramel and Raspberry Sauces

Here in the valley dusk came early, with the ranges that formed the Great Smokies cutting off the sun . . . Colors of bark and beige and rust had been used on the furniture . . . The walls were a light neutral color that added to the sense of stillness. Both ends of the room were solid background, with only clerestory windows set high at one end, lending a translucence to the room. All the rest of the glass was across the front, opening out upon the mountains, decorating the room with a magnificent view . . . the mountains out there running to the horizon in every direction, and the sky painting the ceiling.

Phyllis A. Whitney
The Glass Flame

An ethereal mist kisses Blackberry Farm good morning.

Well-known novelist Phyllis Whitney could have been describing the marvelous Smoky Mountain vista I found at the Inn at Blackberry Farm. The author's words aptly capture the feeling that washes over all who explore Blackberry Farm's main parlor, delightful guest rooms, and vast property.

Raves about the scenery are far from the only praises guests sing while visiting this unique mountain estate. Many memorable poetic verses and song lyrics come to mind and elicit a hankering to hum merrily.

For instance, there are the lyrics from Paul McCartney's song about playing his piano keyboard side-by-side in perfect harmony, which is just what Blackberry Farm is all about: perfect harmony. It is a magical place for an evening of wine and roses.

While the guest house is decorated in Brunschwig & Fils, other designer fabrics, European antiques, and owners Kreis and Sandy Beall's treasured collectibles, this is not a look-but-don't-touch inn. In fact, the emphasis is on activity on Blackberry Farm's 1,100 acres before you earn that evening with candles, flowers, and wine.

Get out those creel baskets and rubber waders, and cast a line into the inn's trout pond. Chef Gregg Reiter will prepare your catch for dinner or breakfast, if you wish. Such casual angling is so much a part of the inn that Kreis has decorated one of the inn's Christmas trees at holiday time in a fishing theme with miniature creels, rods, and lures. If biking suits your fancy, hop onto a mountain bike and tour the surrounding ridges. Grab a walking stick and go hiking with a blanket, nature book, binoculars, and the chef's backpacker picnic of sumptuous and healthy noshes. Play tennis, stroll about the putting green, or just relax on a porch rocker with the panoramic mountain view before you.

Blackberry Farm is a sanctuary for the romantic, the young at heart, and, of course, the discriminating gourmet. Major corporations find this site to be ever so conducive to executive meetings and retreats. Dinner is a voluptuous affair with owner Kreis and inn-keepers Gary and Bernadette Doyle insisting on only the freshest ingredients.

Set under candlelight in intimate dining rooms, a blackberry-patterned Lavinia china by Royal Worcestershire is the canvas for Gregg's artwork, and that of chefs John Charles Fleer and Curtis Smith. Fleer was a private chef to Mary Tyler Moore, and Smith formerly worked at the Old Drover's Inn in New York. The food is New American with a Southern bent. You might find Cajun shrimp or an antebellum bean ragout, and a chocolate bread pudding. There are also some native Tennessee mountain dishes of barbecued smoked pork, briskets, and ribs. "We aren't doing spa cuisine because guests don't want that," says Gregg. "But all of our dishes are prepared with a healthy outlook."

The chef came to Blackberry Farm two years ago with a degree in hotel restaurant management and after a two-year apprenticeship with Dutch master chef Victor Cielisse.

"I think the hardest thing about entertaining at home is the coordination," notes Gregg. "Make notes about what you will need to do when guests arrive, even if you have to put them on the serving trays you're going to use.

"Get to know as many kitchen tips as you can, such as freezing stocks in ice cube trays and storing them in freezer bags so you always have small portions when needed. Get a jump start on your dinner, and you'll begin to really enjoy entertaining."

Although Gary and Bernadette have been running the day-to-day operations of the inn for the past decade, Kreis is very much a part of Blackberry Farm. She is a savvy, elegant hostess with impeccable taste that is reflected in the inn and a separate guest cottage—a one hundred-year-old, post-and-beam house decorated in French

Asparagus Salad with Mountain Trout Cakes

country blues and whites that could make the cover of the most discriminating home and living magazines. Guest rooms in the main house are all named after flowers, and each is a study in individual art.

After dinner on cool, moonlit evenings, the mountains take on another personality. Many inn guests huddle by the bonfire prepared by the Blackberry Farm staff. You can toast marshmallows, have a nightcap, and wrap yourself up in Kreis's woolen blankets while a story is read or gentle banter is exchanged among new friends. At Blackberry Farm it is always an evening of wine and roses—and a whole lot more.

Warm Asparagus Salad with Mountain Trout Cakes

You can make this recipe with crabmeat instead of the trout.

Asparagus Preparation

➤ 24 pencil-thin asparagus shoots, peeled and woody ends snapped

➤ ¼ cup extra virgin olive oil

➤ ¼ cup salad oil

➤ 2 garlic cloves, peeled and quartered

➤ 1 tablespoon freshly chopped rosemary, or ½ teaspoon dried

➤ ¼ cup balsamic vinegar

➤ Salt and pepper to taste

Trout Cakes

➤ 3 eggs

➤ 3 tablespoons heavy cream

➤ 1 tablespoon Dijon mustard

➤ 1 teaspoon Worcestershire sauce

➤ 2 teaspoons Old Bay seasoning

➤ ⅛ teaspoon cayenne pepper

➤ Freshly ground black pepper to taste

➤ 3 tablespoons minced scallions

➤ 2 tablespoons minced parsley

➤ ½ cup mayonnaise (preferably homemade)

➤ 2 pounds fresh trout, boned and poached

➤ ¼ cup finely crushed soda crackers

➤ 1 cup fine bread crumbs

➤ 1 tablespoon or more butter

➤ 2 tablespoons or more oil

➤ Lemon slices for garnish

➤ Fresh tomato slices for garnish

1. Bring a large saucepan filled with water to a boil. Add the asparagus and cook for 5 minutes. Plunge the asparagus into an ice-water bath. Drain well and set aside.

2. In a large skillet heat the oil over medium heat and sauté the garlic and rosemary until the garlic just begins to brown. Remove the garlic. Add the vinegar and seasonings to the pan and set it aside.

3. In a large bowl whisk the eggs. Add the cream, mustard, Worcestershire sauce, Old Bay seasoning, cayenne, and black pepper, and whisk until well-blended. Add the scallions, parsley, and mayonnaise, and mix until well blended. Gently fold in the trout and soda crackers, taking care to break up the trout as little as possible. Form the mixture into 24 small cakes of equal size and coat each cake lightly with the bread crumbs. Place the cakes on a baking sheet, cover with plastic wrap, and chill for 1 hour.

4. In a large heavy skillet over medium heat melt half of the butter and add half of the oil. Add 4 trout cakes, sautéing 3 to 4 minutes on each side until golden brown. Drain on paper towels. Keep warm. Repeat the process with the remaining trout cakes, using the remaining butter and oil, or more if needed. Sprinkle chopped parsley on each cooked trout cake.

5. To assemble, reheat the vinaigrette in the saucepan, but do not boil. Place the asparagus in boiling water and heat through for 1 minute. Slice each spear in half. Arrange 6 half-spears on each salad plate. Pour the vinaigrette over the asparagus. Place 3 trout cakes on each plate. Garnish with lemon and tomato, if desired.

Yield: 8 servings

Sporting gear awaits the adventuresome.

Roasted Quail-Rosemary with Citrus Marinade

❖

- ➤ 24 5- to 6-ounce quail
- ➤ 3 cups olive oil
- ➤ ½ cup balsamic vinegar
- ➤ 3 tablespoons Worcestershire sauce
- ➤ 3 tablespoons soy sauce
- ➤ 2 tablespoons coarse black pepper
- ➤ 2 medium onions, diced
- ➤ 6 cloves garlic, coarsely chopped
- ➤ 1 cup chopped fresh rosemary or 2 tablespoons dried
- ➤ 1 cup orange juice

1. Tie the quail legs together with cotton string. Place the birds in a baking pan.
2. In a medium bowl mix together the remaining ingredients and pour the marinade over the birds. Marinate them in the refrigerator overnight.
3. Preheat ːn to 450°. Drain and reserve the marinade. Place the quail in a roasting pan in the top third of the oven and bake for 10 minutes. Reduce the heat to 400° and bake for 25 minutes. Baste with the marinade every 10 minutes. Remove the strings and serve the quail with the Mushroom Duxelles on the side. Serve at least 2 quail per person.
Yield: 24 quail

Mushroom Duxelle with White Wine

❖

- ➤ ¼ cup (½ stick) butter
- ➤ 2 shallots, chopped
- ➤ 2 pounds domestic mushrooms, cleaned and quartered
- ➤ ¼ cup white wine
- ➤ 1 clove garlic, minced
- ➤ Salt and pepper to taste

In a large skillet melt the butter and sauté the shallots for 1 minute. Add the mushrooms and sauté until tender. Add the white wine. Increase heat and reduce the wine until syrupy. Stir in the garlic and remove the pan from heat. Season and serve.
Yield: 8 servings

Creamy Saffron Risotto

❖

- ➤ ½ cup (1 stick) butter
- ➤ 1 large onion, chopped
- ➤ 1½ teaspoons chopped garlic
- ➤ 1½ teaspoons saffron
- ➤ 3 cups Arborio Italian rice
- ➤ ½ cup dry white wine
- ➤ 7½ cups chicken stock
- ➤ ½ cup (1 stick) butter
- ➤ ¾ cup Parmesan cheese

In a 5-quart saucepan melt the butter and sauté the onion and garlic until transparent. Stir in the saffron. Add the rice, mixing it in well. Add the wine and cook until it evaporates. Stir in the stock, ½ cup at a time, adding each ½ cup as the previous is absorbed. Cook the rice uncovered over medium heat until all of the liquid is absorbed, about 20 to 30 minutes. Remove the pan from the heat. Stir in the butter and Parmesan, and fluff the rice.
Yield: 8 to 10 servings

Roasted Quail Rosemary in regal company

Hearts-a-Bustin' Blackberry Tarts with Caramel and Raspberry Sauces

These are named after a native Tennessee wild-flower and one of the rooms at the inn. The flower compels your attention in early autumn when its wine-colored pods burst open, revealing brilliant red seeds. In this recipe you're building your own free-form tart shells from puff pastry. The tarts sit on top of a bed of sauces and are filled with custard and fresh blackberries or other berries in season. It's really easy to make and yields an elegant, romantic dessert.

Tart Shells
➤ 1 17¼-ounce package frozen puff pastry, thawed
➤ 1 egg
➤ 1 tablespoon heavy cream

Brandied Caramel Sauce
➤ 2 cups sugar
➤ 3 cups water
➤ ½ cup blackberry liqueur

Raspberry Sauce
➤ 1¼ pounds raspberries
➤ ½ cup lemon-lime soda
➤ ¼ cup maple syrup

Custard
➤ 3 eggs
➤ ¾ cup sugar
➤ ⅔ cup sifted all-purpose flour
➤ 1½ cups heavy cream
➤ 4 tablespoons pear liqueur

Assembly
➤ Tart shells
➤ Raspberry and Caramel sauces
➤ 6 cups fresh blackberries or other berries in season

1. Separate the pastry sheets. Cut 24 strips of pastry, each ¼-inch wide. Set them aside.
2. Roll out a sheet of pastry very thin. Cut out heart-shaped pastries, about 3 inches wide and 3 inches long, repeating until 12 hearts have been cut.
3. Preheat the oven to 375°. Cut a piece of parchment paper to fit a cookie sheet. Place the hearts on the parchment. In a small bowl whisk together the egg and cream, and brush the mixture onto each heart. To build the sides of the heart, add 2 pastry strips around the edges of each heart, sealing with egg wash. (Cut off any excess length.) With a fork poke holes in the bottom of the tarts to avoid rising. Place the hearts in the refrigerator for 15 minutes, until chilled. Bake the shells for 20 to 25 minutes, until golden.
4. In a small saucepan over high heat cook the sugar and water until they turn amber in color. Add the brandy and keep the mixture warm.
5. In a blender purée the raspberries with the lemon-lime soda and maple syrup. Strain the mixture and set it aside.
6. In a medium bowl beat the eggs with the sugar until thick and pale yellow in color. Add the flour, mixing well. In a small saucepan heat the cream until boiling. Slowly pour the cream into the egg mixture, whisking con-

Blackberry Tart with Caramel and Raspberry Sauce

stantly. Add the pear liqueur. Strain the custard and set it aside to cool. Fill each tart evenly with custard sauce and top with berries. Reserve some of the custard sauce. Set the tarts aside.

7. To assemble, spoon the raspberry sauce into the bottom of the plate to cover. Add a small amount of custard in the middle of the raspberry sauce. Add a ring of caramel sauce around the edge of the plate. Run the point of a knife from the custard out to the edge of the plate. Repeat around the plate. Then do the opposite between each knife line, bringing the point from the plate edge into the custard so that it forms a "bustin' heart." (See the photo at left on page 90.) Place a tart in the center of each plate. Serve.

Yield: 12 tarts

Everything at Blackberry Farm is a study in still life.

Black Ties and White Lace

Antrim 1844
Taneytown, Maryland

CHEF MICHAEL SELL

Buffet for 50

❖

Spiced Apple and Pepper Chutney

◆

Russian Blinis with Caviar

◆

*Lobster Bisque with White Wine
and Cognac*

◆

Southern Maryland Stuffed Ham

◆

*Lady Baltimore Cake with Blackberry and
Chambord Filling*

A handsome card arrived in the post. The gilded print was an invitation to Dorothy and Richard Mollet's Antrim 1844 plantation inn. Renoir's painting of a refined couple waltzing, *Danse à la Ville*, beckoned me to a black-tie affair. Just what one might expect from the keepers of Antrim. They do everything with fourteen-carat grandeur, right down to the fashioning of china with the inn's logo and a thick gold rim. This was to be a celebration of the inn's success in its first two years of hosting strangers in antebellum luxury.

"They said we were crazy," remembers Dort. "But here we are." In just a short time the inn has garnered the favor of several magazines; the most notable article was an unusually long *Colonial Homes* piece—eleven pages of text and photos—on the beauty of Antrim.

Dort attributes much of this attention to the inn's rich architectural history. Built by a prosperous farmer as the centerpiece of his 450-acre plantation in the mid-nineteenth century, Antrim derives its name from the owner's kinship with County Antrim in Ireland. Slaves constructed the manor house with bricks fired on the property. Many of these bricks form the cinnamon-colored walls of the rustic smokehouse where candlelit dinners invite fireside chats in front of a cozy hearth.

Indeed, the original seventeen-room mansion—with endless examples of distinguished woodwork and massive windows—is truly a study in ideal design. Dort is far too modest when she credits these features, the slave outbuildings, and the gardens as the main attraction, for Dort is an interior designer and a wizard of the sewing machine. She did all of the fabric work at Antrim and coordinated it with bold wallpapers and dramatic artwork. Her own handiwork is another reason Antrim is so heralded.

The inn is graced with prized antiques collected by Richard and Dort, who have made a serious hobby of restoring old homes. All around are oriental dishes, including an assortment of rose medallion bowls. There are antique settles and sideboards, Ming vases, crystal chandeliers, and Persian tapestry.

But for all its stateliness, the Mollets have dreamed up a sophisticated inn that also embodies the lighter side of life. On display in the library, where chef Michael Sell renders his special apple chutney (see recipe) with tea and other libations, are a number of whimsical old head pieces—a pith helmet, a top hat, and a British chapeau. In the second-floor hallway, a wooden butler, affectionately known as James, stands sentinel outside each of the four guest rooms. In the morning he proffers a newspaper, muffins, and coffee only as a prelude

An invitation arrives in the mail.

to a sumptuous breakfast in the grand dining room. At night James is at each door with sherry.

Serving dinner at the inn was not something Dort or Richard had planned; but one request for dinner led to another, and soon Antrim began offering dinner on Saturdays. Overnight guests and the dining public responded so well to the delectables of Michael's kitchen that the inn now serves dinner Thursday through Sunday and hosts weddings and other parties.

The night I was there for their own fête, the Mollets served up smoked salmon, duckling, many more tasty appetizers, and desserts—a specialty of this chef. In fact, when Michael was only fifteen, he was already filling orders for elaborate wedding cakes.

Michael, also an interior decorator, approaches cooking as he does decorating. He uses his imagination to pull various ingre-

gardens. Floral fabrics bloom in the guest rooms where imposing beds—as tall as the top of a traditional stuffed wing chair—enthrone you. And oh, you do not need a proper invitation by post to visit. Just call for a reservation. The ever-faithful James is always in black tie and white gloves to host you, too.

Spiced Apple and Pepper Chutney

❖

Serve the chutney with cream cheese and crackers.

- ➤ *2 quarts tart apples, cored, peeled, and coarsely chopped*
- ➤ *1 cup minced, seeded red and green bell peppers*
- ➤ *1 clove garlic, minced*
- ➤ *1 cup minced yellow onion*
- ➤ *1 pound raisins*
- ➤ *1 pound dark brown sugar*
- ➤ *1 pint cider vinegar*
- ➤ *1 tablespoon each ginger, cinnamon, cloves, and nutmeg*
- ➤ *2 teaspoons powdered mustard*
- ➤ *2 teaspoons salt*
- ➤ *¼ teaspoon crushed, dried red hot chili peppers*

---

1. Preheat the oven to 250°. Stand 4 (1-pint) canning jars and their tops on a baking sheet. Place them in the oven until needed.
2. In a large non-reactive pan combine all of the ingredients. Cover and bring the mixture to a slow boil. Uncover and simmer, stirring occasionally, for 1½ hours, until the mixture thickens.
3. Ladle the hot mixture into the warm jars, filling each within ⅛ inch of the top. Wipe the rims and seal. Cool and store the chutney. **Yield: 4 pints**

dients together, and it always seems to work. "I hardly ever make a dish the same way twice," says the chef, whose style is regional with a European flare. "I just look at something, decide it doesn't have enough color, and then add ingredients that I know will work to give it some added appeal."

With the black-tie menu, Michael advises getting help to serve the food. You may wish to do as they did at Antrim: passing out hors d'oeuvres by the tray-full and then letting guests help themselves to the banquet table for the main courses. Add more favorites of your own to this sampling of party recipes, as Antrim did for their party of fifty. You may want to add to or cut down the recipe ingredients in Michael's menu, depending on how large a party you are giving.

Visiting Antrim inspires imaginings of the privileged side of plantation life. Dwell for a night amid the charms of a romantically restored ice house. Embrace the enchantments of the gazebo and variegated

Lobster Bisque and Antrim's gold-rim china with inn logo

Russian Blinis with Caviar

❖

Blinis are traditional Russian wheat pancakes that often host chopped salmon or puffs of sour cream or crème fraîche. Here they are made bite-size for hors d'oeuvres.

➤ *1 package active dry yeast*
➤ *1½ cups warm water (115°)*
➤ *1½ cups all-purpose flour*
➤ *1½ cups buckwheat (or whole-wheat) flour*
➤ *3 eggs, separated*
➤ *¼ cup melted, unsalted butter*
➤ *⅛ teaspoon salt*
➤ *1 teaspoon sugar*
➤ *1½ cups warm milk (115°)*
➤ *Sour cream or crème fraîche*
➤ *Red and black caviar*

1. In a medium bowl combine the yeast and warm water. Set the mixture in a warm place for 15 to 20 minutes. Slowly add the all-purpose flour. Cover the mixture with a kitchen towel and let it rise in a warm place for 1 hour.
2. In a separate bowl combine the buckwheat flour, egg yolks, butter, salt, sugar, and milk. Add the mixture to the dough. Stir well to blend all of the ingredients. Cover and let the batter rise for 1 hour.
3. Just before cooking, beat the egg whites until stiff. Fold them into the batter.
4. Heat a greased, heavy griddle over medium-high heat. Drop the batter on the griddle by the tablespoon, cooking each pancake until browned on both sides.
5. Allow the blinis to cool slightly. Place a dollop of sour cream or crème fraîche on each blini. Top with red and black caviar.
Yield: 75 blinis

Lobster Bisque with White Wine and Cognac

❖

- ➤ 12 to 14 pounds cooked lobster
- ➤ 4 large white onions, diced
- ➤ 1 bunch celery, diced
- ➤ 6 to 8 medium carrots, diced
- ➤ 3 anchovy fillets
- ➤ 2½ cups dry white wine
- ➤ 4 teaspoons sea salt
- ➤ 4 teaspoons whole black peppercorns
- ➤ 1 teaspoon mace
- ➤ 8 to 10 tablespoons unsalted butter
- ➤ 1 cup grated onion
- ➤ 2 tablespoons all-purpose flour
- ➤ 5 cups half-and-half
- ➤ 5 to 6 cups milk
- ➤ 9 to 10 cups lobster shell broth (see step 2)
- ➤ Salt and freshly ground pepper to taste
- ➤ ⅛ teaspoon cayenne pepper
- ➤ 5 tablespoons cognac (optional)
- ➤ ¼ cup Old Bay seasoning

1. Remove all of the meat from the lobster shells. Dice it and place it in the refrigerator.
2. Crush the shells and place them in a large stock pot with the onion, celery, carrots, anchovies, white wine, salt, peppercorns, and mace. Add water to barely cover. Simmer the broth for 45 minutes, skimming as necessary. Strain through a cheesecloth. There should be 5 to 6 quarts of broth; reserve 9 to 10 cups and freeze the remainder.
3. In a large stock pot melt the butter over medium heat and sauté the grated onion until softened but not browned, about 10 minutes. Sprinkle the flour over the onion and cook for 5 minutes, being careful not to burn the flour. Stir in the half-and-half, milk, and lobster broth. Season with salt and peppers, and cook for 10 minutes, stirring occasionally.

4. Stir in the lobster meat and add the cognac. Heat the soup over low heat for another 5 minutes. Add the Old Bay seasoning. Serve hot in bowls with a sprig of parsley and dusting of paprika.
Yield: 50 ½-cup servings

Southern Maryland Stuffed Ham

❖

The ham may be made up to four days ahead. Go easier on the cayenne if you wish, but the seemingly large quantity given provides a hearty flavor.

- ➤ 1 16- to 20-pound cured ham
- ➤ 2½ pounds fresh kale leaves and tender stems, chopped
- ➤ 2½ pounds fresh cabbage, diced
- ➤ 2 pounds yellow onions, finely diced
- ➤ 4 bunches green onions, finely diced
- ➤ 2 tablespoons celery seed
- ➤ 2 tablespoons mustard seed
- ➤ 1½ tablespoons salt
- ➤ 1 tablespoon freshly ground black pepper
- ➤ ¼ cup cayenne pepper

1. Trim the ham of rind and fat. In a saucepan blanch the kale and cabbage in boiling water for 5 minutes. Drain and reserve the liquid. Run the kale and cabbage under cold water and drain, pressing to extract the excess liquid. In a large bowl mix together the kale, cabbage, onions, celery and mustard seeds, salt, and peppers.
2. Preheat the oven to 325°. Make deep slits in the ham, perpendicular to the bone. Pack the slits with the vegetable mixture, pushing the mixture into each slit until packed firmly. Cover the ham with the remaining stuffing.
3. Wrap the ham in a large piece of tightly

woven cheesecloth, using kitchen twine to secure. Place the ham in a large stockpot with a rack on the bottom to prevent sticking. Cover with the reserved vegetable liquid. Cook the ham for 20 minutes per pound or until the ham is heated through, allowing the stuffing flavors to penetrate.

4. Store the ham in the refrigerator until 2 hours before the party. Remove the cheesecloth. Let the ham sit at room temperature. Slice the ham thinly from the top down toward the base. Serve with cheese and biscuits.
Yield: 1 stuffed ham for buffet of 50

This candle-lit bed is one of Antrim's many unusual sleeping frames.

Lady Baltimore Cake with Blackberry and Chambord Filling

❖

Bite into this heavenly cake and you may feel as though its soft-cloud texture and bejeweled middle are food for the angels. Add cookies and another dessert for your buffet for fifty.

➤ 2½ cups sifted cake flour
➤ 1 tablespoon baking powder
➤ ½ teaspoon salt
➤ ⅔ cup butter
➤ 1½ cups sugar
➤ 1 teaspoon vanilla extract
➤ ½ teaspoon almond extract
➤ ¾ cup milk
➤ 4 egg whites, at room temperature
   Filling
➤ 1 20-ounce can red blackberries, drained
➤ 1 12-ounce jar seedless blackberry jam
➤ ¼ cup Chambord liqueur
   Frosting
➤ 1 cup vegetable shortening
➤ 1 pound confectioners' sugar
➤ 1 teaspoon vanilla extract
➤ ¼ cup water
➤ 1 pound shredded coconut

1. Preheat the oven to 375°. In a medium bowl sift the flour with the baking powder and salt.
2. In a large bowl cream the butter with an electric mixer on high speed and then add the sugar, reserving ¼ cup of sugar. Beat until fluffy. Add the extracts. Reduce the speed to low and mix in the dry ingredients alternately with the milk, ending with the dry ingredients. Set the batter aside.
3. In a separate bowl beat the egg whites until frothy. Slowly add the remaining sugar and beat until very soft peaks form. Fold the egg whites into the batter.
4. Spoon the batter into 2 greased and lined 9-inch round layer cake pans. Bake the cake 25 minutes or until the cake shrinks from the sides of the pan and springs back to the touch. Cool upright on racks. Remove the cake from the pans.
5. In a medium saucepan heat together the filling ingredients over low heat until the jam has dissolved. Remove the pan from the heat and let the filling cool completely.
6. In a large bowl beat together the frosting ingredients except the coconut with an electric mixer until smooth. Frost the bottom layer. Then spread the filling over the layer. Add the second layer and then frost the entire cake. Sprinkle coconut over the top and sides.
Yield: 16 servings

Gourmet Light and Elegant

The Inn at Twin Linden
Churchtown, Pennsylvania

INNKEEPER/CHEF DONNA LEAHY

Dinner for Eight

Artichoke Dill Soup

◆

*Grilled Shrimp and Leeks with
Mustard Sauce*

◆

*Soft-Shell Crab Salad with
Almonds and Pepper Dressing*

◆

*Grilled Pork Medallions with
Roasted Red Pepper Sauce*

◆

*Lemon Poached Pears with
Raspberry Sauce*

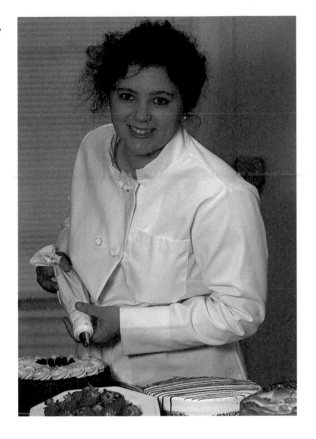

Donna Leahy cooks up so many menus that are wonderfully sinful, I hesitated to ask her to provide light ideas for a menu. But Donna is such a versatile and accomplished chef that I knew I could rely on her to offer a compromise for those watching calories. Here is a menu you can make often without guilt.

At Twin Linden, Donna's meals are less light and lively than they are hearty and lovely. She serves anything from venison pâté followed by apple pheasant-and-sausage strudel baked in pastry for dinner, to cinnamon-butter muffins and apricot-and-cheese-filled French toast with brandied preserves at breakfast.

These are gastronomic productions. In fact, the chef was a video producer before

A view under the twin linden trees

conceived, using only the freshest ingredients. Donna insists on doing it all herself to ensure quality and consistency. So she has no intention of adding to the six dinner tables in the inn's Hunt Club restaurant.

As a result, eating at Twin Linden is almost private dining. You feel as though you're in an elegant but unpretentious home, being served by your very own chef. All this personal attention means public diners sometimes have to wait for the second seating. But even the waiting is something to relish, because the Leahys have two Colonial parlors with classical music, candlelight, and conversation. Once seated, you dine within view of the inn's namesake linden trees, brought here from Europe when the house was built in the mid-1800s. In warm weather, breakfast and dinner are served out amongst the trees in the garden.

Donna is naturally a good cook, with talents she enhanced as an apprentice to chef Tell Erhardt, nationally known for his televi-

she and husband Bob got into innkeeping several years ago in Maine. They opened their first bed and breakfast Down East and later moved south to Pennsylvania Dutch country. The Leahys are blazing a new trail here as one of the first in the area to open a country inn. That is good news for those in search of elegant gourmet dining. But despite the lack of direct competition, Donna hardly rests on her laurels.

Twin Linden dinners are meticulously

Artichoke Dill Soup

❖

A clean, tangy flavor characterizes this delicious soup, which also makes a luncheon dish.

- ➤ 18 unmarinated artichoke hearts, coarsely chopped
- ➤ 6 tablespoons fresh lemon juice
- ➤ 3 cups low- or nonfat plain yogurt
- ➤ 1½ cups defatted chicken stock or broth
- ➤ ½ cup sour cream substitute
- ➤ ¼ cup chopped fresh dill
- ➤ 2 teaspoons freshly ground white pepper
- ➤ Dill sprigs and artichoke hearts for garnish

1. In a large bowl toss the artichoke hearts with the lemon juice. Add the yogurt, stock, sour cream substitute, dill, and pepper. Stir until well combined.
2. Transfer the mixture to a food processor and process until smooth. Remove the soup to another bowl, scraping down the sides of the food processor bowl. Cover and chill for at least 2 hours before serving.

Yield: 8 servings

sion program of years ago and his many appearances on early morning talk shows. While she's cooking during the day, Bob is either tending to innkeeping chores or working at his other job as director of the Center for Underwater Research and Education at Temple University. Underwater photography is his specialty, but the inn is filled with framed photos of Amish environs that show visitors he's just as talented with a camera above water.

The six overnight guest rooms all have decorating themes, and each comes with a Pennsylvania Dutch pretzel and love note from the innkeepers. The Polo Room—in English hunt motif—is adorned with a Ralph Lauren spread that hides dainty Court of Versailles sheets. The Cottage Room is a Victorian hideaway, and the Lancaster Room blooms with the year-round colors of an Amish quilt.

Twin Linden's guest rooms are the icing on the cake after a superb dinner. And yes, you can have your cake and eat it too at Twin Linden, despite Donna's efforts to keep us all in good shape at home with the recipes that follow.

Artichoke Dill Soup

Grilled Shrimp and Leeks with Mustard Sauce

❖

Soak eight 8-inch bamboo skewers in cold water for thirty minutes prior to grilling to prevent burning them.

Marinade

➤ ¾ cup extra virgin olive oil
➤ ¼ cup fresh lemon juice
➤ 3 cloves garlic, minced
➤ 1 tablespoon low-salt soy sauce

Shrimp

➤ 24 extra large shrimp (1½ pounds), peeled (except for tails) and deveined
➤ 8 leeks (white part only), cut into 1½-inch chunks

Dipping Sauce

➤ ¾ cup lowfat cottage cheese
➤ 1 teaspoon Creole or other hot mustard
➤ 2 tablespoons chopped green bell pepper
➤ 2 tablespoons chopped scallions
➤ 2 tablespoons fresh Italian parsley
➤ ⅛ teaspoon cayenne pepper
➤ ¼ cup marinade

1. In a shallow dish whisk together the marinade ingredients. Add the shrimp, cover, and marinate for 20 minutes in the refrigerator. Drain and reserve ¼ cup of the marinade. Alternately mount the shrimp and leeks onto skewers. Cover and chill until ready.
2. Brush with the remaining marinade. Grill or broil 1½ minutes per side.
3. To prepare the dipping sauce in a food processor combine the cottage cheese, mustard, green pepper, scallions, parsley, and cayenne pepper, and process until smooth. Gradually add the reserved marinade, and blend well. Transfer to a serving dish. Cover and chill until ready to use. Serve the shrimp with the dipping sauce.
Yield: 8 servings

Soft-Shell Crab Salad with Almonds and Pepper Dressing

❖

Dressing

➤ ¼ cup fresh lemon juice
➤ ¼ cup rice wine vinegar
➤ 2 cups water
➤ 1 tablespoon finely ground black pepper
➤ 1 tablespoon finely ground white pepper
➤ 1 tablespoon sesame oil

Crabs

➤ 2 eggs
➤ 8 large soft-shell crabs, cleaned and patted dry
➤ All-purpose flour for dredging
➤ 2 cups sliced almonds
➤ 3 to 4 tablespoons canola or corn oil for sautéing
➤ 3 heads Boston or green-leaf lettuce, leaves separated, washed, and dried
➤ 2 heads radicchio or red-leaf lettuce, leaves separated, washed, and dried

1. In a small bowl whisk together the dressing ingredients. Set the dressing aside.
2. In a medium bowl whisk the eggs. Dredge each crab first in the flour, then egg, and finally the almonds. Set the crabs aside.
3. In a medium skillet heat the oil and sauté the crabs 2 at a time until cooked through, about 4 minutes per side. Keep the crabs warming in a 250° oven.
4. To serve, toss the lettuce and divide it among chilled plates. Place 1 crab on each bed of lettuce and drizzle the dressing over the crabs. Serve small bowls of dressing on the side for dipping.
Yield: 8 servings

Grilled Pork Medallions with Roasted Red Pepper Sauce

❖

The so-called "other white meat," pork is dressed in a tasty red sauce here that offers one of its most complementary flavors.

➤ 2 pork tenderloins (about 4 pounds total), cut into medallions and pounded lightly to tenderize

Marinade

➤ ½ cup extra virgin olive oil
➤ 2 teaspoons minced garlic
➤ 2 tablespoons balsamic vinegar
➤ 2 teaspoons freshly ground pepper
➤ 2 tablespoons fresh rosemary leaves (1 teaspoon dried)

Sauce

➤ 10 roasted red bell peppers (see step 2)
➤ 1 cup fresh tomato sauce
➤ 1 tablespoon minced garlic

Lemon Poached Pears with Raspberry Sauce

Pork medallions and grilled vegetables

1. In a shallow dish whisk together the marinade ingredients. Add the pork medallions and marinate for 30 minutes in the refrigerator.
2. To roast the peppers cut them in half and remove the seeds. Broil the peppers 2 to 3 inches from the heat, rotating with tongs until the entire skin is blackened. Transfer the peppers to a paper bag and close the bag tightly to allow the peppers to steam. Remove them after 15 to 20 minutes, and peel off the skins.
3. In a food processor combine the peppers, tomato sauce, and minced garlic. Process until smooth. Set the sauce aside.
4. Preheat the grill or broiler. Grill the pork medallions for 1½ minutes on each side, until cooked through. Keep them warm until all of the medallions are grilled. In a glass, stainless steel, or non-reactive saucepan heat the sauce. Divide the sauce among the serving plates. Arrange the medallions on the sauce and serve.

Yield: 8 servings

Lemon Poached Pears with Raspberry Sauce

❖

- ➤ 8 small pears, peeled, bottoms trimmed so pears can stand
- ➤ Juice and zest of 3 large lemons
- ➤ ⅓ cup lemon curd
- ➤ 8 to 10 cups water
  Sauce
- ➤ 2 cups fresh or frozen raspberries
- ➤ 3 tablespoons sweetened crème fraîche
- ➤ ¼ cup fresh orange juice
- ➤ 2 tablespoons raspberry liqueur such as Chambord (optional)
- ➤ Raspberries and mint leaves for garnish

1. In a large saucepan combine the lemon juice, zest, lemon curd, and water. Add the pears and weight them down with a heat-proof plate so the pears are fully submerged. Bring the liquid to a boil, cover, and reduce the heat to a simmer. Continue cooking until the pears are tender when pierced, about 10 minutes. Remove the pan from the heat. Uncover and allow the pears to cool in the liquid. Refrigerate until chilled. (May be done a day ahead.)
2. In a food processor combine the sauce ingredients, and process until smooth. Refrigerate until chilled.
3. To serve, divide ¾ of the raspberry sauce among the serving plates and place a pear in the middle of each plate. Drizzle the remaining sauce over the pears. Garnish with raspberries and mint leaves.
Yield: 8 servings

Country Inn Cooking at the James Beard House

The White Barn Inn
Kennebunkport, Maine

CHEF EDWARD GANNON

Dinner for Eight

Smoked Mussels on a Croustade with
Honey-Mustard Sauce

◆

Lobster on Fettucine with a Thai Sherry
Vinegar and Honey Sauce

◆

Scallops with Sea-Urchin Hollandaise and
Vegetable Julienne Salad

◆

Chocolate Marquise Tart with Toasted
Hazelnuts and Whipped Chantilly

*I*t was as though I had arrived at a well-known Broadway theater before the curtain went up on opening night. The audience pored over the evening's program with much anticipation, but we had come out of a passion for good food, not acting.

I had driven up to Manhattan that day just to meet White Barn Inn executive chef Edward Gannon and sample his menu on this very special evening. Ed—far from his usual kitchen on the Maine coast—was about to serve one hundred people in the home of the late James Beard, much revered food critic, author, and cook.

The evening was one in a James Beard Foundation series of dinners featuring country inn chefs. The nonprofit foundation also puts on lectures, tastings, and workshops with cookbook authors, visiting foreign chefs, great American chefs, young chefs, new chefs, and hotel chefs to name a few.

James Beard's home, at 167 West 12th Street in New York City, was saved by a group of cooking stars led by one of the nation's top gastronomic legends: Julia Child. In 1985, shortly after Beard's death, Child was concerned with what would happen to her friend's home. She turned to Peter Kump, now president of the foundation and head of the prestigious Peter Kump's New York Cooking School. After much discussion, the two devised a plan to save the home and put it to further use. A number of chefs agreed to host benefit dinners at their restaurants, and eventually enough money was raised to establish the foundation and buy the house. The many functions—such as the country inn chef series—help the organization preserve and maintain the home and slowly acquire many of Beard's possessions, which were auctioned off at the time of his death.

I felt privileged to be a diner at the Beard House, and afterward I had to ask Ed how he felt about being a cook there. "So many great chefs have passed through this kitchen that it was an honor, not just for me but for all of us who came down from the inn," he recalls. "James Beard did a lot for young chefs, as the foundation did for me."

The modest Ed Gannon cooks every day in a place that has aura, tradition, and high marks of its own in the culinary world. The rustic but elegant, four-diamond White Barn is a selected member of the laudable Relais & Chateaux, meaning it is considered one of the world's finest lodging and dining establishments. It is also a favorite of President and Mrs. George Bush, who dine there

Lobster with a Thai sauce over fettucine

after The White Barn had contracted divers to fetch them from deep-blue waters. The smoked mussels and hors d'oeuvres of crab-meat and salmon were also served along with the lobster and the satiny chocolate marquise tart—all from the menu here—plus a stew of pemquid oysters on the half shell with shiitake mushrooms, julienne of leek, and caviar.

It was his pleasure, he says. Ed Gannon is clearly an ambitious, professional cook who plays the role of a luxury country inn or small hotel chef perfectly with his positive and friendly spirit. Ed's wife, Dyanne, who accompanied him to the Beard House, also works at the inn office, and together they are devoted to The White Barn.

Ed came to the inn after serving as a sous chef at the Copley Plaza and the Marquis de Lafayette, two heralded New England auberges. While Ed's sophisticated dishes bring in all the celebrities visiting or living in the quaint seaside town of Kennebunkport, ironically it was never his intent to become a chef. He wanted to be in hotel management and signed up to study at Johnson and Wales University in Rhode Island. "The next thing I knew," recalls Ed, "I was in chef's whites and hair nets. The course required two years of chef's training for the degree. But I had no idea that was part of the curriculum." Ed found he had a natural talent and liking for cooking, which he now realizes was influenced by his grandparents, who lived to cook and eat.

Ed also attributes his success to the education he received working under classically trained chefs. "I took the attitude that I didn't know everything and that I could be humble and learn something."

If there's one thing Ed Gannon has absorbed about cooking that he would like to pass on to home cooks, it is this: "You can cook nearly any recipe. But you must first read through it and understand everything you're going to do before setting out to do it."

Before I left the Beard House that night,

often when staying at their nearby oceanside retreat.

Among the chef's usual specialties that attract such a noteworthy crowd are an open ravioli of rabbit with savoy cabbage, corn, and lardons in a brandy cream; a terrinette of lamb with a rosemary-garlic brochette and a tomato coulis; and char-grilled veal with ribbons of vegetables, shallot confit, and blanched bacon.

Owner/innkeepers Laurie Bongiorno and his wife, Laurie Cameron, are responsible in great part for The White Barn's excellent reputation. The two are hands-on owners of the early nineteenth-century inn. Although handsomely clad as if a part of the audience for the James Beard dinner, they could be found in the kitchen assisting their chef.

On the day before the dinner, The White Barn staff and Ed Gannon traveled down the East Coast, carrying fresh, ice-caressed seafood from various New England ports. The recipe here for the pan-seared scallops was served at the Beard House just a day

A Taste of Maine
at The James Beard House
Monday January 6th, 1992

The White Barn Inn
Kennebunkport, Maine

Our Gratitude for the Cooper

The White Barn Inn

Portland Specialty S

Port Lobster C

Seagram

Switz

Edward Gannon

HAS BEEN SELECTED BY
THE JAMES BEARD FOUNDATION
AS ONE OF THE
Great Country Inn Chefs of 1991

Julia Child
FOUNDER

Peter Kump
PRESIDENT

VICE PRESIDENT

Caroline Stuart

I watched as Ed Gannon came out from backstage for an after-dinner menu-signing for his audience of new-found fans. I couldn't help being excited at the thought of all the many cooking performances that lie ahead for this young chef. Just two days after the James Beard dinner, he was off to Hong Kong in search of oriental cooking techniques to add to his repertoire. Meanwhile, be sure to catch Ed's nightly culinary renditions at The White Barn with his cast of supporting characters. The evening presentations never fail to be a hit.

Smoked Mussels on a Croustade with Honey-Mustard Sauce

❖

Ed Gannon describes this dish as "a basic canapé, featuring the mussel itself." Therefore, he selects quality mussels that are tender but not dry and have been smoked with an apple-and-hickory wood mixture.

➤ 2 tablespoons mayonnaise (preferably homemade)
➤ 1 teaspoon Dijon mustard or more to taste
➤ 1 teaspoon honey or more to taste
➤ 1 baguette, sliced thinly and toasted (or choice of toast rounds)
➤ 24 medium-size smoked mussels
➤ 1 red bell pepper, roasted (see page 174), peeled, and cut into strips

1. In a small bowl combine the mayonnaise, mustard, and honey, blending well.
2. Spread the baguette slices with the sauce and nestle a mussel on top. Garnish each canapé with a strip of roasted red pepper.
Yield: 24 mussels

Lobster on Fettucine with a Thai Sherry Vinegar and Honey Sauce

✣

You will need eight 1½- to 2-pound whole Maine lobsters and 1 pound of fresh fettucine to complete this recipe. The lobster meat is served between the cooked shells of the head and tails, and accented with the whole claw meat (see photo on page 107) over a bed of fettucine and vegetables. This is an optional assembly.

Thai Paste
➤ *1 2- to 3-ounce can Thai red curry paste*
➤ *1 2- to 3-ounce can Thai green curry paste*
➤ *1 bulb garlic, peeled and separated*
➤ *2 red bell peppers, seeded and chopped*
➤ *1 ginger root knuckle, peeled and chopped*
➤ *¼ cup cardamom*
➤ *2 tablespoons turmeric*

Sauce
➤ *1 tablespoon Thai paste, optional (see step 2)*
➤ *1 teaspoon sunflower oil*
➤ *2 tablespoons sherry vinegar*
➤ *2 tablespoons honey*
➤ *3 cups fresh chicken stock*
➤ *2 tablespoons butter*
➤ *Cornstarch to thicken*
➤ *Thai fish sauce (or salt) to taste*

Vegetables
➤ *4 to 5 medium carrots, peeled and julienned into 1½-inch lengths*
➤ *1 ginger root knuckle, peeled and julienned*
➤ *⅛ teaspoon sugar*
➤ *⅛ teaspoon salt*
➤ *1 tablespoon butter*

1. In a stock pot steam or boil the lobsters for 12 minutes. Shell the lobsters, removing all of the meat, reserving all but the tails, knuckles, and claws for making fish stock, if desired. Slice each tail into 5 medallions. Set aside with the knuckles and claw meat.

2. The Thai paste offers this dish a sharp, tasty contrast to the sweet lobster meat. The ingredients are available at Asian markets, but this step may be skipped if desired. In a blender combine all of the Thai paste ingredients and purée until smooth. If necessary add a little oil to moisten it during the blending process. Refrigerate the extra paste up to 1 month or freeze it indefinitely. The paste can be used to heighten the flavor of a vinaigrette dressing or to add to stir-fry vegetables.

3. Fry the Thai paste in sunflower oil. Stir with a whisk to prevent burning. Cook for up to 2 minutes, long enough to release an aroma. Deglaze the pan with the sherry vinegar. Add the honey and reduce the mixture to ¼, stirring constantly. Add the chicken stock and bring the mixture to a boil. Skim the top. Dilute the cornstarch with a little water, and add it to the sauce. Cook the sauce until it is thick enough to coat the back of the spoon, a few minutes. Whisk in the butter. Season to taste with the fish sauce or salt.

4. In a saucepan combine the carrots and remaining ingredients and fill with just enough water to cover. Bring the water to a quick boil and immediately remove the pan from the heat. Drain and keep warm.

5. As the vegetables cook, boil the fettucine until al dente. Drain.

6. Reheat all of the components that have cooled during the preparations. Place a small bed of pasta in the center of each serving plate. Surround the fettucine with some of the seasoned carrots. Arrange the lobster medallions on top of the pasta, add the knuckle meat, and fan out the claws on the sides of the pasta. Nap the lobster with the Thai sauce. Garnish with the head and tail shells, if desired. Serve immediately.
Yield: 8 servings

Scallops with Sea-Urchin Hollandaise and Vegetable Julienne Salad

❖

Scallops and urchin are two of Maine's coastal treasures. Ideally, chef Gannon would have all of us make this dish only with seafood that has come from Maine waters.

Chocolate Marquise Tart

Scallops
➤ 3 *pounds (8 to 10 count) scallops*
➤ ¼ *pound fresh urchin roe*
➤ *Peanut oil for brushing*

Sauce
➤ 1 *tablespoon water*
➤ 3 *egg yolks*
➤ *Puréed urchin roe*
➤ 6 *tablespoons sweet butter, softened*
➤ ½ *teaspoon each lime juice, soy sauce, and fish sauce or more to taste*
➤ ⅛ *teaspoon cayenne pepper or more to taste*

Vegetable Salad
➤ 1 *each carrot, red bell pepper, and zucchini, julienned*
➤ 8 *snow peas, veins removed and julienned*
➤ ½ *tablespoon rice wine vinegar*
➤ 1 *sprig fresh cilantro, finely chopped*
➤ 1 *sprig fresh mint, finely chopped*
➤ ⅛ *teaspoon salt*
➤ 1 *tablespoon peanut oil*

1. Remove the muscles from scallops. Remove 8 nice lobes from the roe. In a blender purée the remainder.
2. In a stainless steel bowl mix together the water, egg yolks, and puréed urchin roe. Froth the mixture with a thin wire whisk. In a double boiler over simmering water heat the sauce, whisking (do not scramble) until thickened. Remove the pan from the heat. Slowly whisk in the butter. Return the pan to the heat and warm through. Season with lime juice, soy and fish sauces, and cayenne. Strain the sauce through a fine sieve. Keep the sauce warm in a bain marie (hot water bath).
3. In a bowl mix together the vegetables, vinegar, herbs, and salt. Taste and adjust the seasonings. Set the vegetables aside.
4. Heat a non-stick skillet to very hot. Brush it with peanut oil. Season the scallops with salt and sear on both sides until light brown. Cook until medium rare.
5. Mound the vegetables onto each plate, haystack-style. Arrange 3 scallops on each plate. Place a dollop of sauce at the base of each scallop.

Yield: 8 appetizer servings

Chocolate Marquise Tart with Toasted Hazelnuts and Whipped Chantilly

✛

Sweet Paste Crust

- ¼ cup sugar
- 1 egg
- ½ teaspoon vanilla extract
- 1¾ cups pastry flour
- ⅛ teaspoon salt
- 1 cup (2 sticks) butter, cold, cut up
- ½ cup toasted chopped hazelnuts (for bottom of shell when assembling)

Marquise Filling

- 10 ounces semisweet chocolate
- ½ cup (1 stick) butter, cut up
- 4 eggs, separated
- 2 tablespoons hazelnut liqueur
- ⅛ teaspoon cream of tartar
- 2 tablespoons sugar

Chocolate Glaze

- 8 ounces semisweet chocolate
- 6 tablespoons (¾ cup) butter, cut up
- 1 tablespoon corn syrup
- 5 teaspoons water

Chantilly and Garnish

- 1 cup heavy cream, chilled
- 1 teaspoon hazelnut liqueur
- 2 tablespoons confectioners' sugar, sifted
- Cocoa powder for garnish
- Toasted, halved hazelnuts for garnish

1. In a bowl mix together the sugar, egg, and vanilla. Set the mixture aside. In a food processor combine the flour and salt. Pulse 2 to 3 times. Add the butter to the flour and pulse until the mixture is crumbly. Add the egg mixture and pulse until the dough comes together. Remove the dough and form it into a ball. Wrap it in plastic and chill it for 1 hour. Divide the dough in half, freezing ½ (for up to a month) to use in another recipe. Roll out the remaining dough to ⅛-inch thickness. Place the dough in a 9½-inch tart shell, and chill the shell for ½ hour.

2. Preheat the oven to 400°. Prick the bottom of the tart with a fork all over, to prevent rising. Bake the shell for 15 minutes, or until golden. Let cool while preparing filling.

3. In a stainless steel bowl melt the chocolate and butter together over a hot water bath. Whisk in the egg yolks and liqueur. Set the mixture aside. In a separate bowl whip the egg whites with the cream of tartar, slowly sifting in the sugar. Beat until stiff peaks form. Fold the egg whites into the melted chocolate. (Be careful not to deflate the whites.) Set the filling aside.

4. In the top of a double boiler over simmering water melt the chocolate, butter, and corn syrup together. Stir in the water. Remove the glaze from the heat.

5. Build the tart by first placing chopped hazelnuts into the bottom of the shell. Use a spatula to pour the marquise filling into the tart, spreading it evenly. With a clean spatula coat the top with the chocolate glaze, spreading the chocolate smooth, like a mirror. Top the tart with thin streaks of melted white chocolate, if desired. Refrigerate the tart until set, about 1 hour.

6. In a large bowl flavor the heavy cream with the liqueur. Add the sugar and whisk to a fluffy chantilly. Remove the tart from the refrigerator and slice it into 8 portions. Garnish with cocoa powder, chantilly, and hazelnuts.

Yield: 8 servings

An Evening in Shenandoah Country

The Joshua Wilton House
Harrisonburg, Virginia

INNKEEPER/CHEF CRAIG MOORE

Dinner for Eight

❖

Smoked Salmon on Apple-Potato Pancake
with Dill Crème Fraîche

◆

Scallop Orzo Soup

◆

Lamb Chops Madeira
with Lentil Relish

◆

Raspberry Cobbler with Raspberry
Grand Marnier Ice Cream

Dinner time at The Joshua Wilton House is signaled by the glow of candlelight against soft lace curtains framing tall, Victorian windows. Three dining rooms, decorated with crisp linens and shining silver, beckon all who enter this pleasant urban country inn to stay for the feast prepared by innkeeper/chef Craig Moore.

Craig owned a restaurant in town prior to the inn. But once he and wife Roberta sampled the bed-and-breakfast and country inns of California's Napa Valley, they wanted a place where they, too, could offer guests a taste of country inn dining right in the heart of Virginia's Shenandoah Valley.

They found the Joshua Wilton House in 1988 and—with help from Craig's family—gutted the entire building before beginning to restore the home to its original condition.

The former fraternity house was in disrepair from the wear and tear you'd expect from collegians—in this case from neighboring James Madison University. Original, but faux, marble fireplaces were brought back to life as were handsome window shutters and imposing mirrors. The house also boasts several gables and turrets that carve out intimate, angled nooks in the dining rooms and in the upstairs guest rooms.

In the kitchen, self-taught Craig tends to be the creative chef, working alongside his chef de cuisine, the classically trained Bill Atwell. "Together, our backgrounds feed off each other," notes Craig.

The Joshua Wilton menu is indeed a collaborative one. The menu provided here includes salmon on a potato pancake. Potato pancakes are a signature of the inn, found here and there with many of the dishes such as a grilled pork tenderloin served with peach chutney on an apple-potato pancake and topped with a Virginia whiskey sauce. Another popular entrée is a grilled yellowfin tuna in a pool of white-and-black-bean chili, and topped with a grapefruit butter sauce. Pasta is a hit, especially the basil linguine smothered in shrimp, scallops, and smoked oysters and a cream sauce of cherry tomato, scallions, and lemon-thyme.

Salads are Roberta's forte. She serves them dinner-plate size and topped with all sorts of choices from Montrachet cheese to smoked duck. Craig enjoys preparing the smoked meats and built his own smoker just behind the inn's kitchen. We cannot all have

Victorian gingerbread frames Joshua Wilton House.

Smoked Salmon on Apple Potato Pancake

smokers at home; so Craig suggests that you ask your butcher for fire-smoked meats, not those that have been smoked by curing the meat.

Joshua Wilton food is fresh and includes meats and poultry purchased from Virginia farms. Everything is served, of course, on Noritake's Shenandoah pattern.

The majority of diners were not inn guests on the night we visited, but my husband and I ambled up a twisting antique flight of stairs to a sitting area along with another pair of overnight visitors, and then retreated to our comfortable room where a restful night followed a most satisfying meal.

Breakfast the next morning was a full-fledged affair—served once again in an elegant manner—in portions large enough to provide the boost needed to go out and explore the surrounding secrets of the Shenandoah.

Smoked Salmon on Apple-Potato Pancake with Dill Crème Fraîche

Craig's recipe for smoking salmon is included in this recipe. The chef prefers smoking his own salmon for the best flavor. If you do not have a smoker, buy quality smoked salmon and skip steps 2 and 3. Prepare the crème fraîche two days ahead and the salmon and potato pancakes a day ahead. The contrast of flavors makes this dish well worth serving to your guests, no matter which way you smoke it!

Dill Crème Fraîche
➤ 1 cup heavy cream
➤ 1½ cups sour cream
➤ ¼ cup buttermilk
➤ ½ tablespoon chopped dill

Salmon Cure
➤ 2 stalks celery, cut into pieces
➤ 2 medium carrots, cut into pieces
➤ ½ medium onion
➤ ¼ cup packed brown sugar
➤ 1 tablespoon sugar
➤ 2 tablespoons salt
➤ 1 tablespoon chopped fresh tarragon
➤ 1 tablespoon chopped dill
➤ 4 6-ounce salmon fillets

Apple-potato Pancakes
➤ 3 medium potatoes, peeled and grated
➤ 1 Granny Smith apple, peeled and grated

To Serve
➤ 1 tablespoon butter
➤ 1 tablespoon olive oil
➤ Caviar

1. In a stainless steel bowl mix together all of the crème fraîche ingredients. Cover the bowl tightly with plastic wrap and let the mixture

Lamb and a fan handmade by the chef's mother

sized patties. Cover and refrigerate until ready to use.

5. When ready to serve, in a skillet heat the butter and oil and sauté the potato pancakes on both sides until golden brown. Place the pancakes on individual serving plates. Cut each salmon fillet in half lengthwise and place one slice on top of each pancake. Pipe the crème fraîche through a pastry bag fitted with the desired tip over each fillet and garnish with caviar.
Yield: 8 servings

Scallop Orzo Soup

❖

> 2 quarts duck or chicken stock or broth
> 2 stalks celery, finely chopped
> ½ Spanish onion, finely chopped
> 1 red bell pepper, seeded and finely chopped
> 1 tablespoon extra virgin olive oil
> 1½ pounds fresh sea scallops, quartered
> 5 Italian plum tomatoes, chopped
> 1 cup tomato juice
> Salt and freshly ground pepper to taste
> ¼ cup chopped fresh basil or 1 tablespoon dried
> ¼ cup cornstarch
> ¼ cup cold water
> 1 cup orzo pasta, cooked al dente and drained

1. In a large stock pot bring the stock to a slow boil. Meanwhile, in a large skillet heat the olive oil and sauté the celery, onion, and red pepper until the vegetables are only slightly firm. Add the scallops, tomatoes, and tomato juice. Season with salt, pepper, and basil.
2. In a small bowl mix the cornstarch with water. Slowly add it to the boiling stock. Boil for 2 minutes, stirring with a wire whisk. Add the sautéed vegetables, scallops, tomatoes, tomato juice, and orzo, and simmer for 10 minutes. Serve hot.
Yield: 8 servings

sit at room temperature for 48 hours. Then refrigerate for 24 hours until firm.

2. In a food processor coarsely chop the celery, carrots, and onion. Add all of the other curing ingredients except the salmon. Place the salmon in a baking dish, pack it with the cure, and refrigerate for 24 hours.

3. Prepare the smoker with charcoal and water-soaked apple and cherry wood branches. Clean the cure from the salmon. Place the fillets in the smoker and smoke until they are firm but still moist. Remove the salmon from the smoker and let it rest. Cover and put it in the refrigerator.

4. In a bowl combine the potatoes and apples. Cover them with water and refrigerate for 24 hours. Remove the potatoes and apples from the bowl by hand, cupping as though forming a hamburger. Squeeze out the water and make pancake patties. Repeat to make 8 even-

Lamb Chops Madeira with Lentil Relish

Lentil Relish

- ➤ ½ green bell pepper, seeded, finely diced
- ➤ ½ onion, finely diced
- ➤ 3 cups lentils, cooked
- ➤ ¼ cup balsamic vinegar
- ➤ ½ tablespoon crushed green peppercorns
- ➤ Salt and freshly ground pepper to taste

Lamb Chops Preparation

- ➤ 8 roasted garlic cloves (see step 2)
- ➤ 24 center-cut lamb chops (have butcher trim bones to 5 inches and remove chine bone)
- ➤ Olive oil for sautéing
- ➤ 1 pound shiitake mushrooms, stems removed and discarded, tops thinly sliced
- ➤ 1 cup Madeira
- ➤ ¼ cup (½ stick) butter, cubed

1. In a small skillet heat the olive oil and sauté the pepper and onion until tender but not browned. In a medium bowl combine the sautéed mixture and the other lentil relish ingredients. Set the mixture aside.
2. Preheat the oven to 450°. Place the garlic cloves in boiling water to cover for 30 seconds. In a small skillet add a tablespoon or so of olive oil, enough to coat the bottom of the pan. Heat the oil until it just begins to smoke. Add the garlic, tossing until coated. Transfer the skillet to the oven and bake until garlic is golden brown, about 6 minutes, turning the garlic each minute. Remove it from the oven and cool. Chop finely. Set the garlic aside.
3. Preheat the broiler or grill. Season with salt and pepper. Broil or grill the chops rare. Place the lamb chops in a shallow baking dish. Bake for 10 minutes or until done to taste.
4. In the bottom of a medium skillet heat a coating of olive oil. Add the garlic and all parts of the mushrooms, and cook until the mushrooms are tender. Season with salt and pepper. Add the Madeira and turn the heat to low. Simmer until the mixture is reduced by half. Add the butter cubes, one by one, swirling the pan constantly over the very low heat. Turn off the heat as you add the last ¼ of the butter. Place 3 chops on each plate and pour the Madeira sauce over each. Top with warm lentil relish.

Yield: 8 servings

Raspberry Cobbler

Raspberry Cobbler with Raspberry Grand Marnier Ice Cream

✦

You can serve the cobbler with quality raspberry ice cream and add a sprinkling of Grand Marnier, but this homemade version is unbeatable, and it is not hard to make. Craig bows to his wife when it comes to the desserts. Roberta brought this recipe to the inn from her childhood days of making ice cream with her grandmother in Ohio. It is a truly delicious ice cream recipe, but the berries can also be replaced with most any fruit.

Ice Cream

- ➤ ¼ cup water
- ➤ 4 cups frozen or fresh raspberries
- ➤ 1 cup sugar
- ➤ Zest of 1 orange
- ➤ 2 cups heavy cream
- ➤ 1 cup half-and-half
- ➤ ½ teaspoon vanilla extract
- ➤ 3 tablespoons fresh lemon juice
- ➤ 2 tablespoons Grand Marnier

Cobbler

- ➤ ½ cup (1 stick) butter
- ➤ 1 cup all-purpose flour
- ➤ 1 cup sugar
- ➤ 1 tablespoon baking powder
- ➤ 2 eggs
- ➤ 1 cup milk
- ➤ 2 cups fresh raspberries

1. In a medium saucepan simmer together the water, raspberries, sugar, and orange zest for 20 minutes. Meanwhile, in a large bowl mix together the cream, half-and-half, vanilla, lemon juice, and Grand Marnier.

2. Strain the cooked raspberry mixture through a fine sieve, using a rubber spatula to press the pulp until all of the juice is extracted. Discard the pulp and blend the liquid into the cream mixture until smooth. Pour the mixture into any cake pan or baking sheet, just to semi freeze it quickly for whipping. Freeze until almost solid. Remove the pan from the freezer and whip with an electric mixer until smooth. Transfer the ice cream to a 2-quart container. Cover and refreeze.

3. Preheat the oven to 350°. Melt the butter in the bottom of a 13 x 9-inch pan. In a large bowl combine the flour, sugar, and baking powder. Add the eggs and milk and stir until smooth, only a few strokes. Pour the mixture over the butter in the baking pan. Do not mix. Evenly sprinkle the raspberries over the batter. They will sink to the bottom. Bake the cobbler for 40 minutes or until the center is firm and does not jiggle. Serve warm with ice cream.

Yield: 8 to 10 servings

Cooking
Inn Season

✤

*Yesterday . . . a resolution was passed . . . that
these United Colonies are, and of right ought to
be, free and independent States . . . solemnized
with pomp and parade, with shows, games, sports,
guns, bells, bonfires, and illuminations—from
this time foreward for evermore.*

John Adams
Letter to his wife Abigail
July 3, 1776

The Inn at Buckeystown, Buckeystown, Maryland

Invitation to Summer

Windham Hill
West Townshend, Vermont

INNKEEPER/CHEF LINDA BUSTEED

Dinner for Four

✥

Garden Pesto Pie

◆

Chilled Tomato Bisque

◆

*Herbed Chicken in
Lemon Cream Sauce*

◆

Mini Broccoli Timbales

◆

*Fresh Fruit Terrine
with Raspberry Coulis*

*J*ust close your eyes
and say, "There's no place like Windham
Hill. There's no place like Windham Hill.
There's no place like Windham Hill," and,
like Dorothy, you can almost transport yourself to a place of your own dreams. The very
sound of the inn's poetic name offers you
the first sense of this mountainside haven's
tranquility. Actually, getting to Windham
Hill was a sojourn of 500 miles for me; but
once here, the drive was soon forgotten and
the trip seemed as easy as closing my eyes
and clicking my heels.

Created by Linda and Ken Busteed,
Windham Hill is one of those inns that is
truly larger than life. The inn is tucked into
a breathtaking mountainscape on 165 plush-
green, historic acres of stone-fenced pastures
and wooded hills that are crisscrossed by

hiking and cross-country ski trails and punc-
tuated by a tiny skating pond. Guest rooms
are found in both the restored brick-and-
frame farmhouse with its quaint twin chim-
neys and the old reinvented dairy barn with
its exposed beams. Wherever you rest your
head, views of the surrounding Green
Mountains are right at eye level, and some
rooms have their own porches for listening
to nature's summer sounds.

Guests amble about the meadows for an
early morning hike. Sometimes you'll find
them out hunting mushrooms under expert
guidance by day or enjoying the strains of
jazz musicians under a summer moon on
musical weekends.

Despite its bucolic setting, Windham
Hill has an air of sophistication, a very
gentle one. Linda's knack for interior design
blends the easy shades of floral prints and
pastels throughout the inn. She approaches
her cooking in the same way, mixing and
matching her creations ever so softly and
serenely. Take as delectable evidence her
shrimp Creole on a bed of spinach fettucine;
her winter pear soup; or her salmon steaks
meunière, which follow a soup of strawberry
bisque. You can read all about them in
Linda's own cookbook, *Dinner at Seven*.

Linda is proud to be featured by Uncle
Ben's Rice in the company's country inn line
of rice dishes. Two boxes—displaying the
inn's picture, write-up and a mushroom-rice
recipe inspired by Windham Hill—sit in her
kitchen as trophies to her talent and accom-
plishments.

Linda's kitchen complements the rest of
her modus operandi. Everything is wiped
clean before another project is started. There
are never any dishes piled up or food scat-
tered about, even when she's preparing the
evening meal, which she tells us is the secret
to easier entertaining. That is just her gentle
way and besides, the kitchen is a combined

culinary work station and check-out desk.
The door is always open to guests.

Linda and Ken are most cordial hosts,
doing whatever it takes to satisfy the needs
of their guests, from serving them a cool
summer drink to recovering a dropped pearl
earring from the trap of a bathroom drain.
(I can attest to both from personal experience.)

A blackboard, decoratively etched with
the evening menu, teases your senses in anticipation of the sumptuous feast served
promptly at seven. Before everyone is seated,
guests gather in the sunroom or the parlor,
enjoying drinks, cheese, and crackers.

The dinner call brings everyone into the
inn's two dining rooms. The dressier room
boasts a silver tea service, chiming pen-
dulum clock, maple breakfront, and a long
and shiny mahogany antique table where as
many as eight guests can gather round to
nurture new-found friendships. The other
room—overlooking the pond—beckons
couples and foursomes to smaller tables.

Dinner is always five satisfying courses,
including Linda's incredible desserts. Her
peanut butter pie is a knockout. Linda told
me that when she first made the dish, most
of the plates came back to the kitchen with
only a few bites missing. "We all tried it,
wondering if something had gone wrong.
The kitchen staff loved it and we realized it
was so rich, we had to cut down the size of
the portions," the innkeeper reports.

Planning each menu begins at least two
weeks ahead. Linda searches her com-
puterized guest records to be sure that no
one at Windham Hill is served the same
meal twice. That has to be her most chal-
lenging chore at the inn; for those who
come once return often, following the twists
and turns of their own yellow-brick road all
the way to the storybook land of Windham
Hill.

Garden Pesto Pie

✜

Frosting the top of this pie with basil gives this delicious recipe its name. You can either spread the pesto entirely over the top or drop it by the tablespoonful around the pie top for another presentation. In the latter instance, place more pesto onto the individual serving plates.

Crust

➤ 1 cup all-purpose flour
➤ ⅛ teaspoon salt
➤ ¼ cup (½ stick) chilled unsalted butter
➤ 4½ teaspoons vegetable shortening
➤ 3 tablespoons ice water

Filling

➤ 1 cup minced onion
➤ 2 tablespoons butter
➤ 1 tablespoon olive oil
➤ 15 ounces ricotta cheese
➤ 4 eggs
➤ ⅛ teaspoon salt
➤ ⅛ teaspoon white pepper
➤ ⅛ teaspoon freshly grated nutmeg

Pesto

➤ 2 cups packed fresh basil leaves
➤ 3 tablespoons pine nuts
➤ 3 cloves fresh garlic
➤ ½ cup grated Parmesan cheese
➤ 5 tablespoons olive oil
➤ Cherry tomatoes and fresh basil for garnish

Garden Pesto Pie

1. Preheat the oven to 375°. In a medium bowl combine the salt and the flour and cut in the butter and shortening until the mixture resembles coarse crumbs. Stir in the ice water until a dough forms. Roll the dough out and press it evenly into a 9-inch tart pan with a removable bottom. Prick the dough with a fork. Overlay the dough with aluminum foil and weigh it down with dried beans or rice. Bake the crust for 10 minutes. Remove the beans and foil and continue to bake the crust for an additional 5 to 10 minutes, until lightly browned. Remove it from the oven.

2. In a small skillet melt the butter and add the olive oil. Sauté the onions until soft. In a bowl whisk together the ricotta, eggs, and seasonings. Add the onions. Spoon the mixture into the crust. Bake for 25 to 30 minutes, until golden.

3. In a food processor purée the basil with the pine nuts and garlic. Add the Parmesan and olive oil, and process until smooth.

4. Spread the cooled tart with pesto. Garnish with sliced cherry tomatoes and additional fresh basil. Slice into wedges and serve.
Yield: 8 to 10 servings

Tomato Bisque for sipping

Chilled Tomato Bisque

❖

The results of this recipe yield a rich, smooth, and tasty pre-dinner drink you can serve with the pesto pie or as a soup at the table.

- ➤ *3 cups tomato juice*
- ➤ *2 tablespoons tomato paste*
- ➤ *5 minced scallions, white and green ends*
- ➤ *⅛ teaspoon thyme*
- ➤ *½ teaspoon curry powder*
- ➤ *Salt and freshly ground pepper to taste*
- ➤ *2 tablespoons fresh lemon juice*
- ➤ *Grated rind of ½ lemon*
- ➤ *1 cup sour cream*
- ➤ *Snipped fresh chives for garnish*

1. In a serving bowl combine all of the ingredients except the sour cream and chives. Chill.
2. Just prior to serving, blend in the sour cream and sprinkle with chives.
   Yield: 4 servings

Chicken and Broccoli Timbales

Herbed Chicken in Lemon Cream Sauce

- ➤ 4 whole chicken breasts, skinned, boned, split, and pounded with a mallet to ¼-inch thick
- ➤ 1 cup all-purpose flour, seasoned with salt and pepper
- ➤ 6 tablespoons (¾ stick) butter
  Lemon Sauce
- ➤ 2 cups heavy cream
- ➤ 4 shallots, minced
- ➤ 8 teaspoons fresh thyme
- ➤ 4 teaspoons fresh tarragon
- ➤ 8 teaspoons grated lemon zest
- ➤ ½ cup fresh lemon juice
- ➤ Salt and pepper

1. Dredge the chicken in the flour. In a large skillet heat the butter over medium heat and

sauté the chicken, turning once, until cooked through, about 8 to 10 minutes. Remove the chicken from the pan and keep it warm.
2. Pour the cream into the hot skillet and increase the heat to medium-high. Deglaze the pan by bringing the cream to a boil and scraping the pan.
3. Add the shallots, herbs, and lemon zest. Cook over medium-high heat, stirring frequently, until the cream is thickened, about 3 minutes. Stir in the lemon juice and cook for 3 to 5 minutes more. Season with salt and pepper. Remove the chicken to a serving plate and spoon the sauce over all. Garnish with fresh herbs.
Yield: 4 servings

Mini Broccoli Timbales

Originally, the word *timbale* meant a "small metal drinking goblet." Today it refers to use of a round, high-sided mold, resulting in a muffin-shaped preparation. Almost any frozen vegetable can be substituted for the broccoli.

- ➤ 10 ounces frozen chopped broccoli, thawed and drained
- ➤ 2 eggs, beaten
- ➤ 2 tablespoons chopped onion
- ➤ 2 tablespoons milk
- ➤ 2 tablespoons melted butter
- ➤ ½ teaspoon salt
- ➤ ¼ teaspoon freshly ground pepper

1. Preheat the oven to 350°. Grease 12 mini muffin cups.
2. In a medium bowl combine all of the ingredients. Spoon the batter into the muffin cups. Set the muffin tin into a lipped baking sheet filled with hot water. Bake the timbales for 35 minutes or until set. Remove the muffin tin from the larger pan and let the timbales cool before loosening the edges and turning them out onto a serving plate.
Yield: 12 timbales

Fresh Fruit Terrine with Raspberry Coulis

❖

- ➤ *1 cup white wine*
- ➤ *½ cup sugar*
- ➤ *3 tablespoons fresh lemon juice*
- ➤ *½ cup water*
- ➤ *5 large ripe peaches, peeled, seeded, and thinly sliced*
- ➤ *2 envelopes unflavored gelatin*
- ➤ *⅓ cup water*
- ➤ *16 small, ripe strawberries, cut in half*
- ➤ *½ cup each raspberries, blueberries, and green seedless grapes, cut in half*

  Raspberry Coulis
- ➤ *1 10-ounce package frozen raspberries*
- ➤ *2 teaspoons cornstarch*
- ➤ *1 tablespoon cold water*
- ➤ *Fresh mint for garnish*

Linda's antique shoes decorate the inn and dessert.

1. In a medium saucepan combine the wine, sugar, lemon juice, and water. Bring the mixture to a boil. Add the peaches and simmer for 15 minutes or until the peaches are very tender. Drain through a colander, reserving the liquids and solids. In a food processor combine 1 cup of the drained liquid and all of the solids, and process until smooth. (Reserve the extra liquid for another recipe, or discard.)

2. In a small saucepan sprinkle the gelatin over ⅓ cup of cold water. Let the gelatin soften for 5 minutes, and then stir over low heat until dissolved. Add the gelatin to the purée filling.

3. Line a 10¼ x 3⅝ inch pan with plastic wrap. Spread ¼ cup of peach purée filling in the bottom. Layer half the strawberries cut-side down, followed by another layer of peach filling. Add a layer of sliced peaches, then more peach mixture. Combine the raspberries and

blueberries and layer them on top. Add more peach mixture, then all of the grapes, and more peach mixture. Add another layer of peaches and strawberries and finish with a layer of peach mixture. Chill the terrine for 1 hour. Cover with plastic and chill for an additional 24 hours.

4. In a small saucepan over low heat bring the frozen raspberries to a boil. Remove the pan from the heat and press the raspberries through a sieve over another small saucepan. Discard the solids. In a small bowl mix together the cornstarch and water. Return the sauce to heat and add the cornstarch mixture. Cook, stirring constantly, until thick. Pour the coulis into a bowl, cover, and chill.

5. To serve the terrine, invert it onto a cutting surface and slice it into ½-inch pieces. Pour a layer of raspberry coulis onto individual serving plates. Place a slice of terrine on top of the sauce. Garnish with mint.

Yield: 8 to 10 servings

Star-Spangled Moments

The Inn at Buckeystown
Buckeystown, Maryland

INNKEEPER/CHEF DAN PELZ

Patriotic Party for Eight

Cream of Red Pepper Soup

◆

*Salad of White
Asparagus Vinaigrette*

◆

*Turkey Legs Baked in Molasses
and Salsa*

◆

*Country-Style Ribs in
Pineapple-Molasses Sauce*

◆

Red Potato and Bacon Salad

◆

Creamed Corn Muffins

◆

*Red, White, and Blueberry
Hurrah Cake*

It is the inn of a thousand clowns—a red-rouge smile here, a weary grin there. A clown in the clouds and one under a big top. They are all part of the collection of whimsical posters, original paintings, and collectible knickknacks assembled over the years by Dan Pelz.

The Buckeystown innkeeper/chef doesn't know what it is about the ubiquitous circus jester that has captured his heart. (It all began during Navy days when he bought his first Emmett Kelly print.) But it is not a stretch to say that Dan himself embodies the jocular spirit of his many caricatures, especially when he is in the kitchen.

That is not to say Dan is one to "clown around" in slapstick fashion at the stove. Instead, his rosy outlook, characterized by a laugh that rises from deep down in his belly, is full of sentiment and romance. "I'm a very sensual person," says the chef. That's what attracts him so to cooking and—I think—to clowns as well.

"I cook by sight, taste, and smell," says Dan. Tutored vicariously by his mother years ago, Dan adapted to cooking so well that his circle of friends caught on to his talent just as quickly. They made him the designated chef for all get-togethers.

For me and other guests of The Inn at Buckeystown, that translates into hearty cooking during the week, with a hint of gourmet on Saturday night only. "My style is 'rustica,'" he opines, borrowing a favorite term—*rustic*—from the Italians. "I take the classic dishes and turn them into my own creations." Dan suggests that his beef Wellington would get the Buckingham Palace seal of approval from the queen, despite his own unconventional twist.

Coupled with the ambience of the inn, Dan's food made The Inn at Buckeystown one of ten selected in 1990 for the Best Inn of the Year award from Uncle Ben's Country Inn Rice. One of his recipes was also featured by the food giant on the back of rice boxes.

The chef gives cooking classes that call for the guests to go out and shop for ingredients. Back at the inn, teams of guests develop a menu, and Dan takes it all into the kitchen where each guest gets a job to perform.

Dan often pontificates, "The meek shall not inherit the earth," when he talks about how to be successful in life and business. But you know he subconsciously applies it to his cooking as well. Dan's dishes are anything but dainty; his food is hearty, plentiful, and full of flavor. He makes a statement with each curried emerald soup that he pours into a bowl and each helping of deviled beef ribs, German duck, prawns scampi, or flounder florentine en croute that is set before his guests. But being the mercurial character he is, dinner—served on tables for eight in Vic-

torian style—is usually accompanied by delicate antique linens, china, and crystal.

Holidays are such a sparkling event at the inn that all foods and decorations change to suit the occasion. The all-American traditional menu featured here may be served to your own guests for any patriotic celebration from presidential birthdays to Memorial Day or July 4th and all the other stars-and-stripes occasions.

Flaming sparklers make a festive addition to your red-white-and-blue party. However, Dan warns that the chemical-laden sparklers should be lit far enough away from food. The inn plays music complementary to each occasion; for this menu the innkeeper recommends the original soundtrack from the Ken Burns' Civil War TV series, as well as albums by The Prague Ragtime Orchestra.

The Inn at Buckeystown is set in a tiny hamlet on the Monocacy River. The village dates to pre-Revolutionary times and is rich in Civil War history. A ride down Buckeystown's main street offers several prime examples of Federal and Victorian architecture, including the inn itself with its tasteful

plaster festoons, Greek columns, and wrap-around porch. It was the inn's architectural splendor that compelled Dan to purchase the building in 1981 after retiring from his position as deputy national director of the Cystic Fibrosis Foundation.

Today Dan—with partner Chase Barnett—offers dining for up to thirty-five guests and six rooms plus two cottages for lodging. The St. John's Cottage—a former church built in 1884—features a loft, fireplace, hot tub, and grand piano.

Ecclesiastical inspiration has always been a part of Dan's life. Before joining the Navy, he spent two years in a monastery. He had only promised to remain silent, but he could never make it a vow. For one thing, Dan couldn't bury his exuberance for life—the sights, scents, and tastes he enjoys so much; so he left the clerical arena for good. His calling to enter the innkeeping profession, however, has resulted in a total commitment that has him performing every day under his very own big top.

Cream of Red Pepper Soup

Cream of Red Pepper Soup

❖

- ➤ 1 pint water
- ➤ 4 large red bell peppers, seeded and chopped
- ➤ 1 large onion, coarsely chopped
- ➤ 2 quarts hearty chicken stock or broth
- ➤ ¼ cup (1 stick) butter
- ➤ 1 quart half-and-half
- ➤ 1 teaspoon each salt and pepper
- ➤ 2 tablespoons cornstarch
- ➤ Fresh chopped dill for garnish

1. In a medium saucepan combine the water, peppers, and onion, and boil until tender. Pour the mixture into a food processor and purée.
2. In a large stock pot heat the chicken stock over high heat. Add the vegetable purée, butter, half-and-half, salt, and pepper. Reduce the heat to simmer. Dissolve the cornstarch in a small amount of cold water. Stir in the cornstarch, and cook the soup until thickened. Serve hot, garnished with dill.
Yield: 8 servings

Salad of White Asparagus Vinaigrette

❖

- ➤ ½ cup olive oil
- ➤ ½ cup (1 stick) butter
- ➤ 32 white asparagus spears, woody ends snapped
- ➤ 1 teaspoon salt
- ➤ 1 teaspoon chopped garlic
- ➤ ¼ cup red wine vinegar
- ➤ 1 cup ice
- ➤ 2 heads Bibb lettuce, cleaned, dried, and torn into bite-size pieces
- ➤ Coarsely ground pepper

1. In a large skillet heat the oil and butter and sauté the asparagus until tender but still somewhat crunchy. Remove the pan from heat. In a bowl mix the asparagus with the salt, garlic, vinegar, and ice. Refrigerate.
2. Serve each plate with 4 asparagus spears on a bed of lettuce, adorned with dressing and sprinkled with pepper.
Yield: 8 servings

Turkey Legs Baked in Molasses and Salsa

❖

It can be barbecue season any time of year with this dish. The turkey is cooked in the oven, coming out with a distinct barbecue-cooked flavor. You can also cook it partially in the oven and then transfer it to a barbecue grill.

- ➤ 2 cups catsup
- ➤ 1 cup hot-flavored salsa
- ➤ ¾ cup dark molasses
- ➤ 1 onion, finely minced
- ➤ ¼ cup fresh lemon juice
- ➤ 8 turkey legs
- ➤ ¼ cup olive oil
- ➤ 2 cloves garlic, mashed
- ➤ Salt and pepper

1. Preheat the oven to 375°. In a large bowl mix together the catsup, salsa, molasses, onion, and lemon juice. Set the sauce aside.
2. Rub the turkey legs with olive oil and garlic. Sprinkle with salt and pepper. Place the legs in a shallow baking pan. Bake for 45 minutes or until browned. Remove the turkey legs from the oven. Skim the fat. Add the molasses-and-salsa mixture to the pan and roll the turkey in the sauce to coat. Cover the pan with foil and return it to the oven for 15 minutes, or finish on a barbecue grill for added flavor.
Yield: 8 servings

Country-Style Ribs in Pineapple-Molasses Sauce

❖

- ➤ 4 meaty racks country-style ribs, cut into 16 equal portions
- ➤ 2 cups catsup
- ➤ 1 cup crushed pineapple
- ➤ ¾ cup dark molasses
- ➤ ¼ cup lemon juice

Bake the ribs at the same time as the turkey and follow the same procedure, but baste the ribs in the pineapple-molasses sauce.
Yield: 8 servings

Red Potato and Bacon Salad

❖

Unlike most potato salads this version is served warm to make the most of the flavors.

- ➤ 8 medium new potatoes
- ➤ 4 slices bacon cooked, crumbled, and fat reserved
- ➤ 1 green bell pepper, minced
- ➤ 3 stalks celery, minced
- ➤ 1 small onion, minced
- ➤ 8 hard-boiled eggs, kept warm
- ➤ ¼ cup red wine vinegar
- ➤ ¼ cup olive oil
- ➤ ½ cup sugar
- ➤ Chopped parsley for garnish

1. Boil the potatoes in their skins until tender. Slice and keep warm.
2. In a large skillet heat the bacon fat and sauté the minced vegetables until translucent.
3. Peel the eggs and dice them finely. Add the eggs to the potatoes. Add the vinegar, oil, sugar, minced vegetables, and bacon. Toss and garnish with parsley. Serve.
Yield: 8 servings

Creamed Corn Muffins

❖

These muffins are high-risers, and the creamed corn is a neat surprise inside.

- ➤ 1¼ cups all-purpose flour, sifted
- ➤ 1 cup cornmeal
- ➤ 1 tablespoon baking powder
- ➤ 1 teaspoon salt
- ➤ ½ cup sugar
- ➤ 1 cup milk
- ➤ ¼ cup vegetable oil
- ➤ 2 eggs, lightly beaten
- ➤ 16 ounces creamed corn

1. Preheat the oven to 400°. In a large bowl mix together the flour, cornmeal, baking powder, salt, and sugar. Stir in the milk, oil, and eggs, incorporating just until wet. Stir in the creamed corn.
2. Pour the batter into 12 greased muffin cups, filling the cups to the brim. Bake the muffins for 25 minutes or until puffed and a tester comes out clean. Let the muffins cool in the pan for 10 minutes before turning out.
Yield: 12 muffins

A Memorial Day picnic on the porch

Red, White, and Blueberry Hurrah Cake

➤ ½ cup (1 stick) butter
➤ 2 cups sugar
➤ 4 eggs, separated
➤ 3 cups all-purpose flour
➤ 2 teaspoons baking powder
➤ ½ teaspoon salt
➤ 1 cup milk
➤ 2 teaspoons vanilla extract
  Topping
➤ ½ cup strawberry or blueberry liqueur
➤ 1 pint heavy cream, lightly sweetened and stiffly whipped
➤ 1 quart strawberries, sliced and lightly sugared
➤ 1 pint blueberries, chopped and lightly sugared
➤ 1 pint each blueberries and strawberries for garnish

Hurrah Cake

1. Preheat the oven to 350°. In a large bowl cream the butter and sugar. Add the egg yolks. Beat until light and fluffy.
2. In a separate bowl beat the egg whites until stiff peaks form.
3. In a medium bowl mix together the flour, baking powder, and salt. Stir the dry ingredients into the creamed mixture alternately with the milk. Mix well. Blend in the egg whites and vanilla. Pour the batter into 2 greased 8-inch round cake pans. Bake the cake for 45 minutes or until a tester comes out clean. Remove the pans from the oven and let the cakes cool in the pans for 5 minutes. Turn out onto racks and cool thoroughly. Split each cake in half to end up with 4 layers.
4. Sprinkle the layers with ¼ cup of the liqueur. Spread each layer with a thin coating of the whipped cream. Divide the strawberries evenly onto 2 layers. Repeat with the blueberries. Stack the cakes alternately on top of each other. Cover the sides and outside top rim with a layer of cream. Place extra sliced strawberries in rows around the top of the cake. Fill in the center with blueberries. Drizzle the sides of the cake with the remaining liqueur.

Yield: 16 slices

Tapestry of Autumn

The Chesterfield Inn
West Chesterfield, New Hampshire

CHEF CARL WARNER

Dinner for Eight

❖

Apple Butternut Squash Soup

◆

Honey Curry Bread

◆

*Grilled Veal Loin Chops
Stuffed with Brie and Scallions*

◆

Puréed Beets

◆

*Flourless Chocolate Cake
with English Custard Sauce*

Only the wise know enough to pull off the road at the sign of the barnyard owl, and I was no fool. This is where The Chesterfield Inn, with its atmosphere of casual elegance, showcases notable New England chef Carl Warner. The chef's nest, where one might find the culinary master brightening the kitchen with a flambé or creating art with dough as though a potter at the wheel, is open to the dining public.

Dinner guests en route to the dining room get an eagle's-eye view of the chef dousing and deglazing, sifting and sautéing. The cook's room of half stainless steel and half cherry cabinets eventually dips down to the oldest part of the 1787 house and into two intimate, candlelit dining rooms. A printed menu, which changes every two months, is handed to the participants, who invariably have trouble choosing between the chef's nightly specials and his current bestsellers.

Perhaps it is because Carl's approach to his work is to make any food taste good. "It doesn't matter whether it's a pizza or a potato," he says with a coy, trademark grin. "I just enjoy putting as much energy and thought into a cheesecake as an omelet."

Carl's tasty victuals linger in the mind long after they have excited the palate. I just had to take home these recipes for an autumn dinner at my house. They are all easy to do and bring rave reviews from my guests. The apple-butternut squash soup is a nice change for a cold night's dinner. I do not care for beets, but I love them in the puréed beets recipe. And the chops filled with Brie make a gourmet entrée that's easy to do. The honey curry bread is so good that Carl has to bake it in nearly every season or guests complain.

Some might take the interference of people passing through their workspace as a nuisance; but Carl, a former school teacher, welcomes culinary queries from those interested in observing his methods. Many guests have left the Chesterfield not only with full bellies but also with a few new kitchen tips to tuck away for their own dinner guests.

A graduate of the Creative Cuisine Culinary School in Cambridge, Massachusetts, Carl came to the inn after cooking in fine Boston restaurants. When not in the kitchen, he is likely to be crafting replica furniture at home, for he is also a cabinetmaker of Early American and Shaker furniture and accessories. The same deft-

ness and attention to detail goes into his culinary work at The Chesterfield Inn.

When it comes time to change the menu, Carl gets out his cookbooks and thumbs through his original recipes to adapt or spin off new ones. Such was the case with the veal and Brie dish. "You can get tired of the same old cooking at home," observes Carl. "Why not look through your own cooking materials and think about tossing together all kinds of interesting ingredient combinations?"

A new dish is often born out of a meeting with innkeepers Judy and Phil Huber, who are omnipresent at the Chesterfield. "We make a ritual out of coming up with some exciting names for new recipes," says Judy. That takes in a host of novel Carl Warner combinations such as baked penne with roasted red pepper, garlic, and Mascarpone cheese; grilled duck breast and leg with Thai coconut milk; ravioli stuffed with whitefish and spinach with scallion beurre blanc; and grilled foccacia with Gorgonzola, caramelized red onions, toasted walnuts, and rosemary.

After dinner, overnight guests retire to attractive, accommodating guest rooms decorated by Judy, who crafted most of the quilts, curtains, and soft accents. The Chesterfield common areas are topped with beamed ceilings and rafters; originally, my room must have been a hayloft in this barn-like building. After dinner, I retreated to my suite with its own fireplace, just one level up from the kitchen.

Next morning, I found Judy at the stove cooking everyone's breakfast. It was off through the kitchen once again and into a glass-enclosed breakfast room for a bountiful morning meal. I could see the sign of the owl once again. So I raised a cup of coffee to salute that wise decision to pull off the road and visit the chef at The Chesterfield Inn.

The sitting room at the inn

Apple Butternut Squash Soup
❖

Filled with a nutty flavor, this soup tastes great any time of year and is a complement to most beef, veal, and poultry dishes.

➤   6   tablespoons (¾ stick) butter
➤   1   large onion, chopped
➤   3   pounds peeled, seeded butternut squash, cut into chunks
➤   8   red apples, peeled, cored, cut into chunks
➤   3   tablespoons sugar
➤   1   tablespoon cumin
➤   1   tablespoon cinnamon
➤   Salt and pepper to taste
➤ 10   cups chicken stock or broth
➤   Sour cream and chopped fresh chives for garnish

1. In a large saucepan melt the butter and sauté the onions until tender. Add the remaining ingredients except the garnishes. Bring the mixture to a boil. Reduce the heat and simmer for 30 to 45 minutes or until the squash is tender.
2. In a food processor purée the soup. Serve it warm with a dollop of sour cream and a sprinkling of chives.
   Yield: 12 servings

Honey Curry Bread
❖

The curry adds just the right hint of flavor to the honey bread.

➤   3   tablespoons dry yeast
➤ 2⅔ cups warm water (115°)
➤   7 to 8 cups all-purpose flour
➤   ½   cup honey
➤   3   tablespoons curry powder
➤   2   teaspoons salt
➤   1   egg, beaten
➤   ½   cup poppy seeds

1. In a small bowl stir together the yeast and warm water. Set the mixture aside for 5 minutes.
2. In a mixing bowl combine the flour, honey, curry, salt, and yeast mixture. Using a dough hook, knead the mixture for 6 to 7 minutes, until smooth and slightly moist. Place the dough in a large greased bowl. Cover the bowl with a kitchen towel and let the dough rise until doubled in size, about 1 hour.
3. Punch down the dough and divide it into thirds. Shape each into a small loaf. Place the loaves on a baking sheet. Cover the loaves and let them rise for 45 minutes.
4. Preheat the oven to 400°. Brush the tops of the loaves with egg and sprinkle them with poppy seeds. Make a ½-inch diagonal slit across the top of each loaf. Bake the bread for 45 minutes or until lightly browned. Cool on wire racks.
   Yield: 3 loaves

Grilled Veal Loin Chops Stuffed with Brie and Scallions

❖

When company is coming at the last minute or when you are late getting home and you want to fix a special dish, this offers a splendid solution!

➤ 1 bunch scallions, chopped
➤ 1 pound Brie at room temperature
➤ 8 8-ounce veal loin chops
➤ Olive oil
➤ Salt and pepper

1. In a medium bowl combine the chopped scallions and Brie, mashing the mixture into a soft paste.
2. Cut a pocket in the side of each chop, using a small paring knife that will make a slit to the bone. Fill each chop with scallion paste.
3. Preheat the grill or broiler. Brush each chop with olive oil and season with salt and pepper. Cook the chops for about 3 minutes on each side. Veal chops should remain slightly pink in the center.
Yield: 8 servings

Puréed Beets

❖

Easy and delicious, this side dish adds depth of color plus nutrition.

➤ 2 pounds fresh beets, roots and ends trimmed
➤ Salt and pepper
➤ 4 cups water
➤ ¼ cup horseradish
➤ 2 tablespoons red wine vinegar
➤ ¼ cup (½ stick) butter
➤ Salt and pepper

Chesterfield Inn and gardens

1. Preheat the oven to 400°. Sprinkle the beets with salt and pepper. In a baking dish cover the beets with the water. Cover the dish. Bake the beets for 90 minutes or until the beets are tender. Discard the water.
2. Peel the beets under cool, running water. (Beets peel easier when they are still hot.) Place the beets in a food processor with the horseradish, vinegar and butter, and add salt and pepper to taste. Process until smooth. Heat the beets until warmed and serve.
Yield: 8 servings

Flourless Chocolate Cake with English Custard Sauce

The cake is rich but light in texture and appears somewhat sunken when baked. This is normal.

Cake

➤ 1 pound semisweet chocolate squares
➤ 1 cup (2 sticks) butter
➤ 9 eggs, separated
➤ 1⅔ cups sugar
➤ 2 teaspoons vanilla extract
➤ ¼ cup Irish cream liqueur

English Custard Sauce

➤ 9 egg yolks
➤ 1⅓ cups sugar
➤ 3 cups milk
➤ 1 tablespoon vanilla extract

Flourless Chocolate Cake

1. Preheat the oven to 350°. In a double boiler over simmering water melt the chocolate and butter.
2. In a mixing bowl beat the yolks and sugar with a wire whisk, about 2 minutes. Add the vanilla and liqueur.
3. In another bowl beat the egg whites until stiff peaks form. Do not over beat or the cake will collapse too much.
4. Fold the yolk mixture into the melted chocolate. Add the egg whites and mix until well combined.
5. Pour the batter into a buttered 9-inch spring-form pan. Bake the cake for 40 to 45 minutes, or until a tester comes out clean.
6. In the top of a double boiler over simmering water whisk together the yolks and sugar for 1 minute.
7. In a medium saucepan scald the milk. Add the hot milk to the egg mixture, whisking momentarily and then stirring with a plastic spatula slowly and steadily, keeping the sides from hardening and the eggs from cooking. When thick enough to coat a spatula, remove the pan from the heat. Add the vanilla, and let the mixture cool to room temperature. Pour a ladleful onto each dessert plate and set a wedge of cake on top.

Yield: 10 to 12 servings

... For These Thy Gifts

Kedron Valley Inn
South Woodstock, Vermont

CHEF TOM HOPEWELL

Thanksgiving Dinner for Eight

Scallop and Wild Mushroom Bisque

◆

Baked Acorn and Butternut Squash

◆

Maple-Glazed Turkey Roulade with
Cranberry-Orange Sauce

◆

Cranberry-Walnut Yeast Bread

◆

Pistachio-Nut Chocolate Mousse Roll

*I*magine a sleigh ride over the river and through the woods to Thanksgiving dinner. Well, it may not happen exactly in that order; but if you are headed for the Kedron Valley Inn at this most festive time of year, there is a good chance you may experience a romantic jaunt through quiet South Woodstock. Horse-drawn sleigh rides begin here as soon as winter snows cloak central Vermont.

The inn is surrounded by local stables. So you can also amble about the meadows and paths on horseback in the warmer seasons by hitching onto a trail ride.

This is indeed a picture-perfect place for a dinner to give thanks for all your blessings, at any time of year.

Kedron Valley guest rooms are romantically appointed with antiques and modern-day amenities. Your stay is a contrast in time, highlighted by innkeeper Merrily Comins's antique quilt collection. There is an old quilt in every room, and many of them are of museum quality. The display revolves around family pieces made by Merrily's maternal relatives during the early 1900s.

The main inn dates from 1822 when it was a stagecoach stop. Merrily and her husband, Max, were living in an apartment in New York City when they traded their fast-paced jobs for the innkeeper's lantern. Max, also a singer and entertainer, found the inn to be an ideal place to play piano and entertain guests, which he does frequently.

Dinner is a four-star performance, orchestrated by chef Tom Hopewell in the inn's two spacious dining rooms. Tom is not one of Kedron Valley's innkeepers, but his love of the inn and the food service makes him a prime player in the Kedron Valley Inn experience. The relationship between this chef and the innkeepers is such a strong bond that Tom's decision-making responsibilities occasionally go beyond matters of food.

"I'm marketing-oriented," Tom told me over breakfast. He has been a chef at the inn since 1986, nearly as long as Max and Merrily have owned it. "So I keep in tune with what's going on as much as possible. I think that an understanding of what the innkeepers are trying to do is important for a chef in this type of food service. It's really a big part of my job."

Tom typifies the country inn chef who is hired by the owners but made to feel a part of the inn, not just someone who shows up for work. Max and Merrily were in search of a good cook when they first took over Kedron Valley, but the chemistry with other chefs wasn't working. Then Tom showed up.

He was a student of the prestigious La Varenne in France and was a sous chef to many European executive chefs. "I wouldn't want to be stuck back in the kitchen with tunnel vision, not being able to contribute to what goes into making Kedron Valley so special," he says. Perhaps that is why the chef's cuisine is a major draw for the inn. Tom's cooking has garnered an impressive amount of regional attention and is always complementary to the inn's atmosphere and activities.

"In France we learned to cook with local ingredients," he says. "I've brought that concept to the inn." The chef spends hours researching where to buy indigenous foodstuffs, including fresh pheasant, milk-fed veal, and goat cheese.

But he does not use his talents at the inn alone. When Tom is not spending leisure time with his son and daughter, he reaches out to the community, offering cooking classes and lectures.

Traditional holiday fare takes on new meaning at Kedron Valley. Tom, who usually cooks classic French and nouvelle Vermont cuisine, passes his magic gourmet wand over typical holiday food and creates a version that is hearty but picturesque. The turkey roulade, for instance, is a great alternative to cooking the big bird every year. Besides, it is a recipe that can be used long after the holidays have passed. I also find that I look to Tom's cranberry-walnut yeast bread now, whenever I serve baked chicken. The pistachio roll is a not-to-be-missed dessert—different and a surprise to your holiday guests. After enjoying your re-creation of Tom's menu, they'll feel as though they, too, have been over the river and through the woods to your house—the next best thing to grandmother's or, of course, to the Kedron Valley Inn.

Acorn squash and turkey roulade

Scallop and Wild Mushroom Bisque

❖

- ➤ ¼ cup quality olive oil
- ➤ 1 tablespoon chopped garlic
- ➤ ¼ cup chopped celery
- ➤ ¼ cup chopped onion
- ➤ ¼ cup chopped carrot
- ➤ 1 pound shiitake mushrooms, stemmed and chopped
- ➤ 1 cup fresh sea scallops, chopped
- ➤ ¼ cup Madeira wine
- ➤ 3 cups heavy cream
- ➤ 3 cups half-and-half
- ➤ Salt and white pepper to taste

1. In a large heavy-bottomed pot combine the olive oil, garlic, celery, onion, and carrot. Cook over low heat, stirring frequently, until tender but not brown, about 5 to 7 minutes.
2. Add the mushrooms, scallops, and wine, and cook over medium heat for 5 to 7 minutes, stirring frequently.
3. In a food processor purée the mixture until smooth.

4. Return the mixture to the pot and whisk in the heavy cream and half-and-half. Heat the bisque through. Season with salt and white pepper to taste.
Yield: 8 servings

Baked Acorn and Butternut Squash

❖

- ➤ 3 medium to large acorn squash, washed
- ➤ 1 medium butternut squash, washed
- ➤ ¼ cup vegetable oil
- ➤ 2 cups water
- ➤ ¼ cup chopped shallots
- ➤ ¼ cup chopped celery
- ➤ ¼ cup chopped carrots
- ➤ 2 tablespoons butter
- ➤ ½ teaspoon allspice
- ➤ Salt and white pepper

1. Preheat the oven to 350°. Stem the squash, cutting ⅓ of the top off each acorn squash. Save the tops. Scrape out the seeds. Cut the butternut squash lengthwise and remove seeds.

2. On a large baking sheet with at least 1-inch sides, place the squash cut-side down. Rub with oil and add the water. Bake the squash for 30 to 40 minutes or until tender. Remove the pan from the oven and let the squash cool. Reduce the oven temperature to 300°. Turn the acorn squash over and scrape ½ of the meat from the inside into a bowl, being careful not to break through the sides. Do the same with the butternut squash, adding it to the bowl.

3. In a 2 quart non stick saucepan melt the butter and sauté the shallots, celery, and carrots until soft, about 3 to 5 minutes. In a food processor combine the squash, sautéed mixture, salt, and pepper. Blend until smooth. Cut a small piece from the bottom of each acorn squash so that they will stand. Fill all of the squash halves with the squash mixture. Bake the stuffed squash until heated through.
Yield: 8 servings

Maple-Glazed Turkey Roulade with Cranberry-Orange Sauce

✤

Pueblo sun corn can be ordered from Fresh and Wild, P.O. Box 2981, Vancouver, WA 98668. Or substitute chopped walnuts.

Roulade
➤ 8 *4-ounce turkey breasts*
   Stuffing
➤ 2 *tablespoons butter*
➤ ¼ *cup chopped celery*
➤ ¼ *cup chopped onion*
➤ ¼ *cup Marsala wine*
➤ 6 *cups cooked wild rice*
➤ ½ *cup chopped pecans*
➤ ½ *cup Pueblo sun corn*
➤ 2 *tablespoons chopped sage*
➤ 2 *tablespoons chopped rosemary*
➤ 2 *eggs*
➤ *Salt and pepper*

Glaze
➤ 1 *cup apple cider*
➤ ⅓ *cup pure maple syrup*
   Cranberry-Orange Sauce
➤ 12 *ounces fresh cranberries*
➤ 1 *cup cranberry juice*
➤ ½ *cup orange juice*
➤ ½ *cup sugar*
➤ ¼ *cup Grand Marnier*
➤ ¼ *cup (½ stick) butter*
   Garnish
➤ *Crème fraîche*

---

1. Pound the breasts to ¼-inch thickness. Set them aside.

2. In a medium skillet heat the butter and sauté the celery and onions until soft. Stir in the Marsala and cook until the liquid is reduced by ½. Set the pan aside to cool.

3. In a 2-quart bowl mix together the celery and onion mixture, rice, pecans, corn, herbs, and eggs. Season with salt and pepper to taste.

4. In a small saucepan stir together the apple cider and maple syrup. Bring the glaze to a boil and cook over medium heat until reduced by ½. Keep warm.

5. Preheat the oven to 350°. Spread each turkey breast with just enough stuffing to be able to roll up the breast. Place the breasts seam-side down in a greased baking dish. Bake the turkey for 25 to 30 minutes, basting frequently with the maple glaze.

6. In a 1-quart saucepan combine the cranberries, juices, sugar, and Grand Marnier. Bring the mixture to a boil. Reduce the heat and simmer for 20 minutes. In a food processor purée the cranberry mixture until smooth. Strain and return it to the saucepan. Over low heat whisk in the butter a little at a time, stirring until melted.

7. Pour some sauce onto half of each plate. Add the crème fraîche in dots and draw the dots out with a knife. (See the photo on page 142.) Slice the turkey breasts on the diagonal into 4 equal slices per roll. Place 2 pieces of the roulade in the center of the plate.
Yield: 8 servings

Cranberry-Walnut Yeast Bread

Thanksgiving dishes tend to be sweet, including the sweet quick breads I make in abundance at this time of year. So I really welcomed this easy yeast bread, which still contains hallmark flavors of the season without the added sugar.

- ➤ *1 package active dry yeast*
- ➤ *¼ cup warm water (115°)*
- ➤ *1 teaspoon sugar*
- ➤ *1½ cups milk*
- ➤ *½ cup water*
- ➤ *2 teaspoons salt*
- ➤ *5½ cups bread or all-purpose flour*
- ➤ *1 cup chopped walnuts*
- ➤ *1 cup chopped fresh cranberries or ½ cup dried*
- ➤ *1 egg*
- ➤ *Water*

1. In a small bowl stir together the yeast, warm water, and sugar. Let the mixture stand for 5 to 8 minutes.
2. In a small saucepan combine the milk, water, and salt. Heat to 115°. Pour the milk mixture into a mixer bowl or food processor with a dough-hook attachment. Add the yeast mixture. As the mixer is running, slowly add the flour, nuts, and cranberries, adding extra flour if the dough is sticky. Mix until smooth and the dough forms a ball. Turn the dough onto a floured surface and knead it for 5 to 8 minutes. Place the dough in a large greased bowl. Cover the bowl with a kitchen towel, and let the dough rise in a warm spot until doubled in size. Punch it down and let it rise again.
3. Preheat the oven to 350°. Divide the dough in half and shape into 2 loaves, or form into rolls and braids if desired. Place the loaves on a greased baking sheet. Beat together the egg and water, and brush the loaves with the mixture. Let the loaves rise until doubled in size.

Bake the bread for 30 minutes, or until golden brown.
Yield: 2 loaves

Pistachio-Nut Chocolate Mousse Roll

I love pistachio nuts, but I rarely see any good recipes that use them. I asked Tom for a dessert with pistachios, and he came up with this smashing dish that is easy to do and is a nice change from traditional Thanksgiving desserts.

Cake

- ➤ *½ cup extra fine granulated sugar, sifted*
- ➤ *3 large eggs*
- ➤ *¾ cup sifted cake flour*
- ➤ *1 cup chopped red pistachios, plus a few whole nuts for garnish*

Decorating the turkey roulade

Pistachio-Nut Chocolate Mousse Roll

Mousse

- ➤ 1½ *cups heavy cream*
- ➤ 2 *tablespoons sugar*
- ➤ 4 *ounces quality bittersweet chocolate*
- ➤ 1 *tablespoon quality dark rum*
- ➤ 2 *egg yolks*

1. Preheat the oven to 425°. Let all of the ingredients come to room temperature.
2. Cut a piece of newspaper about ½-inch larger all around than a jelly-roll pan. Cover the newspaper with waxed paper or foil. Dust with cake flour and set it aside. Cut a piece of waxed paper to fit inside the pan. Brush the paper and the sides of the pan with oil.
2. In a heat proof bowl bake the sugar for about 4 minutes or until hot, but not melting. Break the eggs into a large bowl. Pour the hot sugar into the eggs and beat with an electric mixer at medium speed for 6 to 7 minutes or until doubled in volume.
3. Shake the flour lightly over the mixture. Fold the flour in gently with a rubber spatula until well incorporated. Pour the batter into the prepared pan and sprinkle with half of the nuts. Bake the cake for 9 minutes or until golden brown. Remove the cake from the oven. Run a metal spatula around the sides of the pan, turn the cake onto the prepared working surface, and let it cool.
4. In a small saucepan mix 3 ounces of the cream with the sugar. Bring the mixture to a boil. Add the chocolate, stirring until the chocolate is melted. Stir in the rum and egg yolks. Remove the pan from the heat and cool to room temperature.
5. In a large bowl whip the remaining heavy cream until stiff. Fold the whipped cream into the chocolate mixture. Refrigerate until ready to use.
6. When the cake is cooled, spread the mousse ¼ to ½-inch thick over the cake. Sprinkle with the remaining pistachios and gently press them into the mousse.
7. With both hands, pick up the edge of the newspaper on the longer side and roll up the cake, pushing with the palm of your hand behind the paper. Frost the cake with more mousse. Sprinkle a few whole pistachios on top. Serve with whipped cream, if desired. **Yield: 8 servings**

'Tis the Season

The Checkerberry Inn
Goshen, Indiana

CHEF DOUG MORGAN

Dinner for Eight

❖

Twin Pea Soup

◆

*Roasted Pheasant on Polenta
with Sherry-Pomegranate Sauce*

◆

*Pesto Chicken Dijon in
Lemon-Thyme Velouté*

◆

*Vegetable-Stuffed
Christmas Bouquetiers*

◆

*Amaretto-Filled Chocolate Strawberries on
White Chocolate Fettucine*

We knew we were
closing in on the Checkerberry Inn, but we
passed it altogether, distracted by the en-
chanting sights along the roadway. A
pristine patchwork of harvested farmland
was dotted with the simple homes of the
Old Order Amish. Their quaint, horse-
drawn buggies were out and about, literally
slowing down the fast-lane. Could this
sparsely traveled, timeless route be the road
to a great chef?

Suddenly realizing we had gone too far,
we retraced our steps and soon found our-
selves at the front door of The Checkerberry
Inn. A hand-carved wooden reindeer greeted
us before we met chef Doug Morgan, who
was busy in the kitchen preparing for a holiday dinner party. The late winter afternoon

sun wreathed the inn, casting its light in checkerboards on the floor through large, mullioned windows.

By supper time the whitewashed dining room beckoned us to take our place in front of a glowing fire. We sat on comfortable chairs made from hickory trees. The striking texture and shading of the deep-brown bark framework made an interesting contrast to the bright, bold designer fabrics dancing about the windows and tables.

First, we sampled the inn's sourdough French bread, served in a tiny plate of extra virgin olive oil, enhanced by garlic and herbs and cooked in the microwave for thirty seconds to infuse the flavor. You dip your bread into this, a technique that is only slowly catching on in America but has since made its way to my own table at home. What a perfectly marvelous excuse to buy one of those attractively decorated oil cans! I love

this most civilized, refreshing way of eating bread. And the taste? Well, you'll have to see for yourself! Surprising again, that this fine inn—perched among silos and pastures—is right up to date, even trendsetting.

We sampled many of Doug's dishes, including a marvelous pheasant and holiday ahi (broiled tuna in a pineapple sauce). His pièce de résistance was a dessert of fresh strawberries intertwined with ribbons of white chocolate masquerading as fettucine.

"I just let the food do the talking," says Doug. Indeed, this friendly, conversing, amusing, but always erudite chef creates for the eye and the taste buds. Doug cooked in fine restaurants from Colorado to California and Hawaii before coming to Indiana, where his wife, Charlene, has roots.

Indiana is not California, so matters of taste tend to be somewhat guarded. But Doug is undaunted: "I give them a potato if

Coconut makes good sliding material for this sled of hors d'oeuvres.

that's what they want. But you can bet that it will be the best potato they've ever had."

Doug proved that when he brought out a deliciously flavored dish of red potatoes. He had shaped them like mushrooms (see photo, page 150). The chef showed me how easy it is to create the sculpture. Merely take small red potatoes, clean them, and plunge a hollow tube (¾-inch in diameter) 1 inch into the potato. Cut away excess potato. Pull the tube away and you have a mushroom shape. Cook until tender and season with butter, salt, pepper, and chopped garlic. Roast potatoes in a 400-degree oven until golden brown and tender, about 15 minutes.

Although he has tamed some of his desire to conduct culinary experiments, Doug still feels it is important to offer local diners a taste of the world through his cooking. In fact, he orders much of his specialty seafood sent fresh all the way from Hawaii. Despite the most flamboyant and exotic places he has worked, Doug is in his element here. "People walk through the door and don't expect anything special in these parts." What they find, of course, is the unexpected; and Doug enjoys introducing them to new things.

Innkeeper Susan Graff, who owns Checkerberry with her husband, John, is an interior designer. It shows throughout the inn, built by the Graffs in 1988 and named after the native checkerberry, or wintergreen plant. European and post-modern with oriental and regional sums up the inn's eclectic decorating scheme. Many of the rooms are adorned with Amish straw hats perched in a row above the bed, scrubbed pine furniture, and prints by the masters: Toulouse-Lautrec, Matisse, and more. Only when you catch an earful of one of the twenty-five or so Amish buggies that trot past the inn every day do you remember that you are in the American heartland and not the French countryside.

The white-paneled Checkerberry Suite, with its Pierre Deux fabrics, is as consistently sunny as the weather in Provence, with its canary yellows and royal blues. The suite hosts a large sitting area, two baths, and—like the rest of the inn—panoramic views of the surrounding farmland.

In fact, when the Graffs designed the kitchen, they included a large picture window here as well. As a result, the chef and staff can also enjoy scenes from the land that bears a veritable cornucopia of fresh ingredients used at the inn. Inn food is purchased primarily through local Amish farms. On any day, you can ride past the farms and find signs for everything from eggs to free-range pheasants.

The common sitting room is large and luxurious, highlighted with copper and marble. It includes two powder rooms named Rosemary and Basil, two herbs that bring me back to the dining experience at the Checkerberry.

The sophistication of the inn is evident on the events calendar. It includes celebrations such as a harvest fest for Nouveau wines (Doug's favorites), beer tasting dinners, and a Le Retraite aux Flambeaux celebration to recognize Bastille Day. Goshen is an unusual place for an inn with such a cosmopolitan personality. It is as though the innkeepers heard a voice à la the movie, *Field of Dreams*. As a local writer once scribed: "Build an inn and restaurant, and they will come."

They have come—the discriminating, the adventurous, and, of course, the mercurial Doug Morgan. This worldly cook is becoming every part of the land and the people. When I visited, he was in the midst of restoring a one hundred-year-old Amish house and farm for Charlene and their three children. There is no question that this was indeed the road to a great chef.

Twin Pea Soup

Twin Pea Soup

You will need two 1-gallon pots to make two batches of soup, one green batch and one yellow.

- ➤ 2 cups dry green split peas
- ➤ 2 cups dry yellow split peas
- ➤ 12 cups chicken stock or broth
- ➤ 2 teaspoons thyme
- ➤ 2 cloves garlic, cut in half crosswise
- ➤ 2 teaspoons cumin
- ➤ 4 bay leaves
- ➤ 2 onions, coarsely chopped
- ➤ 2 carrots, coarsely chopped
- ➤ 6 celery stalks, coarsely chopped
- ➤ Julienned ham for garnish

1. Place the green peas in 1 saucepan and the yellow peas in another. Add half of each ingredient to each pan, except the ham. Stir each and bring both to a boil. Reduce the heat to simmer and cook for 90 minutes, stirring every 10 minutes to prevent sticking. The soup is done when the peas soften and the skins dissolve.
2. Pour each soup through a strainer separately, then through a chinois strainer to achieve a satiny smooth texture. Add more stock to thin, if desired. Remove the bay leaves.
3. To serve, simultaneously ladle the green and yellow soups into the serving bowls so that they meet in the middle. Sprinkle with ham.
Yield: 14 cups

Roasted Pheasant on Polenta with Sherry-Pomegranate Sauce

If you are serving this menu exactly, serve either the pheasant or the pesto chicken as an entrée or offer smaller portions of both, so guests can try each one.

Polenta
- ➤ 2 quarts water
- ➤ 2 teaspoons salt
- ➤ 2 cups cornmeal
- ➤ 1 cup cold water
- ➤ 1 teaspoon each fresh basil, thyme, rosemary, and cilantro
- ➤ ¼ cup freshly grated Parmesan cheese
- ➤ ½ red bell pepper, finely diced
- ➤ ½ teaspoon freshly ground black pepper
- ➤ All-purpose flour
- ➤ Vegetable oil
Pheasant
- ➤ 4 small pheasants
- ➤ 1 carrot, chopped
- ➤ 1 large onion, chopped
- ➤ 2 stalks celery, chopped
- ➤ 1 teaspoon fresh thyme
- ➤ 1 bay leaf
Pomegranate Sauce
- ➤ 1 clove garlic, finely chopped
- ➤ 1 large shallot, finely chopped
- ➤ 1 tablespoon butter
- ➤ 1 cup dry sherry
- ➤ 1 tablespoon chopped fresh thyme
- ➤ 1 medium pomegranate, berries reserved and remainder discarded

1. In a large saucepan boil the water with the salt. In a small bowl mix the cornmeal and cold water. Stir the mixture into the boiling water, reduce the heat, and simmer for 10 to

Pheasant and Polenta with Amish-made angels

15 minutes, stirring constantly. Remove the pan from the heat and blend in the remaining polenta ingredients. Pour the batter into 2 9 x 5-inch greased loaf pans. (The batter will only be 2 inches deep in the pan.) Cool overnight.

2. When cold, remove the polenta from the pans and slice it into ¾-inch thick pieces. Dredge the slices in flour. In a large skillet heat ⅛-inch of oil and sauté the polenta. When browned on both sides, remove the fried polenta and cut each piece into diagonal slices. Set the slices aside.

3. Preheat the oven to 425°. Place the pheasant in a large roasting pan with the carrot, onion, and celery. Bake the pheasant for 15 minutes. Reduce the oven temperature to 300° and continue to bake for 25 minutes, or until the birds are browned, basting frequently with the pan juices. Remove the pheasant from the oven and let them cool.

4. Pour the juices from the birds and the pan drippings into a large stock pot. Remove the breasts from the birds, including the first digit of the wing bone. Remove the legs and thighs, and snack on them later. Place the pheasant bones in the pot with the drippings, thyme, and bay leaf. Add cold water to cover. Bring the liquid to boil. Reduce the heat and simmer for 30 to 45 minutes. Strain off the bones and discard them. Boil the remaining stock until reduced by half. Remove the stock from heat and refrigerate it until chilled.

5. One hour before serving, prepare the sauce. In a skillet melt the butter and sauté garlic and shallots until the shallots are transparent. Add sherry, cooking until reduced by ⅔. Add the pheasant stock, and simmer until ready to use. One minute before serving, add the thyme and pomegranate berries.

6. Preheat the oven to 350°. Ten minutes before serving, place the breasts in a shallow pan. Warm the breasts in the oven. Slice and fan them out over the polenta. Add the pomegranate sauce.

Yield: 8 servings

Pesto Chicken Dijon

Pesto Chicken Dijon in Lemon-Thyme Velouté

❖

Chicken

➤ *2 tablespoons fresh basil*
➤ *2 tablespoons freshly grated Parmesan cheese*
➤ *1 clove garlic, peeled*
➤ *2 tablespoons olive oil*
➤ *2 tablespoons pommery mustard*
➤ *1 tablespoon Dijon mustard*
➤ *8 large chicken breasts, pounded to ½-inch thickness*
➤ *Oil for coating*

Velouté

➤ *1 tablespoon freshly chopped thyme*
➤ *1 quart chicken stock*
➤ *1 clove garlic, cut in half crosswise*
➤ *Juice of ½ lemon*
➤ *3 tablespoons cornstarch mixed with just enough water to make a liquid*

1. Preheat the oven to 400°. In a food processor purée the basil, cheese, garlic, and olive oil to make a pesto. Blend in the mustards. Coat the underside of each breast with the mixture, then roll up, coated side in. Brush oil onto the outside of each breast and place them in a baking dish. Bake the chicken for 12 to 18 minutes or until firm. Let the chicken stand for 5 to 10 minutes before slicing, then slice each breast into 5 even pieces.

2. Remove the stems from the thyme and finely chop the leafy part. In a medium saucepan combine the stock, thyme, garlic, and lemon juice. Bring the mixture to a boil. Add the cornstarch mixture, reduce the heat, and simmer until the velouté reaches sauce consistency. Strain and pour it over each chicken breast. Reserve any remaining sauce for another recipe.

Yield: 8 servings

Vegetable-Stuffed Christmas Bouquetiers

❖

These little tomato baskets are most festive.

- ➤ ¼ cup white wine
- ➤ ¼ cup chicken stock
- ➤ ¼ cup white vinegar
- ➤ 2 cloves garlic, mashed
- ➤ ⅛ teaspoon saffron
- ➤ ½ head cabbage, quartered, cored, and sliced into thin strips
- ➤ ½ head cauliflower
- ➤ ½ head broccoli
- ➤ 5 medium red but hard tomatoes

---

1. In a large pot combine the wine, chicken stock, vinegar, garlic, and saffron and simmer until well combined, about 5 minutes. Add the cabbage and cover tightly. Simmer until all of the liquid disappears, stirring frequently, about 1 hour or longer. When done, remove the cabbage from the pot and cool.
2. Par-cook the cauliflower, in rapidly boiling salted water for about 5 minutes, then add the broccoli. Remove the vegetables from the pot when they are tender but still crisp. Plunge them into ice water to stop the cooking process. Drain. Break the cauliflower and broccoli into flowerettes.
3. Core the tomatoes and flatten the ends by shaving them slightly with a knife so they sit nicely on plates. Cut each tomato in half, scoop out the pulp and discard it. Fill each tomato with cabbage, cauliflower, and broccoli.

Yield: 10 bouquetiers

Amaretto-Filled Chocolate Strawberries on White Chocolate Fettucine

Strawberries on White Chocolate Fettucine

Chocolate Fettucine
- ➤ 7 ounces white chocolate, melted
- ➤ ¼ cup light corn syrup
- ➤ Confectioners' sugar

Strawberries
- ➤ 24 large ripe strawberries, washed and patted dry
- ➤ Amaretto liqueur
- ➤ 8 ounces dark sweet chocolate, melted

Strawberry Sauce
- ➤ 24 ripe strawberries

1. In a small bowl mix together the white chocolate and corn syrup until a soft dough forms. On a parchment or waxed paper surface gently roll out the dough by hand to ⅛-inch thickness. Cool until hardened in the refrigerator. Then run the chocolate through a pasta machine fitted for fettucine cut. (If you don't have a pasta maker, cut the chocolate into thin strips to resemble cooked fettucine, about ⅓-inch wide.) While cutting, let the strips fall into a pile of the confectioners' sugar to prevent them from sticking. Refrigerate them for later use.
2. Using a cooking syringe, inject 24 of the strawberries with a squirt of Amaretto. Dip each strawberry into the melted dark chocolate. Place the berries on parchment or waxed paper on a baking sheet and cool them in the refrigerator.
3. Purée the remaining berries until smooth. Sift through a chinois or other fine strainer. Cover each plate with a layer of sauce. Add a few fettucine noodles and top with 3 chocolate-dipped strawberries per plate.
Yield: 8 servings

Winter Warmer from the Adirondacks

The Interlaken Inn
Lake Placid, New York

INNKEEPER/CHEF CAROL JOHNSON

Dinner for Eight

Mushroom Strudel with
Potato Leek Sauce

◆

Cream of Chestnut Soup

◆

Cornish Game Hens with
Apricot Grand Marnier Sauce

◆

Praline Sweet Potatoes

◆

Apple Tarts with Caramel Sauce

*T*he name means "land between the lakes," and you couldn't describe the location of this hilltop inn any better. Interlaken Inn is perched high above Mirror Lake, with views of it from third-floor rooms. Also within walking distance is Lake Placid.

The winters are long but full of activity and the remembrances of 1980, when the area hosted the Thirteenth Winter Olympics. Visitors can go "zigging" and "zagging" down the same bobsled course that was used during the games; peer up in disbelief at daredevil ski jumpers; take in an ice hockey match; skate romantically on frozen lakes; swoosh down a toboggan run; and mount the trails themselves, hiking or skiing cross country.

This wealth of activities draws the "outdoor crowd," as Carol Johnson describes her guests. In her and husband Roy's 1906 inn, they cater to the ambitious, active types who want an atmosphere of casual comfort. Whether coming off a snowy slope or a spectator's bleacher, Interlaken guests retire to spacious rooms, some with sitting areas and all decorated by a wide-brimmed hat on the door. A carafe of sherry on each room's desk or dresser takes the nip off any blustery afternoon.

Carol has a flair for decorating, and she hand-painted a trailing vine up the scissored main staircase. She is always working on a new project in one of the rooms. When I visited, she was resurfacing ceilings with a raised-print Victorian wallpaper. It will complement the original, magnificently patterned tin ceilings in the dining room and the large foyer.

The inn was known as a cottage at the turn of the century. By today's standards, it is a very big cottage! The building houses twelve guest rooms, several common areas, and open-air and closed porches for guest rooms and the morning meal.

After shedding heavy winter apparel, Interlaken visitors stop by Roy's cocktail lounge—complete with his golf souvenirs—for a drink and the innkeeper's wealth of personal anecdotes. Others relax by a fire in the living room. Dinner is served in an intimate dining room where this sportsman like crowd sheds its competitive personality for the gentility of a quiet evening with candlelight and gourmet fare.

Carol serves up a five-course dinner, and the pageantry of luscious foods floats out in such dishes as sautéed veal with tomatoes and Gruyère cheese served with a mushroom sauce, veal with brandied peaches, poached salmon with a champagne sauce, or Southwestern chicken in a puff pastry.

Your menu for a winter dinner party can start with a fondue and some warm beverages by the fire before you seat your guests at the dinner table. You can make an extra recipe of Carol's potato leek sauce from the mushroom strudel. Add some Gruyère

cheese and wine and heat through in a fondue pot, serving with cubes of French bread
to dip in the hot sauce.

The cream of chestnut is one of the more
unusual soups I have come across. Years ago
when I researched an article on cooking
with chestnuts, I missed this idea altogether,
but I did discover that chestnuts are an
energy-rich and highly nutritious food.
They contain high proportions of starch and
potassium, plus vitamins B and C. So I
highly recommend this bowl of creamy
brew.

Cornish hens are a favorite of mine for
serving guests because they make such a
complete and impressive dish. While we
have pictured them family-style here, you
can serve one per plate on top of a bed of
rice and vegetables.

Carol's apple tarts not only look elegant,
but they taste divine. You will find them
easy to construct and a pleasure to serve.
Creating desserts is a favorite pastime for
Carol and her son, Kevin Gregg, who together make a house specialty that looks too
good to eat. It consists of a vine-like basket
formed from dark chocolate and filled with
the lightest, tastiest white chocolate mousse
I've ever encountered.

They make everything fresh at Interlaken, including their own salsa. When I say
"they," I'm talking about the family. While
Carol is the main menu-planner and chef,
daughter Kathy is the assistant manager;
daughter Karri serves as part of the wait
staff whenever she is home from college;
and Kevin, a Culinary Institute of America
graduate, blends the best of his technical
schooling and his mother's experience in the
kitchen. Roy, who lived for many years
in California's Napa Valley, acts as the
sommelier. He accompanies his delightful
selection of wines with effervescent stories
of their origin.

In 1912 the Lake Placid newspaper re-
ported on the many merits of the original
building that is now Carol and Roy's place.
Forrest B. Guild, the property's original in-

Arch was handpainted by the chef.

vestor, was hailed in the article for attaining
"a standard of excellence . . . that will be
difficult to rival" in his design for the "finest
and most commanding location for homes
that is to be found in Lake Placid." In all
they do at Interlaken—from the cooking to
the cosseting of their guests—they are
"returning to that era," says Carol. And it is
true today that when you have a family running a country inn together, it is a special
breed of inn.

They work as a team at Interlaken,
blending fine culinary performances with
award-winning hospitality. The true spirit of
country innkeeping cheers you on, and you
cannot help but applaud the Johnson family
as they go for the gold every day.

Mushroom Strudel with Potato Leek Sauce

❖

You will be making four whole strudels, cutting each into four even pieces. Serve one piece per guest. Wrap and refrigerate any extra slices for your next day's lunch.

Mushroom Strudel

Potato Leek Sauce
- ➤ 3 *baking potatoes, peeled and quartered*
- ➤ 2 *leeks (white part only), sliced*
- ➤ 2 *cups chicken stock or broth*
- ➤ ½ *cup heavy cream*

Strudel Filling
- ➤ ¾ *cup (1½ sticks) butter, melted*
- ➤ 6 *cups minced mushrooms, tops and stems*
- ➤ 1 *teaspoon salt*
- ➤ ¼ *teaspoon curry powder*
- ➤ ½ *cup sherry*
- ➤ ¼ *cup chopped shallots*
- ➤ 1 *cup sour cream*
- ➤ 1½ *cups dry bread crumbs*
- ➤ 1 *16-ounce box frozen phyllo dough, thawed*
- ➤ *Sour cream and chopped parsley for garnish*

1. In a medium saucepan over medium heat cook the potatoes and leeks in chicken stock until tender. Spoon into a blender and purée, while adding the cream. Return the sauce to the saucepan and keep it warm while preparing the strudel.
2. In a large skillet over medium heat melt the butter and sauté the mushrooms with the salt, curry, sherry, and shallots until the mushrooms are wilted and liquid is gone. Let the mixture cool. Add the sour cream and ½ cup of the bread crumbs.
3. Place a sheet of phyllo dough on a bread board. Brush it lightly with some of the melted butter, and sprinkle with a coating of bread crumbs. Repeat this process until you have 4 layers.
4. Preheat the oven to 350°. Spoon ¼ of the mushroom mixture onto the narrow end of the dough. Turn the long sides of the dough in about 1 inch to seal the filling, and roll up jelly roll-style. Brush the roll with butter and sprinkle with more of the crumbs. Place it on a lightly greased baking sheet and score with 4 knife marks for slicing through later. Repeat the above process to make 3 more strudels. Bake the strudels for 25 minutes or until golden brown. Slice each strudel into 4 pieces. Spoon some of the potato leek sauce onto each serving plate. Place a slice of the strudel on top. Garnish each piece with a dollop of sour cream and chopped parsley.
Yield: 4 strudels, 16 slices

Cream of Chestnut Soup

❖

For a more casual party I would serve this soup by the fire in attractive mugs or punch cups before sitting down to the dining table. You might even want to roast the nuts at the fire as appetizers in a perforated chestnut pan or a wire basket. When buying chestnuts, select heavy, hard, and shiny nuts.

➤ 2 pounds fresh chestnuts, peeled (see step 1) or 2 8-ounce jars chestnuts, peeled and drained

➤ ¼ cup (½ stick) butter

➤ 2 carrots, peeled and diced

➤ 1 small onion, minced

➤ 1 clove garlic, minced

➤ 3 scallions, chopped

➤ 3 stalks celery, chopped

➤ 5 cups chicken stock or broth

➤ 2 tablespoons brown sugar

➤ 1 teaspoon nutmeg

➤ Salt and pepper to taste

➤ 2 cups heavy cream

➤ ⅓ cup hazelnut liqueur

---

1. Preheat the oven to 400°. Cut an X into the rounded part of the chestnut. Roast the nuts on a baking sheet for 5 minutes. Remove the nuts from their shells using a small paring knife and peel away the shell and membrane. It works best to only do a few nuts at a time, for they must be kept warm to ensure easy peeling.
2. In a large saucepan melt the butter over medium heat. Add all of the vegetables and sauté until soft but not browned, about 5 minutes. Add the chestnuts, broth, brown sugar, nutmeg, and seasonings. Reduce the heat and simmer for 40 minutes or until the chestnuts are soft.
3. In a food processor purée the soup. Return it to the saucepan, add the cream and liqueur, and stir until heated through.
Yield: 8 servings

Cornish Game Hens with Apricot Grand Marnier Sauce

❖

➤ 8 18-ounce Cornish game hens, washed and dried

➤ Salt and freshly ground pepper to taste

➤ 3 tablespoons freshly chopped rosemary (1 tablespoon dried)

Sauce

➤ 1½ cups dried apricots, quartered

➤ 1½ cups applesauce

➤ ¾ cup firmly packed brown sugar

➤ 1 teaspoon cloves

➤ 2 teaspoons cinnamon

➤ 2 teaspoons grated orange zest

➤ 1½ cups dry white wine

➤ ¼ cup Grand Marnier

➤ Fresh sprigs of parsley and rosemary for garnish

---

1. Preheat the oven to 350°. Place the hens on a rack in a large sheet pan, breast side up. Season inside and out with salt, pepper, and rosemary. Roast the hens for 1 hour or until golden brown.
2. In a medium saucepan combine the apricots, applesauce, sugar, spices, zest, and white wine. Simmer uncovered for 30 minutes, stirring occasionally. Add the Grand Marnier and continue cooking for 10 minutes, stirring occasionally.
3. Spoon 1 cup of the sauce over the hens and roast them for an additional 30 minutes. Keep the remaining sauce warm to serve with the hens.
Yield: 8 servings

Cornish Hens and Praline Sweet Potatoes

Praline Sweet Potatoes
✥

This delicious dish also goes nicely with lamb and pork.

➤ 4 *cups cooked mashed sweet potatoes*
➤ 1 *cup packed brown sugar*
➤ 3 *eggs, beaten*
➤ ¼ *cup (½ stick) butter*
➤ 1 *teaspoon vanilla extract*
　　Topping
➤ 1 *cup packed brown sugar*
➤ 1 *cup chopped pecans*
➤ 1 *cup grated coconut*
➤ ⅓ *cup butter*
➤ ⅓ *cup all-purpose flour*

1. Preheat the oven to 350°. In a large bowl mix the sweet potatoes, sugar, eggs, butter, and vanilla.

2. In a separate small bowl mix the sugar, pecans, coconut, butter, and flour. Pour the potato mixture into a buttered casserole. Top the sweet potatoes with the crumb mixture. Bake the sweet potatoes for 30 to 40 minutes or until golden.
Yield: 8 servings

Apple Tarts with Caramel Sauce
✥

➤ 1 *17¼-ounce package puff pastry sheets*
➤ 1½ *cups slivered almonds*
➤ ⅓ *cup confectioners' sugar*
➤ 2 *tablespoons white corn syrup*
➤ ¼ *cup heavy cream*
➤ 4 *Granny Smith apples, cored and thinly sliced*
➤ 1 *egg, beaten*
➤ *Quality caramel sauce*

1. Preheat the oven to 400°. Cut the puff pastry into 8 6-inch circles and set it aside.
2. In a food processor finely chop the almonds. Add the sugar, syrup, and cream until well blended.
3. Place 2 tablespoons of the almond mixture in the center of each circle. Place the apple slices on top in a circle. Brush the pastry that's around the apples with the egg wash. Place the tarts on a lightly greased baking sheet. Bake the tarts for 15 minutes or until golden. Remove them from the oven and let them sit a few minutes. Drizzle caramel sauce on top and serve.
Yield: 8 servings

Apple Tarts and the chef's collection of hat pins

❖ WINTER WARMER FROM THE ADIRONDACKS ❖
159

From This Night Forward: New Year's Eve

Richmond Hill Inn
Asheville, North Carolina

CHEF JOHN BABB

Dinner for Eight

Smoked Salmon Chowder

•

*Provolone and Sun-Dried Tomato Terrine
with Pesto Dressing*

•

Lobster Ravioli in Saffron Sauce

•

Champagne-Raspberry Sorbet

•

*Shrimp with Apples and Snow
Peas in a Wine and Mustard
Cream Sauce*

•

Lemon Zest Tart

My first real taste of the elegance of Richmond Hill began while walking through the great hall of raised-panel oak and up the grand stairs to tour the historic bedrooms, named after prominent North Carolina citizens. The mansion has been masterfully renovated into a classic country house hotel high atop a hill.

Dinner offered a second sampling of Richmond Hill graciousness. My table was on the enclosed porch where I could behold the mountainous Asheville skyline on a fiery dusk canvas. As I opened the menu, I was awestruck by something that made it clear why this is such a special place.

It was not the chef's impressive bill of fare—the salmon mousseline with smoked mountain trout, the shrimp in strawberry

A portrait of Gabrielle Pearson watches over Richmond Hill's living room.

sauce, or the crayfish pasta pillows in basil tomato coulis. Having just visited with chef John Babb, I wasn't surprised to find these and other culinary treasures on his table d'hôte. John has worked from coast to coast, orchestrating diets for prize fighters and other celebrities, including Frank Sinatra, Gerald Ford, and Richard Nixon. Classically trained under the seasoned whisk of European chefs, he says, "It was my love of eating that got me interested in food. I just followed my palate, and my career evolved."

No, the menu had me spellbound for another reason. It was not even the rundown of New Year's Eve dinner selections or the summary of upcoming special events, which included English Evenings. These Richmond Hill events begin with tea or traditional lagers, ales, and stouts along with British videos, chess matches, and copies of *The London Times*. All these are offered be-

fore guests sit down to authentic English fare of leek and braised celery soup, lamb chops with Welsh onion cakes, Yorkshire pudding, and baked Devonshire apple dumplings.

What actually caught my eye were the two oval-framed portraits on either side of the menu. One depicts Gabrielle Pearson, the original hostess of the manor, from whom the inn's restaurant—Gabrielle's—now takes its name. The facing portrait shows her husband, Richmond, who built Richmond Hill in 1889. The more I studied the inn's past and present, the more I felt that this tableside tribute to the Pearsons is an intriguing one.

Richmond Pearson was a twenty-year veteran of the North Carolina Supreme Court and a foreign diplomat. These roles found the Pearson family entertaining all the time. Hosting overnight guests and spreading a bountiful table before these visitors was especially important to Mrs. Pearson.

A burly but soft-spoken individual who could be actor John Goodman's double, John Babb approaches food with a genteel reverence and careful attention to detail. Far be it from him to cook pasta in anything but a flavored liquid—as he explains in the recipe for lobster ravioli. And he is most concerned that we cook his raviolis "ever so sublimely."

John loves entertaining, and says Richmond Hill affords him just the right size and atmosphere to pursue his dreams as a culinary host. In this New Year's Eve menu, he balances the seafood with the lemon tart, which he explains is a palate-pleasing end to any fish dinner. The ravioli, he adds as a tasty starch. And the sorbet is a festive intermezzo for the new year ahead.

Jake and Marge Michel, the current owners of Richmond Hill, are the new breed of Pearsons, if you will. They purchased the mansion and the surrounding forty acres in 1987 through the auspices of their other business, The Education Center in Greenville, North Carolina. Their purchase and subsequent restoration work came not long after the local preservation society had saved the aging home from demolition and moved the one and one-half-million-pound structure six hundred feet to a new, permanent resting place.

The Michel's daughter, Susan, is the very capable and refreshingly unpretentious innkeeper of Richmond Hill. Oddly enough, the attitude and personality of each member of the Michel family reminded me of something else I had seen and read at the inn. When Marge Michel entered the room, I had to look twice. Surely, I thought, she resembles the woman in the menu whose original oil portrait hangs in the grand oak hall as it probably has for much of the time since it was painted in Paris in 1888. Indeed, the features and coloring of Gabrielle Pearson and Marge are similar; and from what I've read and observed, they also share the quality of a gracious and happy heart.

Jake, a former school teacher, told me he always wanted an historic building. Along the way to Richmond Hill, he left his elementary school teaching post to start a publishing and distribution company for teaching aids. Today the company is a leader in supplying educational materials to grade schools nationwide. Richmond Pearson was also a strong proponent of education. In 1887 he was instrumental in establishing the Asheville public school system.

Records from the estate best illustrate the fascinating parallels between the two families. One passage describes Richmond Pearson as "cultivated, well-read, and a well-educated gentleman who was handsome, agreeable, and humorous." That seems to sum up not only Jake Michel but the character of the entire inn today. This, too, is a stunningly handsome place, one that any sojourner will find most pleasant and filled with good cheer.

Beyond these correlations, there is one I find to be even more enthralling. Chef John Babb's birth date falls on the same day of the year as that of Richmond Hill's former host and food aficionado, Gabrielle Pearson. That seems to me to be almost predestined, and very apropos at that. Don't you agree?

Soup and terrine

Smoked Salmon Chowder

❖

- ➤ 2 strips bacon
- ➤ 2½ cups finely chopped onion
- ➤ ¼ cup all-purpose flour
- ➤ 4 large white potatoes (about 1½ pounds), peeled and cut into ½-inch cubes
- ➤ 2 cups fish stock
- ➤ 1 pound smoked salmon, cut into ¼ x ⅛-inch strips
- ➤ 2 quarts heavy cream (or milk)
- ➤ ¼ cup (½ stick) butter
- ➤ Salt and pepper to taste

1. In a medium skillet cook the bacon, stirring frequently, for about 5 minutes. Add the onions and cook for another 5 minutes. Add the flour, stirring briskly to blend. Add the potatoes and fish stock.
2. Simmer for 30 minutes. Add the salmon, cream, butter, salt, and pepper. Bring the chowder just to a boil. Remove the chowder from the heat and serve.
Yield: 12 servings

Provolone and Sun-Dried Tomato Terrine with Pesto Dressing

❖

Tomato Mixture
- ➤ 1½ cups sun-dried tomatoes, drained
- ➤ 4 cloves garlic
- ➤ ½ teaspoon salt
- ➤ ½ teaspoon black pepper
- ➤ 1 tablespoon freshly chopped basil
- ➤ 1 tablespoon freshly chopped oregano
  Pesto Dressing
- ➤ 2 cups prepared pesto
- ➤ 1¼ cups mayonnaise
- ➤ Juice of 1 lemon
- ➤ ½ teaspoon each salt and pepper
  Assembly
- ➤ 24 slices Provolone cheese, cut into ⅛-inch thickness
- ➤ 2 cups finely chopped ripe black olives
- ➤ Basil, edible pansies, lettuce for garnish

1. In a food processor purée the tomato mixture ingredients.
2. In a bowl combine the pesto, mayonnaise, lemon juice, salt, and pepper until well incorporated. Set aside.
3. Line a 2-quart round dish with plastic wrap. Coat the wrap with non-stick cooking spray. Place a layer of Provolone on the bottom of the dish. Follow with a layer of olives, Provolone, tomato mixture, and Provolone again. Repeat this process, pressing each layer down after adding the Provolone. Unmold the terrine and remove the plastic wrap.
4. Cut the terrine into 8 even wedges. Place each wedge in the center of a salad plate. Drape the pesto dressing over the terrine wedges and add garnish.
Yield: 8 servings

Lobster Ravioli in Saffron Sauce

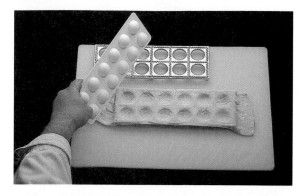

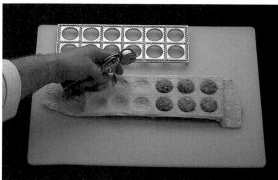

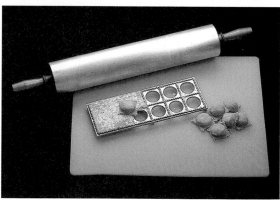

Lobster Stuffing

- ➤ 8 ounces lobster-tail meat, finely chopped
- ➤ 2 tablespoons finely minced celery
- ➤ 1 clove garlic, minced
- ➤ 1 scallion, finely minced
- ➤ 2 tablespoons finely minced red bell pepper
- ➤ 1 egg, beaten
- ➤ 2 tablespoons seasoned dry bread crumbs
- ➤ 2 tablespoons Parmesan cheese
- ➤ 1 tablespoon finely chopped parsley
- ➤ ¼ teaspoon salt
- ➤ ⅛ teaspoon pepper
- ➤ 1 tablespoon heavy cream

Saffron Sauce

- ➤ 1 tablespoon butter
- ➤ 1 tablespoon chopped shallots
- ➤ 4 ounces crème fraîche
- ➤ 4 ounces heavy cream
- ➤ 1 tablespoon saffron
- ➤ ¼ teaspoon salt
- ➤ ⅛ teaspoon pepper
- ➤ ¼ cup sherry

Ravioli Dough

- ➤ 6 eggs, beaten
- ➤ 6 tablespoons water
- ➤ 3 teaspoons salt
- ➤ ⅛ cup soybean or olive oil
- ➤ 4 cups all-purpose flour
- ➤ Egg wash

Court-bouillon Poaching Liquid

- ➤ 1 sprig fresh thyme or 1 teaspoon dried
- ➤ 2 cups white wine
- ➤ 1¼ cups water
- ➤ 3 bay leaves
- ➤ Juice of ½ lemon
- ➤ 10 black peppercorns

- ➤ *1 clove garlic*
- ➤ *2 sprigs parsley*
- ➤ *1 teaspoon salt*
- ➤ *½ stalk celery, coarsely chopped*
- ➤ *2 tablespoons green onion tops*

1. In a large bowl mix together ingredients for the lobster stuffing. Cover and refrigerate.
2. In a small skillet melt the butter and sauté the shallots. Add the crème fraîche and heavy cream. Add the saffron, seasonings, and sherry. Reduce the heat, keeping the sauce warm until ready to serve.
3. In large mixer bowl combine the eggs, water, salt, and oil with a dough hook. On low speed gradually add the flour until the dough forms a ball. Add more oil if needed to keep the mixture from sticking to the bowl. Remove the dough to a clean surface and cover it with a kitchen towel. Let the dough rest for 15 minutes.
4. Turn the dough out on a floured board and roll it very thin. Make ravioli sheets with a ravioli press. (See the photos on page 164). Shape raviolis with a ravioli cutter. Place a generous teaspoonful of the lobster stuffing in the center of each individual ravioli. Coat with egg wash and place a second sheet on top for a cover. Press the dough together and cut out the raviolis.
5. In a stock pot combine all of the ingredients for the court-bouillon. Add the pasta just before the bouillon comes to a boil. Allow the ravioli to cook until tender, about 6 to 8 minutes. Do not boil. Carefully remove the ravioli with a slotted spoon.
6. Place some saffron sauce in the well of the plate and spread evenly. Place 4 raviolis per plate.

Yield: 32 ravioli

Ravioli (left) and Shrimp with Apples and Snow Peas

Champagne-Raspberry Sorbet

❖

Scoop the sorbet into a wide-rimmed champagne glass and serve between the salad and entrée.

- ➤ 1¼ cups fresh or frozen/thawed raspberries
- ➤ ¾ cup sugar
- ➤ 1 cup water
- ➤ 1 cup champagne

---

1. In a food processor purée the raspberries. Pour the liquid through a chinois to remove the seeds. Set aside.
2. In a medium saucepan combine the sugar, water, and champagne, and bring the mixture to a boil. Add the raspberry purée and simmer for 4 to 5 minutes. Return the mixture to the food processor and blend until frothy. Pour the mixture into a pan and place it in the freezer.
3. When half frozen mix the sorbet vigorously with a whisk until frothy. Return it to the freezer until solid.
   Yield: 1 quart

Shrimp with Apples and Snow Peas in a Wine and Mustard Cream Sauce

❖

- ➤ 1 cup (2 sticks) butter
- ➤ 64 to 80 medium shrimp, peeled and deveined
- ➤ ¼ cup chopped garlic
- ➤ ¼ cup chopped shallots
- ➤ ⅔ cup Riesling wine
- ➤ 2 cups crème fraîche
- ➤ ½ cup grainy mustard
- ➤ 40 snow peas, ends snapped and veiny strings removed
- ➤ 40 slices red apple, cut ¼-inch thick
- ➤ 1½ pounds fettucine pasta, cooked and drained
- ➤ ½ teaspoon dried oregano
- ➤ ½ teaspoon dried basil
- ➤ Salt and pepper to taste
- ➤ Dill sprigs and lemon slices for garnish

---

1. In a large saucepan melt half the butter and sauté the shrimp in 1 tablespoon of the garlic

and shallots. Add the wine, crème fraîche, and mustard, and simmer for 5 minutes. Add the peas and apples, and cook for 5 minutes. more. Keep warm.

2. In a large skillet melt the remaining butter and sauté the remaining garlic and shallots, adding the fettucine just long enough to heat through. Mix in the herbs, and add salt and pepper to taste.

3. Place the pasta on dinner plates and top it clockwise with alternating shrimp, snow peas, and apple slices. Drizzle the remaining sauce from the saucepan over all. Artfully add the dill and lemon.

Yield: 8 servings

Lemon Zest Tart
❖

Lemon Zest Tart

Pastry Shell

➤ *2 cups unbleached, all-purpose flour*

➤ *2 tablespoons sugar*

➤ *½ teaspoon salt*

➤ *½ cup plus 2 tablespoons (1¼ sticks) butter, cut into bits and chilled*

➤ *2 tablespoons shortening*

➤ *¼ cup ice water*

Tart Filling

➤ *Zest of 3 lemons*

➤ *½ cup fresh lemon juice*

➤ *¼ cup (½ stick) butter, softened*

➤ *4 eggs*

➤ *5 egg yolks*

➤ *1 cup sugar*

➤ *2 tablespoons unflavored gelatin*

➤ *2 tablespoons boiling water*

1. In a food processor combine the flour, sugar, and salt, and process to blend. Drop in the butter and pulse again 3 or 4 times. Add the shortening and process until the mixture resembles coarse crumbs.

2. With the machine running, add the ice water 1 tablespoon at a time. When the mixture forms lumps, remove it from the bowl and quickly press the dough into a patty. Cover the dough with plastic wrap and chill for 30 minutes.

3. Preheat the oven to 400°. Roll the dough out to fit into a 10-inch tart pan. Mold the pastry into the pan. Bake the shell for 12 to 15 minutes until golden. Allow it to cool.

4. In a heavy enameled saucepan combine the lemon zest, lemon juice, butter, eggs, yolks, and sugar. Stir to blend the ingredients well. Cook the mixture over low heat, whisking constantly until slightly thickened.

5. Dissolve the gelatin in the boiling water and add it to the lemon mixture. Cool the filling by setting the pan in cold water. When cool, spread the filling into pastry shell and chill for 2 to 3 hours before serving.

Yield: 8 servings

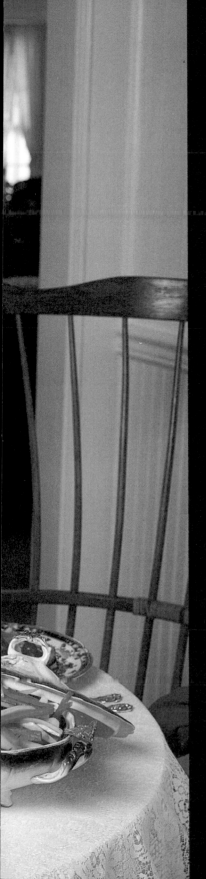

Regional Classics

When thinking about who we are, we must remember that America was discovered by the Europeans while in search for food . . . and ever since the Europeans began moving between the New World and the Old, there has been such a thing as American ethnic food . . ."

Jeff Smith
The Frugal Gourmet Cooks American

The Windflower, Great Barrington, Massachusetts

From the Land of Adobes and Pueblos

Inn of the Anasazi
Santa Fe, New Mexico

CHEF PETER ZIMMER

Dinner for Eight

*Roasted Corn Broth with
Pork Potstickers*

◆

*Salad of Fire-Roasted Peppers
on Navajo Flatbread*

◆

*Cinnamon and Chili-Crusted Scallops
with Mango Salsa*

◆

*Snapper Fillets in Tortilla Crust
with Cilantro-Lime Salsa*

◆

*Venison Chili with Cheddar Quesadillas
and Tobacco Onions*

◆

Squash Blossom Tarts

Anasazi. The name means "the ancient ones" and refers to the ancestors of today's Pueblo Indians living in and around Santa Fe. As you walk into the Inn of the Anasazi, you cannot help but feel it is a most fitting moniker. A sense of mystery and excitement prevails, much as it does when you come upon the ruins of an abandoned Pueblo in this area. Soothing, cave-like walls of softly brushed maize tones embrace your way through angled entryways, not unlike the gateways to ancient Indian villages. Doors painted and carved in patterns reminiscent of Navajo rugs beckon you to explore the gathering rooms where guests enjoy kiva fireplaces, private butler service, books, and board games.

Designed tastefully in materials true to the region, the inn is actually a new construction, built with a sensitivity to the environment, the land, and the people. The adobe-plaster base walls emit a sensual glow, as they were painstakingly coated by hand with beeswax. Water streams down a two-story wall built to replicate ruins at nearby Chaco Canyon. The floors of local flagstone are the perfect surface to catch the thump of cowboy boots that still stride proudly about these parts. Ceilings consist of ponderosa pine and cedar; and even a time capsule, housing everything from food to children's drawings, is embedded in the center of the building.

Guests are greeted in the lobby with hot apple cider or ginger-lemonade and the pure and natural sounds of native American flute music by noted regional artist R. Carlos Nakai.

During my visit I heard one guest ask, "Is this a bed and breakfast?" Though the inn has fifty-nine rooms, I chuckled to myself, fully understanding why the question was asked. Everything they do at the Inn of the Anasazi gives it the earmarks of a much smaller inn in the country. For instance, when you retire to your luxurious room at night, you feel as if in the hands of a most caring bed and breakfast innkeeper. Bed materials are natural fibers, woven blankets, and cotton; rich Mexican tiles decorate the bathroom walls and floors. Toiletries are organic, and their containers bear the petroglyphs—or primitive figures—that are used as symbols of the inn. Someone has turned down the sheets for you and left a gift on your pillow: either a sweet dessert or a printed native American bedtime story you can take home as a remembrance.

The inn is owned by Robert D. Zimmer's hotel development and management

company. His son, Peter, is the chef. You will discover it is an inn with an emphasis on the organic and natural in food and materials. You see, all things about the Inn of the Anasazi offer guests a feeling of well-being.

Chef Peter Zimmer's menu is an intriguing collection of cowboy, new Southwest, Hispanic, and Pueblo Indian flavors. You might find roasted acorn squash with ancho cream, giant ravioli with winter squash and walnut pesto, buffalo-style quail, and vegetable empañadas.

The ninety-six-seat dining room bears still further resemblance to an old adobe. More petroglyphs highlight one wall, while windows with real twig shutters fill another. Waiters wear boots and bolos with white shirts.

Breakfast is its own unique combination of hearty foods such as sourdough French toast with chili-roasted pecans, and molasses or mess o' pork chops with tortillas and chili cheese grits.

For all the meals Peter prepares, nearly 90 percent of his ingredients are organic and come from small local farms. "It's a way of trying to serve the best available and also help nurture these small farmers into thriving businesses for their families," says Peter. He concedes that it is more time consuming and not as cost effective to deal with the independent, non-commercial farmers, but says the benefits outweigh the tribulations. "I can ask these families to custom grow a certain type of vegetable, according to my needs and desires, and begin to build a continuing source of products for the inn," explains the chef.

The menu he has given me here is fun to prepare. Southwestern is an increasingly popular fare that I know your guests will enjoy as mine do. Most of the ingredients are easy to find, especially in gourmet shops. Serve one or a small portion of each of the three entrees—the scallops, chili, or snapper fillets.

Cooking was not something Peter initially desired to do with his life. Even though he was washing dishes in restaurants at thirteen, he had dreamed of playing jazz bass in a combo at the early age of seven. But as he graduated from bottle-washer to potato-peeler, Peter found he was one of the best at whatever he did and soon realized a stronger calling to cooking than making music.

Peter was just nineteen when he opened his first restaurant with a partner, shortly after already helping open the renowned Mansion at Turtle Creek in Texas. At twenty he became one of the youngest executive chefs ever, and was voted one of the top ten new chefs in America.

"Tourism can affect and influence so many people. I feel it's part of my role here to introduce them to cultural diversity and a holistic approach to living," says Peter. "I'm committed to this style of cooking now. We care about what we do to the earth as well as the soul."

And what about the wandering guest's question regarding the inn being a bed and breakfast? Strictly speaking, the answer is no; but in theory, perhaps so. The Inn of the Anasazi is actually in the new category of luxury country inn. This means it is more like a small hotel but still has a special dedication to guest service and amenities, not at all unlike its much smaller kin: the traditional bed and breakfast or country inn.

The ancient ones would no doubt be impressed with the Inn of the Anasazi's respect for the individual and its modern-day approach to their time and ways, a cultural heritage few in Santa Fe want to forget. This little "city of holy faith" will make you a believer in its customs, as it does for me every time I visit. Partaking of the food and the ambience of the Inn of the Anasazi will help you imagine what it must have been like long ago—and experience what it can still be like today.

Navajo Flatbread hosts roasted peppers and lettuce. Corn broth with potstickers (rear).

Roasted Corn Broth with Pork Potstickers

⚜

Broth

- ➤ 10 ears grilled yellow corn, cut off and cobs reserved
- ➤ 1 yellow onion, diced
- ➤ 4 poblano chilies, diced
- ➤ 1 celery stalk, diced
- ➤ 2 tablespoons olive oil
- ➤ 2 cloves garlic
- ➤ 1 gallon chicken stock or broth
- ➤ 2 bunches cilantro, chopped
- ➤ Salt and pepper to taste

Potstickers

- ➤ ½ pound ground pork
- ➤ 1 tablespoon minced ginger
- ➤ 1 tablespoon minced garlic
- ➤ 2 tablespoons soy sauce
- ➤ 1 tablespoon sesame oil
- ➤ 1 tablespoon chili flakes
- ➤ 1 bunch green onions, sliced
- ➤ 1 bunch cilantro, chopped
- ➤ 3 eggs
- ➤ 1 package wonton wrappers
- ➤ Salt and pepper to taste
- ➤ Egg wash (1 yolk and 2 tablespoons water mixture)

1. In a stock pot heat the olive oil and sauté the corn, onion, chilies, and celery in olive oil for 3 to 5 minutes. Add the garlic, chicken stock, and corn cobs, and boil for 15 to 20 minutes or until tender. Remove the cobs. Stir in the cilantro, and season to taste. Keep the broth warm.
2. Combine all of the potsticker ingredients except the wonton wrappers and egg wash. Place a hearty tablespoon of the mixture in the center of each skin. Brush the wonton edges with egg wash. Fold corner to corner to form a triangle. Press the edges together to seal. Fold the 2 opposite corners around a finger. Moisten with egg wash and press together to seal. (See wonton photos on page 240.) Steam the potstickers until the skins are tender. Place the corn broth in soup bowls and two potstickers in each bowl.

Yield: 8 servings

Salad of Fire-Roasted Peppers on Navajo Flatbread

Herb Vinaigrette

- ➤ 1 cup olive oil
- ➤ 1 cup balsamic vinegar
- ➤ 1½ tablespoons each chopped basil and parsley
- ➤ 1½ teaspoons minced garlic
- ➤ Juice of 3 lemons

Fire-roasted Peppers

- ➤ 4 each red, green, and yellow bell peppers
- ➤ 4 poblano chilies
- ➤ 2 tablespoons olive oil

Flatbread

- ➤ 2½ cups all-purpose flour
- ➤ ¾ cup dry milk powder
- ➤ 2½ teaspoons baking powder
- ➤ ½ teaspoon salt
- ➤ 2½ tablespoons butter, softened
- ➤ ¾ cup cold water
- ➤ 1 tablespoon butter
- ➤ 1 red onion, thinly sliced
- ➤ 1 pound shiitake mushrooms, sliced
- ➤ 6 sage leaves, chopped or ½ teaspoon dried
- ➤ 2 tablespoons olive oil
- ➤ Mixed salad greens

1. In a small bowl combine the vinaigrette ingredients. Set the dressing aside.
2. Rub the peppers and poblanos with oil, and roast them over a wood grill or open-flame burner until charred and blackened. (Or

Cinnamon and Chili-Crusted Scallops with Mango Salsa

Scallops with the spices of the region

blacken under the broiler.) Place each pepper in a paper bag and let it steam for 10 minutes. Peel off the skin, remove the seeds and membranes, and cut into 3-inch triangles. Marinate the peppers in vinaigrette for 2 to 3 hours.

3. In a food processor combine the flour, dry milk, baking powder, and salt. Add 2½ tablespoons of butter and the water. Process 2 to 3 minutes. In a 12-inch skillet melt 1 tablespoon of butter and sauté the red onions and mushrooms for 3 minutes. Add the sage. Add this mixture to the dough, mixing until combined. Let the dough rest for 15 to 20 minutes.

4. On a floured board roll out the dough to ¼-inch thickness. Cut into 8-inch rounds or 1½-inch base triangles by 3 inches long (see the photo on page 173). In a 6-inch skillet heat olive oil and sauté the flatbread for 30 to 40 seconds on each side until golden brown. Cut the rounds into quarters and arrange the wedges or triangles on the plates with the roasted peppers and mixed salad greens. Serve with the herb vinaigrette.

Yield: 8 servings

Mango Salsa
- ➤ 1 cup, peeled, seeded, and diced mango
- ➤ 2 poblano chilies, diced
- ➤ 1 red onion, diced
- ➤ 1 tablespoon honey
- ➤ 1 tablespoon olive oil
- ➤ 1 bunch cilantro, chopped
- ➤ 1 red bell pepper, diced
- ➤ Salt and pepper to taste

Cinnamon-Chili Mix for Crust
- ➤ 2 tablespoons Spanish or red paprika
- ➤ 2 tablespoons sugar
- ➤ 2 tablespoons cayenne pepper
- ➤ 3 tablespoons crushed coriander seeds
- ➤ 2 tablespoons salt
- ➤ 2 tablespoons cinnamon

Scallop Preparation
- ➤ 1 tablespoon olive oil, or more for sautéing
- ➤ 40 jumbo sea scallops
- ➤ Leafy greens

1. In a medium bowl combine all of the mango salsa ingredients until well mixed. Set the salsa aside.
2. In a separate bowl combine the cinnamon-chili crust ingredients.
3. Dust the scallops with the cinnamon-chili mix until completely covered. In a 12-inch skillet heat the olive oil and sauté them in batches for 2 to 3 minutes on each side or until the desired tenderness.
4. Place the greens on serving plates and top with 3 to 5 scallops. Add a dollop of mango salsa by each scallop.

Yield: 8 to 10 servings

Snapper Fillets in Tortilla Crust with Cilantro-Lime Salsa

✤

In this recipe, tortillas are used in place of bread crumbs.

Cilantro-lime Salsa

➤ 2 cups yellow corn, cut off the cob
➤ 1 tablespoon olive oil
➤ ½ tablespoon balsamic vinegar
➤ 1 each red and green bell pepper, diced
➤ 2 medium red tomatoes, diced
➤ Juice of 6 limes
➤ ½ teaspoon minced garlic
➤ ½ bunch parsley, chopped
➤ 1 bunch cilantro, chopped
➤ Salt, pepper, and cayenne pepper to taste

Snapper Fillets

➤ 8 5-ounce snapper fillets
➤ 2 cups all-purpose flour
➤ 4 eggs, beaten
➤ 12 6-inch corn tortillas, cut into ¼-inch strips
➤ ½ cup olive oil

1. In a medium bowl combine all of the salsa ingredients. Season to taste. (It should be spicy.) Set the salsa aside.
2. Preheat the oven to 350°. Dust the fillets on both sides with flour. Dip in egg, then in the tortillas. Press firmly so that the tortillas crust the fish. In a 12-inch skillet heat the olive oil and sauté the fish for 40 seconds on each side. Place the fillets on a baking sheet. Bake the fillets for about 5 to 7 minutes, until the fish is heated through and the tortillas are fused to the fish.
Yield: 8 servings

Venison Chili with Cheddar Quesadillas and Tobacco Onions

Tobacco onions are a preparation of red onions that remind one in appearance of a cowboys' chewing tobacco. The resemblance ends there! They are delicious.

Chili

➤ 1 tablespoon olive oil
➤ 3 pounds boneless venison leg, cut into 1-inch pieces
➤ 1 tablespoon chopped garlic
➤ 1 cup each cooked plain and blue posole (or hominy)
➤ 1 each roasted red and yellow bell peppers, cut into 1-inch pieces
➤ 3 roasted poblano peppers, cut into 1-inch pieces
➤ 2 red onions, cut into 1-inch pieces
➤ 1 bunch fresh sage, chopped or 2 tablespoons dried
➤ ½ bunch thyme, chopped or 1 tablespoon dried
➤ 1 tablespoon chili powder
➤ 2 cups veal or beef stock or broth
➤ Juice of 5 limes
➤ Salt and pepper to taste

Tobacco Onions

➤ 2 cups all-purpose flour
➤ 1 tablespoon cayenne pepper
➤ 1½ teaspoons salt
➤ 5 red onions, sliced paper thin
➤ 2 cups vegetable oil

Quesadillas

➤ 6 18-inch flour tortillas
➤ 2 tablespoons butter, melted
➤ 2 cups grated white Cheddar cheese
➤ ½ cup hot green chilies, diced

1. In a 12-inch skillet heat the olive oil until smoking. Sear the venison. Add the remaining chili ingredients except the stock, lime juice, salt, and pepper. Quickly deglaze with stock. Season to taste. Reduce the liquid by half. Return the venison to the chili. Add the lime juice and keep the chili warm.
2. In a 3-quart bowl combine the flour, cayenne, and salt. Break the onion rings apart and dredge them in the flour mixture until lightly covered. Shake off the excess flour. In a 4-quart saucepan heat the oil and fry half the onions until golden brown. Drain them on a paper towel. Repeat the process with the remaining onions.
3. Preheat the oven to 350°. Brush the tortillas with butter. Sprinkle the cheese and green chilies evenly on one half of each tortilla. Fold the tortillas and place them on a baking sheet. Bake until the cheese melts, about 3 to 5 minutes.
4. To assemble each serving, pour the venison chili into serving bowls and arrange the quesadillas around the bowl, points sticking out. Place a small amount of tobacco onions in the center.

Yield: 6 servings

A venison chili night in the Sangre de Cristo mountains is warmed by an inn fire.

Squash Blossom Tarts

❖

If you've ever traveled the Southwest, you have no doubt seen kiosks and jewelry shops selling turquoise Indian jewelry, and you may even have come home with a squash blossom necklace. Squash blossoms are the bright yellow edible flowers of squashes that grow prolifically in this region. They are also available at farm stands and in supermarkets in summer in many areas of the country. In the Southwest squash blossoms are used in a variety of other dishes, such as salads.

Pastry Shells
- ➤ 2⅔ cups all-purpose flour
- ➤ ½ cup shortening
- ➤ ½ cup (1 stick) softened butter
- ➤ 1 teaspoon salt
- ➤ ½ cup ice cold water

Squash Custard
- ➤ 2 cups sugar
- ➤ 2 tablespoons all-purpose flour
- ➤ 1 tablespoon yellow cornmeal
- ➤ 2 teaspoons cinnamon
- ➤ ½ cup (1 stick) butter, melted
- ➤ 3 eggs, beaten
- ➤ ½ cup buttermilk
- ➤ 2 teaspoons vanilla extract
- ➤ 1 cup cooked, mashed acorn or butternut squash

Squash Blossoms
- ➤ 8 squash blossoms, yellow part only, rinsed clean
- ➤ 1 egg
- ➤ ¼ cup water
- ➤ ½ cup yellow cornmeal for dipping, or more
- ➤ Oil for frying
- ➤ 2 tablespoons or more sugar for coating
- ➤ 1 teaspoon or more cinnamon for dusting
- ➤ Sweetened whipped cream for topping

1. In a large bowl combine the flour, shortening, butter, and salt with your hands until coarse crumbs form. Add the water to moisten and form a dough. Do not overwork the dough. On a floured surface roll the dough out to ⅛-inch thickness. Cut into 8 4-inch circles and place them in tart shells.
2. Preheat the oven to 350°. In a medium bowl mix together the sugar, flour, cornmeal, and cinnamon. Blend in the melted butter and then the eggs.
3. In another bowl blend together the buttermilk, vanilla, and squash until smooth. Add the squash mixture to the flour mixture. Pour the mixture into the tart shells. Bake the tarts for 30 to 40 minutes or until the shells are nice and brown.
4. While the tarts are baking beat together the egg and water. Dip the squash blossoms into the egg mixture and then into the cornmeal, coating the blossoms. In a skillet heat enough oil to deep-fry the squash blossoms, and fry them for about 30 seconds. Roll the fried blossoms in sugar, and sprinkle them with cinnamon. Place a blossom on each tart. Add a dollop of whipped cream.

Yield: 8 servings

Dining in Paradise

Kilauea Lodge
Volcano Village, Hawaii

INNKEEPER/CHEF ALBERT JEYTE

Dinner for Eight

❖

Coconut Cream of Celery Soup

◆

Hawaiian Sautéed Ahi (Tuna)
in Caper Sauce

◆

Broiled Mahi Mahi with
Mango-Chutney Sauce and
Macadamia Nuts

◆

Baked Seafood and Ham
Zucchini Gratin

◆

Tropical Vanilla Mousse
with Fresh Papaya

*A*lbert Jeyte never imagined that after thirty years in the theater business and an Emmy award, he would someday trade his makeup artist's case for a cupboard full of cooking utensils. But his life changed in 1980, when—after serving as makeup artist to such stars as Anthony Hopkins—Hollywood called Albert from his native Germany to Hawaii to work on the "Magnum P.I." series.

When the television show took its final curtain call some seven years later, Jeyte had no intention of leaving paradise. On the night he won his Emmy, he was out celebrating when a young lady asked him to dance. Her name was Lorna, and they were soon married. But since Hawaii is not Hollywood, there was not any work for a make-up artist of his caliber. While Albert was search-

Rainbow Falls in Hilo

ing for a new business, he stumbled upon Kilauea Lodge, formerly a YMCA camp.

The Jeytes bought the lodge on the spot and turned dormitory rooms into guest suites, hung the bed and breakfast sign out, and hired a chef. In less than a year, Albert fired his cook, packed a suitcase for France, and went off to cooking school himself.

Today he and Lorna bid you, "e komo mai," or "welcome to our home." This "home" offers twelve attractive guest rooms in the shadow of Pele's continuing wrath— Volcanoes National Park—only a mile from the inn. While the Hawaiian goddess of fire may rule the nearby park, there's anything but a fearsome inferno of smoke spewing from the lodge's chimney. Instead, there is a gentle, warming hearth in the dining room; and only aromatic cooking flames emanate from the kitchen at Albert's nouveau *kama ina,* or cross between a European ski lodge and an old Hawaiian plantation house. In fact, the hearth is the inn's hallmark—with its own story to tell.

Known as the Fireplace of Friendship, it was constructed with stones from around the world, including the Dead Sea, Mount Vernon, and the Acropolis. It is also embedded with international coins and artifacts and local tools such as a kukui nut grinder. The fireplace was built in 1937 when the YMCA founded the mountain retreat.

It is little wonder Albert traded his makeup brushes for a toque. Kilauea Lodge is situated in paradise, all right. At dawn or dusk, the silence is pervasive; and if you listen, you may hear the rumblings of Pele— at least in your imagination.

You won't find such touristy luau fare as poi and roasted pig at Kilauea Lodge. After a day of hiking across the black lava and hopping around hot steam vents in the nearby park, my husband and I were ready to be pampered with fine food and romantic dining. The lodge's dining room with its wood floors, beamed rafters, and cedar ceiling, was a welcome sight as the tropical moon crested overhead. The room took on a warm glow; and when the food was brought to the table, we knew this was Hawaii at its most gracious.

Albert offers a selection of native seafood as well as beef, lamb, and fowl. His mouth-watering entrées tip their hat to the people, their livelihoods, and the land—the factors he considers when devising new dishes. Prawns Mauna Loa is shrimp from Hawaiian waters—sautéed with shallots, mushrooms, and basil served on a bed of pasta. When I visited, I enjoyed broiled rack of lamb with a sweet papaya apple-mint sauce laced with rosemary and the paupiettes of beef, which are juicy rolls of sliced prime rib stuffed with mushrooms, beef, cheese, and fresh herbs deep-fried in a brown sauce. The menu also has a Germanic influence, hosting hasenpfeffer, or braised rabbit, with bacon in a brandy sauce, and a specially prepared Jeyte sauerbraten.

Desserts—such as the Macadamia Nut Pie—also have a touch of native ingredients. If you want to make this pie at home, merely substitute the sweet and crunchy macadamia for the pecans in a traditional pecan pie recipe. And of course, don't forget to make the coffee a cup of Kona.

I asked Albert to include the recipe for mahi mahi, as this fish has become more widely available on the mainland. As a result, many of us can use more recipes for preparing this seafood. I have served Albert's menu to friends, and I highly recommend it. You may want to set the table with anthurium or bleeding-heart flowers and use post-cards from Hawaii as placecards. As your guests arrive, drape leis over their heads and wish them, "e komo mai," in the spirit of chef Albert Jeyte and his Kilauea Lodge.

Coconut Cream of Celery Soup

❖

This recipe also makes a plain cream of celery soup. Just delete the coconut syrup and add another cup of heavy cream.

➤ 10 cups chicken stock or broth
➤ 3 pounds celery, stalks cleaned and cubed
➤ 2 pounds russet potatoes, peeled and cubed
➤ 2⅛ cups milk
➤ ½ cup coconut syrup
➤ ½ cup heavy cream
➤ 1½ teaspoons celery salt
➤ 1 teaspoon white pepper
➤ 1 cup (2 sticks) butter
➤ Finely chopped parsley for garnish

1. In a 4-quart stock pot bring chicken broth to a boil.
2. In a food processor purée the celery and potatoes until very smooth. Add the purée to the boiling broth and beat with a wire whisk for 2 minutes. Add the milk and coconut syrup. Bring the soup to a fast boil, then reduce the heat to low and let it simmer. Add the celery salt and pepper, and stir to blend. Cover the pot and let the soup simmer for 40 minutes, stirring frequently.
3. Remove the pot from the heat. Pour the soup through a strainer into a 4-quart bowl. Discard the heavy purée. Cut the butter into ½-inch cubes and add it to the soup. Whip the soup until the butter is dissolved. Ladle it into individual soup bowls. Garnish with parsley.

Yield: 8 to 10 servings

Broiled Mahi Mahi

Hawaiian Sautéed Ahi (Tuna) in Caper Sauce

❖

Tuna is one of Hawaii's most sought after sea-food dishes. This recipe is meant to be served as an appetizer for the menu presented. But you may also serve this as an entrée over a rice pilaf with a yield for four.

➤ 4 8-ounce tuna pieces, each ½-inch thick
➤   All-purpose flour for coating
➤ 1 tablespoon butter
➤ 2 teaspoons minced garlic
➤ 2 teaspoons minced shallots
➤ 1 teaspoon chopped parsley
➤ 2 tablespoons dry white wine
➤ 2 tablespoons water
➤ 4 teaspoons capers
➤ 4 slices lemon, seeds removed

1. Lightly coat the fish in the flour and set it aside.
2. In a 9-inch skillet melt the butter over moderate heat, and sauté the garlic, shallots, and parsley until tender. Add the tuna to the skillet and sauté it for 2 minutes on each side. Add the wine, water, capers, and lemon slices. Reduce the heat to low and simmer for an-

other 5 minutes or until the fish is cooked to the desired tenderness. Squeeze the juice from the lemons into the liquid and discard the lemons. The sauce should be smooth and creamy.
3. Remove the fish from the pan and place it on a serving dish. Cut each piece into 8 appetizer-size pieces. Spoon the sauce over each piece and serve.
Yield: 4 entrée or 8 appetizer servings

Broiled Mahi Mahi with Mango-Chutney Sauce and Macadamia Nuts

❖

➤ 8 8-ounce pieces mahi mahi
➤   Softened butter
     Mango Chutney Sauce
➤ 2 cups mango chutney
➤ 3 ounces white Chablis wine
➤ 2 tablespoons cider vinegar
➤ 6 tablespoons packed brown sugar
➤ 1 ounce sherry
➤ ½ teaspoon white pepper
➤ ¼ cup lilikoi juice or guava juice (optional)
➤ ¼ cup pineapple juice
➤ ½ cup chopped macadamia nuts
➤   Chopped parsley for garnish

1. In blender or processor purée the mango chutney until smooth and creamy. Pour the chutney into a medium saucepan and add the sauce ingredients except the nuts. Stir over low to moderate heat. Reduce the heat and simmer for 10 minutes, stirring frequently. Keep the sauce warm.
2. Brush both sides of the fish with butter and broil it on both sides until cooked and slightly brown.
3. Place the fish on serving dishes and spoon 3 teaspoons of the sauce over the middle of each. Sprinkle the nuts over the sauce and top with parsley.
Yield: 8 servings

Baked Seafood and Ham Zucchini Gratins

These tasty mounds are a complement to a sea-food entrée. You can make the stuffing mix the day before. The liquid smoke ingredient does not come from the breath of Pele, Hawaiian goddess of fire; it is an artificial flavor that gives the food a smoky taste.

The lodge is surrounded by natural beauty.

Stuffing Mix
- 6 tablespoons (¾ stick) butter
- 1 bunch celery, cleaned and diced, leaves removed
- 1 large onion, finely chopped
- 4 teaspoons finely minced garlic
- 8 large mushrooms, diced
- 2 teaspoons dried thyme
- 1 teaspoon white pepper
- 3 bay leaves

Stuffing Mix Additions
- 2 teaspoons Worcestershire sauce
- ½ teaspoon liquid smoke
- ¾ cup diced crab meat
- 1 cup bay shrimp, chopped
- 3 ounces smoked ham, finely diced
- 5 tablespoons all-purpose flour
- 4 ounces sliced mild Cheddar cheese
- 1½ cups mayonnaise

Zucchini Preparation
- 6 large zucchini (2 inches in diameter)
- Salt, pepper, and paprika
- ½ cup sliced Swiss cheese
- ⅔ cup grated mild Cheddar cheese
- ⅔ cup grated Parmesan cheese
- 1 bunch parsley, finely chopped

1. In a 10-inch saucepan combine the stuffing ingredients. Simmer over moderate heat for 15 minutes. Add the next 5 ingredients and continue simmering for a few minutes. Add the flour and simmer for 5 more minutes, stirring frequently. Turn off the heat and fold in the cheese. Let the stuffing cool. Fold in the mayonnaise. Remove the bay leaves.

2. Preheat the oven to 400°. Wash the zucchini and cut off the ends. Cut them into 1¼-inch rounds and scoop out the center of each piece, leaving a ¼-inch bottom. Steam the zucchini for 8 minutes or until tender. Do not over-steam. Let cool.

3. Arrange the zucchini pieces close together in a 10 x 8-inch oven-proof glass baking dish. Sprinkle lightly with salt, pepper, and paprika on the inside of each piece. Fill each piece with the stuffing. Place the slices of Swiss cheese on top of the stuffed zucchini. Gener-ously sprinkle the grated Cheddar cheese over all. Bake the zucchini for 15 to 20 minutes or until the cheese bubbles and has light brown spots on top. Remove the zucchini from the oven and arrange it on a serving plate. Sprinkle with the Parmesan cheese and parsley.

Yield: 8 to 10 servings

Tropical Vanilla Mousse with Fresh Papaya

❖

- ➤ 3 to 4 ripe papayas
  - Mousse
- ➤ 1½ teaspoons unflavored gelatin
- ➤ 2½ tablespoons cold water
- ➤ 2 cups plus 2 tablespoons heavy cream
- ➤ 8 egg yolks
- ➤ 1½ cups superfine sugar
- ➤ 2 tablespoons vanilla extract
  - Garnish
- ➤ 8 teaspoons chopped bittersweet dark chocolate
- ➤ 8 strawberries
- ➤ 8 vanilla wafers
- ➤ Mint leaves

Anthurium grows naturally at the inn.

1. Cut the papayas into ½-inch thick slices to fit a wide-mouth stemmed glass. Remove the seeds and skin and cut each slice in half.
2. In a small bowl soften the gelatin in cold water.
3. In a large bowl whip the cream until stiff peaks form.
4. Bring 5 cups of water to a boil in a large double boiler or a pot large enough to hold a 9-inch stainless steel bowl. Place the egg yolks in the bowl over the boiling water, gently stirring in the sugar and vanilla. Turn the heat down to a gentle boil. Whip constantly until the egg mixture thickens but is still creamy. Remove the bowl and add the gelatin. Stir until dissolved. Let the mixture cool, stirring frequently.
5. Fold the whipped cream into the egg mixture and blend well. Spoon a little of the mousse into each glass and place 4 halves of the papaya slices opposite each other on the sides of the glass. Fill each glass with more mousse. Sprinkle with chocolate. Refrigerate until chilled. Add a strawberry, a vanilla wafer, and mint leaf to each glass before serving.

Yield: 8 servings

Traditional Recipes from New England

Windflower
Great Barrington, Massachusetts

CHEF CLAUDIA RYAN

Dinner for Six

Three-Cheese and Langoustine Rolls

•

Chowder Maize with Bell Peppers

•

Roast Duckling with Plum Sauce

•

Casserole of Root Vegetables

•

Brandied Chocolate Apricot Torte

*T*he planning for dinner at the Windflower often begins outside the inn at a fresh produce and gourmet market. Chef Claudia Ryan and innkeeper Barbara Leibert sashay up and down the aisles of Guido's, a large domestic and imported produce and gourmet market in nearby Pittsfield, as they inspect their selections. I went along on one of their shopping jaunts to see firsthand what it takes to buy for an inn-full of guests.

The mother-daughter team skillfully scoured the bountiful wooden bins of richly colored fruits and vegetables, as though in their own Disney World of sorts. They filled carts to overflowing with the exotic and the common: jícama, baby squash, porcini, and motsu. My mouth watered as I imagined how they would prepare the resulting cornucopia. It was two and three and four of everything and double-digit pounds of this and that. Every so often, Claudia and Barbara would take a break from their foraging to convene an impromptu planning session at mid-aisle. "What if we did this?" Claudia would suggest. Or "What if we did that?" Barbara would counter, as the two explored new menu ideas.

Claudia went about selecting everything with a suspicious eye, passing up anything already prepared, such as fresh pastas and breads—items they make from scratch at Windflower. The chef rejected anything with character flaws but welcomed anything that might challenge her creativity in the kitchen.

"I prefer it this way," Claudia says of these personal shopping forays. "We don't buy things by the case-load unseen and then shipped to our back door." In fact, the daily milkman is one of the few delivery services allowed at the Windflower kitchen. Even when the answer to "Guess who's coming to dinner?" is as many as fifty or sixty guests and preparation time is at a premium, Claudia believes a visit to Guido's is well worth the fifteen-mile trek. "This is all part of why it's so special being the chef at a small inn," she says. Obviously, it begins with discriminating shopping. The cooking at Windflower is regional with a gourmet flair. Even Claudia's brisket is cooked to a delicate tenderness and served with a dressing of sherried sauce. Her salmon is so tender, you think you are eating a savory mousse.

During the Berkshire winters, Claudia depends solely on Guido's to help put the freshest produce before her guests; but in summertime, she makes the journey a bit less frequently. When the warm weather rolls into western Massachusetts, she relies on husband John's personal victory garden.

Vegetables—as fresh as they can be—are a mainstay of the inn. John, who is the evening host, is also Windflower's resident Mr. Greenjeans by day, a professional arboriculturist. He knows his plants and soils as well as trees. And in summer his exper-

tise translates into legendary salads, containing four or five varieties of lettuce and a host of obscure, tiny vegetables, all grown organically.

Fruit is also produced in Windflower gardens or garnered from local farms and wild meadows. Berries are plucked from the nearby Mount Washington area. Claudia and John pack the car with lunch and their children, Jessica and Michael, and ride to where the waters fall and the mountains rise to pick berries for the evening dessert or the next day's breakfast.

Our dinner at Windflower began in one of the inn's common rooms, where my husband and I worked a few pieces into a jigsaw puzzle of the New England countryside. There were langoustine rolls, and we could order wine to fuel our activity.

We were soon seated in front of a fire in the dining room. Duck, so indicative of New England, was on the menu. When they brought out the dainty fingerbowls, I figured we were in for a treat. I was right.

We enjoyed a bottle of wine from the underground wine cellar, which is managed by Claudia's father, Gerry. "We don't charge much more than we pay for the wines," he says. "We really want people to enjoy them and not be prohibited from buying a bottle because of price. That's just the way we do it here." By the way, Windflower's sommelier and resident storyteller recommends you serve a quality merlot to complement his daughter's duck dish.

Remember to provide your own fingerbowls with this or any other menu. It is a nice touch. Add a slice of fresh lemon or a fragrant flower. Guests really appreciate this handy old and gracious way of wiping clean a sticky palm or two.

Yes, they still do things the old-fashioned way in this part of Great Barrington; and Windflower is a classic example of a traditional country inn where the family is omnipresent, providing just the right amount of doting. The rambling nineteenth-century house has a most unusual drop-

A lawn of falling autumn leaves graces Windflower.

ceiling staircase; the dining room features Currier and Ives prints and original watercolors by Gerry; and wainscoting highlights both the dining room and several guest bathrooms. Some of the rooms are done in designer fashions, but most are donned with family heirlooms and country accents.

Windflower has been a country inn for a long time. The two generations of inn-keepers live side by side in separate houses on the ten-acre Windflower property, just a few yards from the inn and the swimming pool. The Leiberts were innkeepers and owners of The Tulip Tree Inn in Chittenden, Vermont, before they started Windflower. This time they asked their daughter and son-in-law to join them. Barbara did the cooking at Tulip Tree and, of course, still works in the kitchen here. Claudia received her unofficial culinary degree from years under her mother's influence, as well as training on

the job with Austrian and French chefs at The Woodstock Inn in Vermont, the Ritz-Carlton in Boston, and a few of the premier restaurants on Martha's Vineyard.

Following the splendid Windflower dinner, we retired to one of those spacious and inviting rooms. After taking a bubble bath (many rooms here have claw foot tubs) and employing the inn's complimentary lufa sponge, I curled up to peruse a floor-to-ceiling bookcase full of the chef's food magazines dating to 1974. Although they were meant for guests to explore, too, I thumbed through their textbook pages gingerly, knowing I had a part of the chef's past in my hands.

As we continued to enjoy all of the fruits of Windflower's labor, I put aside the copies of food journals, glanced at my contented husband, and voiced my usual expression of passion for an endearing inn: "It just doesn't get any better than this."

Three-Cheese and Langoustine Rolls

❖

Langoustines resemble crayfish. Serve one roll per person as an appetizer or two for a light supper or lunch.

➤ 2 tablespoons olive oil
➤ 6-8 sprigs parsley, finely chopped
➤ 3 scallions, finely chopped
➤ 12 ounces thawed langoustines, drained
➤ 2 tablespoons Marsala wine
➤ ½ teaspoon dried thyme
➤ 8 ounces cream cheese at room temperature
➤ 15 ounces ricotta cheese
➤ 4 ounces Feta cheese, crumbled
➤ ½ teaspoon Pickapeppa sauce
➤ ¼ cup (½ stick) butter
➤ 1 16-ounce box (about 24 sheets) phyllo dough

1. In a large skillet heat the olive oil and sauté the parsley, scallions, and langoustines over medium heat. Add Marsala and thyme, and cook until lightly browned, about 5 minutes.
2. Remove the langoustines, parsley, and scallions to a bowl, leaving the seasoned liquid in the pan. Reduce the liquid to half over high heat. Pour the sauce over the langoustines and set them aside to cool.
3. Beat together the three cheeses with the Pickapeppa sauce. Add langoustine mixture.
4. Preheat the oven to 350°. Butter a baking sheet. Stack 2 sheets of phyllo together and brush lightly with butter. Place 3 heaping tablespoons of the filling approximately 2 inches in from the shorter end of the phyllo. Fold the sides in over the filling and roll up. Place the roll on the prepared baking sheet and repeat until all of the phyllo and filling are used up.
5. Brush the rolls with melted butter. (They may be wrapped and frozen at this point.) Bake the rolls for 20 minutes or until the tops are light brown and crisp to the touch.
Yield: 12 to 14 rolls

Chowder Maize with Bell Peppers

❖

The addition of red potatoes renders this a hearty corn chowder. If fresh corn is not in season, make the soup with canned corn. Substitute fresh corn with one 16-ounce can each of creamed corn and whole-kernel corn. Add all corn to the pot after the vegetables are puréed. Skip the first part of step three about puréeing the fresh corn with cream.

➤ ¼ cup (½ stick) butter
➤ 1 cup chopped onion
➤ 2 cups sliced red potatoes
➤ 3 stalks celery, sliced into chunks
➤ 1 quart chicken stock
➤ 1 each medium red and green bell pepper, minced
➤ 2 pounds cooked corn niblets removed from cobs
➤ ½ cup light cream
➤ 1 cup half-and-half
➤ 1 teaspoon Pickapeppa sauce
➤ 4 slices crisply cooked bacon, crumbled
➤ Salt and freshly ground pepper to taste

1. In a heavy 4-quart saucepan with cover melt the butter and cook the onion, potatoes, and celery until onion is translucent but not browned, about 10 minutes.
2. Add the chicken stock and simmer for 30 minutes or until the vegetables are soft. Pour the soup into a food processor and purée. Return it to the pot. Add the peppers and cook for another 10 minutes.
3. In a food processor purée half the corn with the light cream. Add this and the remaining corn to the pot and cook for 20 minutes. Add the half-and-half, Pickapeppa, and bacon. Heat through, and season with salt and pepper. Serve hot.
Yield: 12 to 14 servings

Nothing puzzling about making the chef's Langoustine Rolls

Roast Duckling with Plum Sauce

❖

Great care and nurturing goes into this preparation. No wonder it is so popular here. No doubt it will be a hit at your table. Cook the ducks a day ahead.

Plum Sauce
- ➤ 2 1-pound cans purple plums
- ➤ 18 ounces red currant jelly (homemade preferred)
- ➤ ½ cup cassis
- ➤ ½ cup duck stock

Ducklings
- ➤ 3 4- to 4½-pound ducklings, cleaned
- ➤ 1 orange, cut into wedges
- ➤ 1 medium onion, cut into wedges
- ➤ Salt, garlic powder, pepper, paprika to taste
- ➤ Sprinkling of dry white wine

Windflower's corn chowder and a hungry menagerie

1. Pit the plums. In a medium saucepan combine all of the plum sauce ingredients, including the syrup from the plums. Simmer over medium heat for about 1½ hours. The sauce should be thick. It will keep well for weeks in the refrigerator and is also wonderful on chicken and pork.
2. Preheat the oven to 350°. Set the giblets aside in a 2-quart saucepan to make a stock. Remove the fat from the duck cavities and from the neck flap. Rinse and drain the ducks and place breast-side-up on racks in a foil-lined roasting pan. Squeeze the orange wedges over the ducks and place the squeezed wedges between the ducks and in their cavities. Place the onion wedges in the same areas. Sprinkle the ducks with seasonings.
3. Place the ducks in the oven. After 15 minutes, prick their skins, being careful not to pierce the meat. Cook for another 30 minutes.
4. Remove the ducks from the pan and drain off the fat, including the fat in the duck cavities. Place the ducks breast-side-down and sprinkle again with seasonings. After 15 minutes prick the skin again. Return the ducks to the oven and cook for 45 minutes. Remove them from the oven and repeat the draining process. Replace the ducks breast-side-down and pour a splash of white wine over each duck. Cook for 15 minutes.
5. Turn the ducks breast-side-up and again splash with wine. Cook for 15 minutes.
6. Ducks will be done when they are well browned and have slightly puckered skin, about 2 hours and 15 minutes. Drain the fat from the cavities and place the ducks on cooling racks. Chill them in the refrigerator overnight.
7. Cut the ducks into serving portions, either in half or in quarters. Let them come to room temperature. Heat the duck in a 400° oven for 30 to 40 minutes, or until heated through and brown and crisp. Serve with plum sauce.
Yield: 6 servings

Brandied Chocolate Apricot Torte

Casserole of Root Vegetables

❖

➤ *1 pound parsnips, peeled and cut into 1-inch pieces*

➤ *2½ pounds white potatoes, peeled and cubed*

➤ *1 small celery root (optional), peeled and cubed*

➤ *¼ cup melted butter*

➤ *¾ cup buttermilk*

➤ *Salt and freshly ground pepper to taste*

1. In separate saucepans cook the parsnips, potatoes, and celery root in boiling salted water until very tender. Make sure the centers of the parsnips are soft.

2. Preheat the oven to 350°. Drain the vegetables and mash them together in a large bowl with 3 tablespoons of the melted butter and all of the buttermilk. Blend with an electric mixer until smooth. Add salt and pepper.

3. Brush a 4-quart casserole with the remaining melted butter and fill with the vegetable mixture. Pour any remaining melted butter over the vegetable mixture. Bake for 30 minutes or until golden brown and crusty on top. **Note:** For a special presentation, pour the mixture through a pastry bag fitted with a rosette pattern and pipe onto a cookie sheet. Bake at 350° on a buttered baking sheet for about 15 to 20 minutes or until golden.
Yield: 6 to 8 servings

Brandied Chocolate Apricot Torte

❖

- ➤ 1 9-inch chocolate cake layer
- ➤ ¼ cup apricot brandy
- ➤ 2½ cups heavy cream
- ➤ 1 pound semisweet chocolate, finely chopped
- ➤ 3 ounces dried apricots, finely chopped
- ➤ 2 tablespoons apricot fruit preserves
  Frosting
- ➤ ¾ cup heavy cream
- ➤ 6 ounces semisweet chocolate, finely chopped
- ➤ 1 tablespoon apricot brandy
  Apricot Purée
- ➤ 4 ounces dried apricots
- ➤ 1 cup water
- ➤ ½ cup plus 3 tablespoons apricot nectar
- ➤ 1 tablespoon apricot brandy
  Assembly
- ➤ Whipped cream
- ➤ Chocolate curls

1. Line a 9-inch springform pan with plastic wrap, allowing the wrap to hang over. Place the cake layer in the bottom, and brush with 2 tablespoons of the apricot brandy. Set the pan aside.
2. In a small saucepan bring 1 cup of the heavy cream to a boil. Add the chopped chocolate and stir until melted. Cool the mixture to room temperature, about 1 hour. Do not let the mixture get too stiff.
3. Whip the remaining 1½ cups of cream and fold it into the cooled chocolate with the apricots, 2 tablespoons of brandy, and the preserves. Pour the mixture over the cake layer. Smooth the top and cover with the plastic wrap. Chill the torte in the refrigerator for several hours or overnight.
4. Lift the torte out of the pan, and remove the plastic wrap. Place it on a serving plate. In a small saucepan bring the cream to a boil. Add the chocolate and stir until melted. Add the brandy. Chill the frosting until thick. Frost the torte.
5. In a small saucepan simmer the apricots in the water and nectar until very soft, about 40 to 60 minutes. In a food processor purée the apricots and liquid, and add the brandy. The mixture may be thinned with more water, nectar, or brandy if necessary. Ladle the purée onto dessert dishes and place a piece of the prepared cake in the center of each. Top with whipped cream and chocolate curls, if desired.
Yield: 8 to 10 servings

Southern
Nights

Glen-Ella Springs Inn
Clarkesville, Georgia

INNKEEPER/CHEF BARRIE AYCOCK

Dinner for Eight

Black-Eyed-Pea Salsa Dip

◆

Okra and Tomato Soup

◆

Herbed Rainbow Trout Pecan

◆

Braised Cabbage with Bell Peppers

◆

*Fried Green Tomatoes
Hollywood Style*

◆

Sweet Georgia Peach Custard Pie

A chilling, misty
rain accompanied my drive through the
Chattahoochee National Forest to the edge
of the Blue Ridge Mountains. Despite the
somber skies, I could count my lucky stars,
for travelers of the past had to reach the
historic Glen-Ella Springs Hotel by horse-
drawn buggy or wagon from the local train
station. As I rounded corners over the same
old dirt roads, the modern-day comforts allowed me to focus on the lush terrain
beyond the drenched roadway.

Of course, it was water that drew the
visitors here in those days gone by. Glen-Ella
Springs Inn, which dates to the 1870s, is
tucked between verdant meadows of grass
and scenic hills of evergreen in a tranquil
valley scalloped from tip to toe by moun-
taintops and streams. In its prime, the hotel

was a summer getaway for Atlantans seeking the "curative" waters of the springs and the thrilling sight of Tallulah Falls, only a few miles from the hotel. That sense of nineteenth-century resort is still what Glen-Ella is about today, although innkeepers Bobby and Barrie Aycock have revived the long-neglected monument as a country inn.

Upon initial inspection, Bobby, a building contractor by trade, deemed the hotel's structure to be sound and manageable before the Aycocks bought it in 1986. The couple was tiring of city life in Atlanta, and Barrie wanted to serve her food to the public, motivation enough for the two to risk reopening the inn in their own style. However, their subsequent rejuvenation of Glen-Ella still meant adding plumbing and electricity and cleaning up the inn's signature heart-pine floors and paneling.

Bobby also rebuilt the many porches, which now host bending willow rockers. The back porches double as delightful sun decks with views of the surrounding mountains. All this restoration work has earned the Aycocks recognition from The Georgia Trust for Historic Preservation and a spot on the National Register of Historic Places.

Originally, the old hotel had twenty-seven guest rooms. The Aycocks added private baths bringing the number down to sixteen "to offer the best possible world for our guests," says Barrie.

Barrie's desire to run a restaurant sent her to cooking and management school. Her dinners at Glen-Ella can be as southern as the regular menu here, or as new American as lobster baked in white wine and lemon sauce with a trademark appetizer of chicken livers with Marsala and country ham or fried breaded Brie.

The menu features the inn's most popular entrée of trout, caught locally. The combination of lime and pecans adds a handsome flavor to the dish, and Barrie apologizes for the Bisquick. "I'd ordinarily shy away from prepared biscuit mix, but there's just something in this packaged mix that makes this taste just right."

Barrie has cooked or eaten fried green tomatoes in a number of different ways since childhood in the South. She finds the recipe included in this menu and featured in *Fried Green Tomatoes*—the highly successful movie with Jessica Tandy and Kathy Bates—to be one of the best. "The secret is in the way food stylist Cynthia Hizer Jubera combined flour and cornmeal as the dredging substance. Usually, this dish is made with only one of these ingredients," says Barrie, "as southern cooks disagree over how to dredge the tomatoes." In addition, sugar isn't always a part of the recipe for fried green tomatoes, but Barrie advises that it is a positive addition.

The chef is big on theme dinners, and I am sorry I missed her "Evening with Basil" bash. I mention it here as I think it is a great idea to use at home for a summer party. At Glen-Ella, it started with champagne garnished with piccolo basil and fruit followed by a cinnamon basil pâté and artichokes and basil dip. The soup was chilled cantaloupe and tomato with chopped sweet basil; a green salad was bathed in an opal basil vinaigrette. Entrées were a grilled jumbo shrimp wrapped with—what else—basil leaf and prosciutto ham and a chicken breast stuffed with goat cheese and basil. A yeast bread was baked from scratch with a spiral filling of chopped basil, olive oil, and Parmesan cheese. Still to come was dessert of blueberries in puff pastry with a flashing finish of basil sabayon sauce.

Alas, it wasn't basil season when I visited Glen-Ella. But the warmth of the quietly lit heart-pine walls, the fire in the rustic stone hearth, and the promise of a new season around the corner when the inn would be alive with bathers by the pool and iced-tea sippers in the rockers were all I needed to feel that I would not want to be anywhere else on this day.

A different twist for black-eyed peas

Black-Eyed-Pea Salsa Dip
❖

Barrie loves experimenting with different ways to prepare black-eyed peas. This one is a winner. Even those who do not care for the peas shouldn't shy away from this clever rendition.

- ➤ ½ *pound dry black-eyed peas*
- ➤ 1 *teaspoon salt*
- ➤ ½ *teaspoon cayenne pepper*
- ➤ 1 *bay leaf*
  Salsa
- ➤ 1½ *cups cubed ripe tomatoes*
- ➤ 1½ *tablespoons seeded and finely chopped jalapeños*
- ➤ 2 *tablespoons minced fresh cilantro*
- ➤ 1 *tablespoon lime juice*
- ➤ 3 *tablespoons minced onion*
- ➤ ½ *teaspoon salt*

1. Wash and pick over the peas. In a small saucepan cover the peas with 2 inches of water. Bring the water to a boil and cook for

2 minutes. Remove the pan from the heat and let it sit for 1 hour. Return the pan to the heat and add the salt, cayenne pepper, and bay leaf. Cook over medium heat until the peas are tender, about 30 to 45 minutes. Drain and let the peas cool.
2. In a medium bowl mix together the salsa ingredients. Add the peas. Taste the salsa and adjust the seasonings. Store in airtight jars. Serve with tortilla chips.
Yield: 4 cups

Okra and Tomato Soup
❖

Okra looks so appetizing, especially when you can get it fresh at local markets. I like having a recipe such as this one to remind me to serve okra more often. Not being southern-born-and-raised, I rarely think of weaving okra through my family meal plans. I do now.

- ➤ ¼ *cup virgin olive oil*
- ➤ ½ *teaspoon mixed dried oregano, thyme, and basil*
- ➤ ½ *teaspoon dried red pepper flakes*
- ➤ 1 *bay leaf*
- ➤ 3 *cups sliced fresh (or frozen) okra*
- ➤ 1 *medium onion, chopped (1 cup)*
- ➤ 46 *ounces tomato juice*
- ➤ 14 *ounces crushed Italian peeled tomatoes*
- ➤ 2 *cups water*

1. In a large stock pot warm the olive oil over very low heat. Turn off the heat and add the herbs, red pepper, and bay leaf. Stir and let the pan sit on the stove for 15 minutes to flavor the oil.
2. Add the okra and onions and simmer on low for about 30 minutes, until the onions are very soft and the okra is tender. Add the remaining ingredients and heat through. Remove the bay leaf and serve.
Yield: 8 to 12 servings

Herbed Rainbow Trout Pecan

❖

This is the inn's most popular entrée and offers me yet another easy, but still delicious way to prepare something I rarely think about cooking.

➤ 8 6-ounce fillets rainbow trout
➤ 2 cups Bisquick mix, seasoned with salt and pepper
➤ ½ cup (1 stick) butter
➤ 2 limes
➤ ½ cup chopped toasted pecans
➤ ¼ cup mixed chopped fresh parsley, basil, and oregano

1. Preheat the oven to 325°. Dredge the fillets in the biscuit mix.
2. In a skillet heat 2 tablespoons of butter and sauté 2 fillets skin-side-up over moderate heat until browned. Turn and brown the other side. Sauté the remaining fillets 2 at a time, adding more butter as needed, until all of the fillets are browned. (The fish may be prepared 30 minutes in advance up to this point. Hold at room temperature and place it in the oven 5 minutes before serving.) Place the fish skin-side down in a baking dish. Squeeze lime juice over the fish and sprinkle it with pecans and herbs. Bake for 6 to 8 minutes or until the fish flakes easily with a fork.
Yield: 8 servings

Braised Cabbage with Bell Peppers

❖

Cabbage is an important crop in Clarkesville. Being in a mountainous region, the land is steep, allowing the cabbage to grow well. There is even an annual cabbage festival in a nearby village.

➤ 1 head cabbage (about 2 pounds)
➤ 2 each large red and green bell peppers
➤ Butter for sautéing
➤ 1 large onion, sliced into rings and cut in half
➤ 1 cup chicken stock or broth
➤ 1 cup water
➤ ½ teaspoon minced fresh garlic
➤ ½ teaspoon red pepper flakes

A great way to enjoy okra

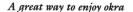

1. Cut the cabbage into quarters and remove the core. Place cut side down on a cutting board and cut into ¼-inch-thick slices.
2. Core and seed the peppers, slicing into ¼-inch-thick strips.
3. In a large skillet heat the butter. Sauté the cabbage, peppers, and onion just until the vegetables begin to wilt. Add the stock, water, garlic, and pepper flakes. Simmer briefly, just until the vegetables are tender but still crisp. Serve warm.

Yield: 8 to 12 servings

Fried Green Tomatoes Hollywood Style

❖

Fried green tomatoes were new to most of the cast of the movie by that name. So while on the set one night, the movie's food stylist created her own version and gave the actors and crew a taste of one of the South's most famous dishes (see more about this on page 194). Barrie thought it would be more of a treat to offer us a recipe inspired by the movie version, instead of her own recipe. But she stresses that it is best to use unripened vine tomatoes instead of green tomatoes. She admits that is only possible in June, when she picks them right off her own vines at the inn. We have doubled the recipe to serve with the rest of this dinner-for-eight menu.

➤ *2 cups cornmeal*
➤ *1 cup all-purpose flour*
➤ *2 tablespoons sugar*
➤ *4 pounds (8 to 10) green tomatoes, sliced ½-inch thick*
➤ *Oil or solid vegetable shortening for frying*
➤ *Salt and black pepper to taste*

1. In a shallow bowl mix the cornmeal, flour, and sugar. Dredge both sides of the tomatoes in the mixture, pressing the slices firmly into the mixture to coat well.
2. In an iron skillet heat ¼ inch of oil or shortening over medium-high heat. Add the tomatoes a few at a time, without crowding. Fry for about 2 minutes or until golden brown. Turn and cook on the other side. Season to taste and serve.

Yield: 8 servings

Sweet Georgia Peach Custard Pie

Crust

- ➤ 1½ cups all-purpose flour
- ➤ ½ cup sugar
- ➤ 1 teaspoon baking powder
- ➤ ½ cup (1 stick) butter
- ➤ 1 egg
- ➤ 1 tablespoon peach schnapps or other peachy liqueur (or water)

Filling

- ➤ 6 tablespoons sugar
- ➤ 1 tablespoon all-purpose flour
- ➤ 2 eggs
- ➤ ¾ cup sour cream
- ➤ ¾ teaspoon vanilla extract
- ➤ ⅛ teaspoon grated fine lemon zest
- ➤ ⅛ teaspoon nutmeg
- ➤ ⅛ teaspoon salt
- ➤ 1 tablespoon peach schnapps or other peachy liqueur
- ➤ 6 ripe freestone peaches, peeled and sliced into ¼-inch-thick slices
- ➤ ¾ cup apple jelly, melted

1. Preheat the oven to 350°. In a food processor combine the crust ingredients and process until just combined. (Do not let the dough form a ball.) Pat the mixture into a greased 9-inch by 1½-inch-deep pie plate, pressing the dough evenly into the bottom and up the sides of the dish.

2. In a large bowl mix together all of the filling ingredients except the peaches and jelly. Pour it evenly into the pie shell. Arrange the sliced peaches over the filling in a swirled pattern. Bake the pie for 20 minutes. Remove it from the oven and spoon warm apple jelly over the pie to glaze. Bake for another 30 minutes or until the glaze is set. Cut into wedges and serve warm.
Yield: 8 servings

Country Home Cooking with Horns Aplenty

The Birchwood Inn
Temple, New Hampshire

INNKEEPER/CHEF BILL WOLFE

Dinner for Eight

Orange Anise Bread

◆

Copper Carrot Relish

◆

Colonial Peanut Soup

◆

Avocado Chicken and Cheese Bake

◆

Cranberry Pudding

No matter the time of year, dinner guests find festively lit candles in each window as they approach this former roadside tavern. The Birchwood's lights, which say welcome, symbolize the hospitality offered by this quaint New England inn. I encourage you to practice this cheerful custom all year, too. (Many homeowners do so in southeastern Pennsylvania.) Electric candles are inexpensive to use; and whenever we have a dinner party or expect a guest for any reason, we turn on our candles as innkeepers Judy and Bill Wolfe do at their 1775 inn.

The Birchwood stands adjacent to the town common in Temple, a quintessential New England small town where all I had to do was raise the window of my guest room just a tad to hear nearby cows mooing in the

early morning. The inn has quite a legacy, dating to its early days as a tavern for men on horseback as well as those traveling by coach.

Itinerant artist Rufus Porter stopped by for a drink in 1825 and ended up adorning the dining room walls with his trademark weeping trees and rolling landscape. The Wolfes had the valuable mural restored in 1978 when they bought The Birchwood. Now the main dining room is named in honor of the artist.

Another well-known man of the arts who stopped by to assuage his thirst and rest his head was writer Henry David Thoreau. He made his way to The Birchwood in 1852 and later wrote about the wild berries that grew along its path. There are several reminders of Thoreau around the inn today, and Bill uses berries from some of those same bushes in his kitchen, making his own sauces, jams, and preserves.

But Rufus Porter is the kindred spirit with Bill Wolfe. The painter was also a musician of the fiddle, fife, and drum; and he even dabbled in railroading, inventing the elevated railway two decades before the first one was built. Music and railroading are two avocations Bill shares with Porter. The inn-

keeper's hobby trains—displayed on tracks in the main dining room and the common area—could be interpreted as a subtle tribute to Porter's interest in railroading. Rufus Porter was a free spirit and his own man. So is Bill Wolfe, as you will see from his cooking philosophy.

The Music Room—complete with old instruments from generations of Wolfe family musicians—is one of seven Birchwood guest rooms decorated in individual theme motifs. Music always fills the inn, whether it is a live performance by former music teacher and vocalist Bill or a recorded selection from his library of the classics. Beethoven tracks go well with the chef's baked-and-stuffed flank steak or spinach lamb loaf and a Vivaldi violin concerto seems well-suited for his sole Birchwood or émincés of veal. Perhaps a few notes from a Wynton Marsalis trumpet would be most complementary to Bill's chicken sausage gumbo. All these culinary numbers can be found in the cookbook Bill and Judy wrote, *The Birchwood Sampler.*

The innkeeper/chef started cooking during grade school, when he first discovered a natural aptitude for putting together an after-school snack he had to make instead of simply unwrap. That freedom to raid the kitchen and experiment honed the skills of a chef who turned up his nose at cooking school. "The thought of it was too regimented for me. I wanted to learn as I went along and not be influenced in any one direction," explains Bill.

The desire to share his lifetime enjoyment of cooking propelled Bill and Judy toward innkeeping.

Bill's kitchen is a small, homey galley where he is within counter-length reach of the telephone and guest reservations book. Behind the kitchen is another work area: an unheated room you might call Bill's sugar shack. Here Bill carries on an age-old German folk custom: barley candy making.

When the New Hampshire air turns very cold, he mixes a brew of sugar, water, vine-

Authentic Rufus Porter walls

gar (instead of barley), and a touch of cinnamon oil over the kitchen stove and boils it up to a froth just under 300°. (Temperature is crucial so the liquid does not harden before reaching his treasured collection of molds in the outer room.) Then he throws on a coat, rushes to the shed, and quickly pours the syrup into the waiting cast-iron molds. In minutes he has an assortment of colorful, transparent candies in shapes of everything from a pair of scissors to a steamship. The candies were originally used as Christmas tree ornaments, but today Bill gives them to holiday diners as they leave the inn.

The molds belonged to Bill's great-great-grandfather, a commercial baker and confectioner. A hundred years of tradition have stayed with Bill; so has his great-great-grandfather's propensity for working in the food business.

Bill and Judy's blackboard menu changes nightly at the Birchwood—including any thing from veal to venison and lobster to shrimp tortellini. Bill's approach is not that of a gourmet chef. That would not be true to Bill Wolfe or tradition at the Birchwood. These innkeepers insist that everything, like the music and the past, plays here in harmony. And it does!

Copper Carrots and the chef's steam engines

Orange Anise Bread

❖

➤ 1 package active dry yeast
➤ 1/2 cup warm water (115°)
➤ 1/2 teaspoon sugar
➤ 1/2 cup orange juice
➤ 1/3 cup honey
➤ 2 eggs
➤ 2 tablespoons oil
➤ 2 teaspoons salt
➤ 1 teaspoon anise seed
➤ 4 teaspoons grated orange peel
➤ 1 cup cottage cheese
➤ 5 cups or more all-purpose flour

1. In a large bowl dissolve the yeast in the warm water with the sugar. Set the mixture aside until the yeast bubbles and activates, about 5 to 10 minutes.
2. Add the orange juice, honey, eggs, oil, salt, anise, orange peel, and cottage cheese, and beat well with an electric mixer. Add 2 cups of the flour and beat for 2 minutes. Continue beating while gradually adding 3 more cups of flour. Add up to 1 cup more, enough to make the dough pull away from the sides of

the bowl. Turn the dough out onto a floured surface and knead it until smooth. Place it in a greased bowl. Cover the bowl with a kitchen towel and let the dough rise until doubled in size. Punch it down and knead a few times. Divide the dough in half. Cover the dough and let it rest for 10 minutes. Shape it into loaves. Place the loaves into 2 9 x 5-inch loaf pans and brush the tops with melted butter. Cover and let rise to double.
3. Preheat the oven to 375°. Bake 30 minutes or until golden brown. Cool on a rack.
   Yield: 2 loaves

Copper Carrot Relish

❖

➤ 1/2 cup red wine or cider vinegar
➤ 1 cup canola or vegetable oil
➤ 1/2 teaspoon salt
➤ 10 ounces condensed tomato soup
➤ 1 clove garlic, minced
➤ 2 pounds carrots, cooked and julienned
➤ 1 onion, julienned
➤ 1 green bell pepper, julienned

In a small bowl mix together the vinegar, oil, salt, soup, and garlic. Place the vegetables in a serving bowl or relish dish, and toss with the dressing.
Yield: 1 1/2 quarts

Colonial Peanut Soup

❖

➤ 1/4 cup (1/2 stick) butter
➤ 1 medium onion, finely chopped
➤ 2 stalks celery, finely chopped
➤ 3 tablespoons all-purpose flour
➤ 2 quarts chicken stock or broth
➤ 2 cups smooth peanut butter
➤ 1 3/4 cups light cream
➤ Chopped peanuts

1. In a medium saucepan melt the butter and sauté the onion and celery until transparent. Blend in the flour. Add the stock and bring it to a boil. Remove the pan from heat.
2. Pour the stock through a strainer. Return the stock to the pan. Reserve the vegetables for another recipe. Add the peanut butter and cream. Blend well and heat through. Pour the soup into bowls and garnish with peanuts.
Yield: 8 servings

Avocado and Chicken Cheese Bake

❖

➤ *4 large boneless chicken breasts, skinned and halved*
➤ *Salt and pepper*
➤ *¼ cup or more all-purpose flour*
➤ *½ cup (1 stick) butter*
➤ *½ cup chopped onion*
➤ *1 clove garlic, minced*
➤ *8 large mushrooms, chopped*
➤ *2 tablespoons all-purpose flour*
➤ *1 teaspoon celery salt*
➤ *½ teaspoon freshly ground pepper*
➤ *½ cup chicken stock or broth*
➤ *½ cup white wine*
➤ *1 avocado, peeled, pitted, and mashed*
➤ *1 cup grated Monterey Jack cheese*

1. Pound the chicken between waxed paper with a mallet to flatten. Sprinkle each piece with salt, pepper, and flour. In a large skillet melt half of the butter and lightly brown the chicken. Remove the chicken from the skillet and set it aside.
2. Preheat the oven to 350°. In the same skillet melt the remaining butter and sauté the onion, garlic, and mushrooms until lightly browned. Stir in 2 tablespoons of the flour, the celery salt, pepper, stock, and wine. Cook until thickened, about 4 to 5 minutes.
3. Stir in the avocado and ½ cup of the cheese. Arrange the chicken breasts in a baking dish. Spoon the mushroom mixture over the

Avocado Chicken and music everywhere

chicken and sprinkle with the remaining cheese. Bake for 10 to 15 minutes or until the chicken is cooked through. Serve over a bed of orzo pasta or rice.
Yield: 8 servings

Cranberry Pudding

❖

This is one of those desserts that is so easy to make, it allows you to spend more time on an entrée and the rest of the meal.

➤ *2 cups heavy cream*
➤ *3 tablespoons sugar*
➤ *1 teaspoon vanilla extract*
➤ *8 slices pumpernickel bread, crumbled*
➤ *2⅔ cups whole cranberry sauce*

1. In a large bowl whip the cream until stiff peaks form. Gently add the sugar and vanilla.
2. In clear dessert dishes alternate layers of the bread crumbs, cranberry sauce, and whipped cream. Chill at least 2 hours before serving.
Yield: 8 servings

Foreign O'Fares

We have almost forgotten what it means to work so hard for our food. But still, in many countries, people labor with their hands to produce food to stay alive, rather than being able to buy it packaged off a shelf. It reminds us of how much it meant when food was shared by one family to another, even though it called for a personal sacrifice by those who could ill afford it. Offering a foreigner a seat at your table with food you have prepared, however humble or grand, is the greastest gift you can give.

Mary Lee Papa
The Shire Inn

October Country Inn, Bridgewater Corners, Vermont

A North African Feast

October Country Inn
Bridgewater Corners, Vermont

INNKEEPER/CHEF PATRICK RUNKEL

Dinner for Eight

Near East Peanut Chicken Soup

◆

Yemarina Yewotet Dabo
(Ethiopian Honey Bread)

◆

Moroccan Flatbread

◆

Raita (Cucumber and Yogurt) Salad

◆

Spicy North African Lentils

◆

Tajine of Lamb and Green Beans

◆

Date-Nut Cakes with
Orange Custard Sauce

I had spoken to inn-keeper Richard Sims several times by phone before I visited October Country Inn. Thanks to his name, familiar-sounding voice, and invigorating personality, I conjured up an image of Richard Simmons, the ani-mated exercise/diet king; but when I finally walked through the door of the inn, a taller, stockier, and bearded Richard Sims—non-VIP—greeted me. The only traits that con-tinued to feed my Hollywood image of Richard were his refreshing style and per-sonable manner. In fact, Richard's character and chef Patrick Runkel's fabulous food lit-erally flavor this very special inn with some of the most sincere hospitality and tasty din-ing you will find at any country inn.

The menu that follows is only one of the ethnic spreads Patrick creates for guests, who do not know what's for dinner until it marches out piping hot through the kitchen's saloon-style doors and into the inn's two inviting country/Colonial dining rooms. It really does not matter what is on the plates. Patrick, who serves most of the dishes family style, masterfully creates and blends foods of any language. He is a formidable presence in the kitchen, totally in control of the foreign ingredients he is uniting. The inn's lively spirit is ever-present in the kitchen where an occasional guest may sit at a large antique wooden table to witness the chef in action.

I was entertained watching Patrick cook up the African meal. He did so with great presence, verve, and alacrity—confident of his mixture of herbs and spices, grinding all of them fresh into iron pots and skillets as though he had been at this for decades. Actually, the former special education teacher learned to cook on the job and at cooking classes. He has only been ardently at the stove since 1987 when he and Richard bought the inn (named for the month it was purchased by former owners).

As you explore the ingredients for the recipes, which are mostly from Morocco and North Africa, you will note that they are primarily low-fat. This is not unusual for dishes from many non-American cultures. However, I am sure that the recipes were also influenced by Patrick's days spent working in a health-food market. The chef researched the cuisine primarily in cookbooks and developed his own adaptations. I found preparing this meal at home to be easy and most rewarding. Do not be afraid to try it yourself just because the foods are unfamiliar; the ingredients are readily available, and the methods of preparation are easy. I enjoyed exploring the use of various spices and found the probable origin of the

The inn's guest book and bread dough art by the chef

bonnet-shaped flatbread especially interesting. Many African breads were originally designed to serve also as eating utensils. Richard conjectures that this may have been one such bread.

Also on the list of fascinating ethnic adventures at October Country are the signature cuisines of Russia, Scandinavia, Greece, Mexico, and India. More traditional Italian and French meals are big hits, as is the gourmet Mexican. The global list continues to grow as the ethnic meals become increasingly popular with guests. The inn's cornucopia logo is an appropriate one; the food is bountiful and full of surprises.

Guests always find cookies, tea, and coffee sitting out in the hospitality nook. A varied collection of mugs—sent to the inn by guests—allows you to take your pick according to your mood. Believe me, this is a ritual at October Country! The innkeepers often can be caught cordially nosing in on guests, curious to see what mugs will leave the shelf. I arrived on a snowy afternoon and drank Celestial Seasonings Bengal Tiger tea at Richard's suggestion. I selected a rather serious mug that depicted a snow scene and had a soothing winter poem to help me kick off my high heels and relax for the afternoon. By next morning—in my Reeboks—I had switched to a Gary Larson "Far Side" cartoon cup. Whimsy is found in appropriate places from the kitchen to the nook, and the large sitting room filled with puzzles, games, books, a wood stove, and fireplace.

This is a most thoughtful inn, and not far from my idea of heaven on earth. On winter mornings, there is a printed report from the innkeepers, highlighting the skiing conditions and open trails in the area. In summer, news of weather conditions assists the many bikers who relax here while on tour.

Guest rooms are cheerfully decorated with pretty wallpapers and painted trims. Antiques abound in this old farmhouse with its wide-board floors. The decor is homey

Tale of two breads: Honey and Moroccan

yet tasteful and coordinated. The ambience is casual but crisp, with feel-good things all around, such as feathered pillows to rest one's weary head on at night and jacquard-style throws for an afternoon nap on the sofa.

You can tell by the volume of guest book entries this inn has collected that visitors leave regretfully. Who said a bit earlier that the innkeepers are not VIPs here? The unlined pages of book after book are filled with endearing notes, accented by an abundance of colorful artwork from the amateur to the artistic. Richard and Patrick encourage their guests' thoughts by putting colored markers in obvious places. It seems everyone is inspired to reach for a pen. Even this hard-nosed former newspaper reporter had something to say before moving on: "Extra! Extra! Read all about it in *Great Cooking with Country Inn Chefs*, I wrote in my best Times-Roman typeface. And now you have.

Near East Peanut Chicken Soup

❖

In that part of the world peanuts are a very popular food used prolifically in everyday cooking. This soup is divine. You'll want to serve it over and over again!

- ➤ 2 tablespoons olive oil
- ➤ 2 medium onions, chopped
- ➤ 4 cloves garlic, mashed
- ➤ 2 large red or green bell peppers, chopped
- ➤ 28 ounces canned tomatoes, coarsely chopped
- ➤ 8 cups chicken stock or broth
- ➤ ¼ tablespoon black pepper
- ➤ ¼ teaspoon crushed hot pepper flakes
- ➤ ½ cup uncooked long-grain rice
- ➤ 1½ cups cooked chicken, chopped
- ➤ ⅔ cup smooth unsalted, sugarless peanut butter

1. In a large saucepan heat the oil and sauté the onions, garlic, and peppers. Add the tomatoes, stock, pepper, and hot pepper flakes. Simmer the soup uncovered over low heat for about 1 hour.
2. Add the rice and chicken and simmer for 20 minutes or until the rice is tender. Whisk in the peanut butter and mix until completely smooth. Heat the soup through. Thin with more chicken stock, if desired.
Yield: 8 servings

Yemarina Yewotet Dabo (Ethiopian Honey Bread)

❖

The sweeter flavor of this savory bread is a perfect accompaniment to the spicier dishes.

- ➤ 1 package active dry yeast
- ➤ ¼ cup lukewarm water (115°)
- ➤ 1 egg
- ➤ ½ cup honey
- ➤ 1 tablespoon coriander
- ➤ ½ teaspoon cinnamon
- ➤ ¼ teaspoon cloves
- ➤ 1½ teaspoons salt
- ➤ 1 cup lukewarm milk
- ➤ ¼ cup (½ stick) unsalted butter, melted
- ➤ 4 to 4½ cups all-purpose flour

1. In a small bowl dissolve the yeast in lukewarm water. Set the mixture aside until the yeast starts foaming, 5 to 10 minutes.
2. In a large bowl beat together the egg, honey, spices, salt, milk, and butter with a wire whisk.
3. Gradually add the flour, ½ cup at a time, using enough to make a soft dough. Turn the dough onto a floured surface and knead it for 5 minutes or until the dough is smooth and elastic. Add more flour if the dough is too sticky to handle. Shape it into a ball and place it in a buttered bowl. Cover the bowl with a kitchen towel and let the dough rise until doubled in size, about 1½ hours. Punch the dough down and knead it again for 1 to 2 minutes. Shape it into a ball and place it in a deep 3-quart buttered soufflé or baking dish, completely covering the bottom of the dish. Let the dough rise until doubled.
4. Preheat the oven to 300°. Bake the bread for 50 to 60 minutes or until the bread is browned on top. Turn out onto a rack to cool.
Yield: 1 loaf

Moroccan Flatbread

❖

Once put together, this bread resembles a wide-brimmed hat.

- ➤ 1 tablespoon active dry yeast
- ➤ ¼ cup warm water (115°)
- ➤ 3 cups all-purpose flour
- ➤ 1½ tablespoons sugar
- ➤ 1 teaspoon salt
- ➤ ⅓ cup dry powdered skim milk
- ➤ 1½ tablespoons vegetable oil
- ➤ 1 cup warm water (115°)
- ➤ 1 egg yolk, beaten with 1 teaspoon water
- ➤ ¼ cup sesame seeds

1. In a medium bowl dissolve the yeast in warm water. Set the mixture aside until the dough starts foaming, 5 to 10 minutes.

2. In a food processor pulse together the flour, sugar, salt, and dry milk a few times to mix well.

3. Add the oil and warm water to the yeast mixture. Start the processor slowly, pouring the oil-yeast mixture through the feed tube until the dough balls up. Process about 30 seconds more to knead. Turn the dough onto a floured surface and knead by hand for a few more minutes. Place the dough in a large buttered bowl. Cover the bowl with a kitchen towel and let the dough rise until double in size. Punch the dough down, cover, and let it rest for 10 minutes. Pinch off ¼ of the dough, shape it into a ball, and set it aside.

4. On a greased, round pizza pan shape the large piece of dough into a flat round cake. Poke a hole in the center, and enlarge the hole to about 4 inches. Flatten the small ball of dough into a circle about 10 inches in diameter. Place the circle in the center of the hole and flatten it slightly to fill the hole. Lightly brush with olive oil, cover with plastic, and

Tajine of Lamb over couscous and spicy lentils

refrigerate for 6 hours or overnight.

5. Preheat the oven to 350°. Remove the loaf from the refrigerator and let it stand at room temperature for 15 minutes. Brush with beaten egg-and-water mixture and sprinkle with sesame seeds. Bake the bread for 30 to 40 minutes or until the loaf is a deep golden brown and sounds hollow when tapped. Cool slightly on a wire rack before cutting.

Yield: 1 loaf

Raita (Cucumber and Yogurt Salad)
❖

Patrick provides this salad both as a vegetable and palate cleanser, which may be kept in a separate dish on the side throughout the meal.

➤ 3 large cucumbers, peeled, seeded, and sliced into rounds about ½-inch thick

➤ 2 cups plain yogurt

➤ 1½ teaspoons cumin seeds

➤ 1½ teaspoons finely chopped mint

---

1. In a serving bowl mix together the cucumbers and yogurt.
2. In a hot cast-iron skillet toast the cumin seeds without oil until lightly browned. Shake the pan to prevent scorching. Remove the pan from heat and let it cool. Pound the cumin seeds with a mortar and pestle to a coarse grind. Stir the ground cumin seeds and mint into the cucumbers and yogurt, and chill.

Yield: 8 servings

Spicy North African Lentils
❖

Lentils have been a staple food in North Africa since the African provinces were the storehouses of Rome. This recipe makes use of red lentils, but the dish ends up looking more yellow-green than red.

➤ 3 cups orange lentils

➤ 1½ teaspoons salt

➤ 6 tablespoons olive oil

➤ 1½ large onions, minced

➤ 1½ teaspoons each grated ginger, mashed garlic, coriander, turmeric, crushed cumin, and cardamom

➤ ¾ teaspoon cayenne pepper

➤ Tomato and lemon slices for garnish

---

1. In a medium saucepan cover the lentils with water. Add the salt and cook until tender, about 30 minutes. Drain and mash the lentils slightly.
2. In the same pan heat the oil and sauté the onions until golden. Add the spices and simmer for about 5 minutes. Add the lentils, stirring well. Heat through. The dish should be thick, as a purée. Adjust the consistency if necessary by adding a little water or chicken stock. Add garnish.

Yield: 8 servings

Tajine of Lamb and Green Beans

❖

A tajine is a deep-glazed, earthenware dish with a conical lid. It is used for preparing and serving a variety of recipes that are cooked slowly and result in a ragout, such as October Country's lamb stew. Serve this dish over a bed of Moroccan pasta or couscous, a semolina-based starch discovered by the French in Algeria during Charles X's conquest. Couscous is the national dish of Algeria, Morocco, and Tunisia.

➤ 6 tablespoons olive oil
➤ 4 pounds lamb stew meat, cubed
➤   Salt and freshly ground pepper
➤ 4 onions, chopped
➤ 2 cloves garlic, chopped
➤ 2 teaspoons cumin
➤ 1 teaspoon each: ginger, turmeric, thyme
➤ 2 bay leaves
➤ ⅛ teaspoon cayenne pepper
➤ 2 cinnamon sticks
➤ ¾ cup freshly chopped parsley
➤ 8 tomatoes, peeled and chopped
➤ 6 tablespoons tomato paste
➤ 1½ cups water
➤ 2 pounds green beans, sliced lengthwise
➤ 2 tablespoons toasted sesame seeds

1. In a large casserole dish heat the oil and brown the meat (in batches, if necessary). Remove the lamb from oil and season it with salt and pepper. Set it aside.
2. In the same casserole sauté the onions and garlic until lightly browned. Add the spices, parsley, tomatoes, tomato paste, and water, and blend well. Add the reserved lamb. Cover the casserole and simmer for 1½ to 2 hours

or until the meat is tender. Stir occasionally.
3. In a saucepan blanch the green beans in boiling salted water until nearly tender. Preheat the oven to 400°. Add the beans to the casserole. Bake the tajine for 15 minutes or until the beans are tender. Remove the tajine from the oven. Remove the bay leaves and cinnamon sticks. Sprinkle with sesame seeds.
Yield: 8 servings

Date-Nut Cakes with Orange Custard Sauce

❖

Patrick goes African-gourmet with this recipe. Pastillas, a national dish, are also served with dessert-type fillings, but he makes this dish in honor of the continent's prolific use of dates and nuts.

Cake
➤ 1 teaspoon baking soda
➤ 1 cup boiling water
➤ 1 cup chopped, pitted dates
➤ 1 tablespoon butter, softened
➤ 1 cup sugar
➤ ½ teaspoon salt
➤ 2 eggs, well beaten
➤ 1 cup all-purpose flour
➤ 1 cup coarsely chopped walnuts
   Orange Custard Sauce
➤ 4 egg yolks
➤   Zest of 1 orange
➤ 6 tablespoons sugar
➤ ⅛ teaspoon salt
➤ 2 cups scalded milk, hot
➤ 1 teaspoon vanilla extract
➤   Orange segments or zest for garnish

Dessert of Date-Nut Cakes with Orange Custard Sauce

1. Preheat the oven to 325°. Grease a 12-cup muffin pan. In a small saucepan dissolve the baking soda in boiling water. Add the dates. Remove the mixture from the heat and set it aside to cool.
2. In a large bowl combine the butter, sugar, salt, eggs, and flour. Mix well. Add the date mixture and walnuts, and beat until well-blended. Pour the batter into the muffin cups, filling each ¾ full. Bake the cakes for 40 to 50 minutes or until a cake tester comes out clean. Let the cakes cool on racks.
3. In a heavy-bottomed pan whisk the egg yolks just enough to blend. Add the zest, sugar, and salt. Slowly pour in the hot milk, stirring constantly. Cook over medium heat until the custard coats the spoon. Remove the pan from heat. (Do not let the mixture boil or the eggs will curdle.) Stir in the vanilla and strain the custard sauce into a bowl or pitcher. Cool to room temperature, then cover and chill. The custard will thicken as it cools. Pour the custard on serving plates and top with a date-nut cake. Garnish with 3 orange segments per serving.
Yield: 12 cakes

Ciao, Italian

The Shire Inn
Chelsea, Vermont

INNKEEPER/CHEF MARY LEE PAPA

Dinner for Six

Crostini Mascarpone with
Smoked Salmon and Caper Sauce

◆

Farfalle Pasta with Pancetta and
Basil Cream Sauce

◆

Grilled Tuna with Roasted Peppers
and Anchovy-Parsley Purée

◆

Toasted Almond Chicken with
Amaretto and Porcini Mushrooms

◆

Baked Amaretti-Stuffed Pears
with Toasted Almonds

◆

Chocolate-Dipped Cherry and
Walnut Biscotti

Υou might think
this quite an ambitious menu. But in Italian
families, it is typical to have an appetizer
followed by a pasta and then two entrées
before dessert is served, as Mary Lee Papa
has in this menu with the tuna and chicken
dishes. When I was growing up, I thought
all families ate this way. You see, my grand-
mothers and mother always set bountiful
tables, even for everyday meals, and I
wondered why my friends would act so
surprised, "Do you always eat this way?"
Nonetheless, the food was irresistible. So
when either grandmother insisted, *"Manga!
Manga!"* or "Eat! Eat!" they couldn't
ignore it.

This is the size meal we enjoyed at most
family gatherings. Sometimes even more
dishes were included. You will want to add
at least a green salad and some crudites with
or without a dip, or an antipasto with vege-

tables, cheeses, anchovies, olives, artichoke hearts, and caponata (an eggplant condiment).

The Shire Inn offers its guests much more than Italian specialties. But regardless of the cuisine Mary Lee is serving on any given day, it is always five courses and nearly as all-inclusive as the menu she has given us. Mary Lee's husband, Jim, is Italian, so the chef bows to his heritage when she cooks up an Italian dinner, often calling on traditional recipes from Jim's mother. As a result, the historic Shire Inn is certainly up on modern-day preferences. According to a 1992 National Restaurant Association study, Italian food is still the most popular on restaurant menus.

Otherwise, a non-ethnic meal here might include Mary Lee's pear-and-leek soup, a salad with maple and coriander dressing, a Grand Marnier sorbet, lemon poppy veal with fresh vegetables, and a decadent chocolate cake.

You will find Mary Lee's Italian bill-of-fare exciting, starting with the crostini, which—when served in Italy—is a sign of hospitality. Actually, it is a recipe you can serve as a welcoming food with any menu. The pancetta in the pasta recipe is something you do not want to miss; but if you must, you can substitute with bacon. Just don't tell any culinary aficionados that you did so. Serve a sherbet or sorbet as a palate cleanser before the entrées.

Mary Lee and Jim run the inn at the same time they are raising three elementary school-age children. The Papas opened the Shire Inn in 1986. "We were tired of being apart," explains Mary Lee. The family was living on Long Island, and Jim's New York City job had him traveling overseas several months out of the year. When the couple found the 1832, six-bedroom, red-brick building, "We fell in love with it and the town of Chelsea," recalls the chef.

The inn, with its circle-head door frame, certainly commands attention from the vil-

lage street; and, once inside, I found a library/parlor area and an intimate dining room with only a few tables where Mary Lee serves her meals for up to eighteen inn guests and public diners.

The chef studied at The New England Culinary Institute in Montpelier, Vermont, where she continues to take classes that help her keep the inn's menus fresh and new. In 1991, a group of thirty-two Estonians visited the area, and Mary Lee decided to demonstrate the state's hospitality to them. She called her idea "Connecting Through Cooking" and created a menu with foods donated by the culinary institute. Mary Lee served a fall harvest menu with traditional New England dishes. "The focus of the event was the understanding of cultures through such a common, linking element as food," states the innkeeper/chef. "Here were these Estonians who were becoming a free nation, and I felt that the best way to show our friendship and caring was through food."

Of course, Mary Lee really espouses that philosophy all year long at her inn—no matter who stops by. The message of hospitality she always sends is the same in any language: *"Manga! Manga!"* And they do.

Crostini Mascarpone with Smoked Salmon and Caper Sauce

❖

Crostini means "crust" in Italian, and in Italy it is often served on round toasts. This is an easy bread-based hors d'oeuvre to prepare and may be made with a variety of toppings such as anchovy or bean pastes. Here Mary Lee Papa combines a soft dessert cheese with salmon and a delicate sauce. It's delicious!

Crostini is served as a gesture of welcome.

Crostini
➤ 6 slices Italian bread, cut ¼-inch thick
➤ Extra virgin olive oil

Caper Sauce
➤ 1 cup milk
➤ ¼ cup (½ stick) butter
➤ 2 tablespoons all-purpose flour
➤ 1 cup chicken stock or broth
➤ Salt and white pepper
➤ ⅓ cup heavy cream
➤ 3 tablespoons capers
➤ 2 teaspoons caper liquid

Topping
➤ 8 ounces Mascarpone cheese
➤ 4 ounces smoked salmon, very thinly sliced
➤ 1 red onion, thinly sliced
➤ Fresh or dried rosemary

1. Preheat the oven to 375°. Brush the bread moderately on one side with olive oil and place it in a single layer, oiled side up, on a baking sheet. Bake for 15 to 20 minutes or until the bread is lightly toasted and crisp. Turn the bread over, brush with oil, and bake for another 15 to 20 minutes or until the bread is toasted and crisp.

2. In a saucepan warm the milk over low heat. In a separate, heavy saucepan melt the butter. Add the flour to the butter all at once and cook until mixture bubbles. Gradually pour in the broth and the heated milk, whisking constantly. Cook for 2 minutes over low heat, stirring constantly, until the sauce is creamy and thickened. Remove the pan from the heat. Add the salt and pepper to taste. Stir in the heavy cream, capers, and caper liquid. Do not cook the capers in the sauce, as it may cause the sauce to curdle.

3. Spread each baked crostini with a layer of Mascarpone. Top with ½ ounce or so of salmon, a slice of onion, and sprinkle with rosemary. Serve warm caper sauce drizzled on top or on the side.
Yield: 6 servings

Farfalle Pasta with Pancetta and Basil Cream Sauce

✣

You can use almost any style of pasta to make this dish. We chose the bow-ties as they make for an attractive, inviting plate; I would also recommend mafalda-style macaroni. Serve this after the crostini and a garden salad and before the entrées.

➤ *1½ pounds farfalle (bow tie) pasta*
➤ *¼ cup (½ stick) butter*
➤ *4 garlic cloves, minced*
➤ *10 ounces smoked pancetta, julienned*
➤ *3 scallions, minced*
➤ *1 cup white wine*
➤ *2 cups heavy cream*
➤ *Salt and freshly ground pepper to taste*
➤ *5 tablespoons finely chopped fresh basil*
➤ *2 tablespoons finely chopped fresh parsley*
➤ *Grated Parmesan cheese*

1. In a large saucepan cook the farfalle until al dente. Drain and set it aside.
2. In a large skillet heat the butter over moderate heat and sauté the garlic. Add the pancetta and cook until just crisp. Drain the fat from the pan and return the pan to heat. Add the scallions and deglaze with wine, reducing the wine to half. Add the cream, seasonings, and herbs, and blend well.
3. Toss the pasta with the cream sauce and top with Parmesan.
   Yield: 6 servings

Tasty Farfalle Pasta with Pancetta and Basil Cream Sauce

Grilled Tuna with Roasted Peppers and Anchovy-Parsley Purée

Purée

- ➤ ½ cup plain bread crumbs
- ➤ 3 tablespoons white wine
- ➤ 2 egg yolks that have been poached in water
- ➤ 1½ cups finely chopped fresh parsley
- ➤ 5 anchovy fillets, chopped
- ➤ 3 garlic cloves, chopped
- ➤ 2 teaspoons capers, chopped
- ➤ 2 cups olive oil
- ➤ Salt and white pepper

Roasted Peppers

- ➤ 6 red bell peppers
- ➤ Olive oil
- ➤ 3 garlic cloves, minced

Tuna

- ➤ 6 yellowfin tuna steaks (7 ounces each)
- ➤ Olive oil
- ➤ Freshly ground pepper

1. In a small bowl soak the bread crumbs in wine. In a food processor combine the egg yolks, parsley, anchovies, garlic, and capers until well-blended. Squeeze the wine from the bread crumbs and add it to the egg mixture. Add the olive oil and blend until creamy. Add the seasonings. Let the mixture stand up to an hour to allow the flavors to blend.
2. Split the peppers in half lengthwise and clean out the seeds. Place them skin-side-up on a broiling pan or skin-side-down on a grill. Sprinkle with olive oil and garlic. Grill or broil the peppers for about 5 minutes, and slice them into thin strips.
3. Brush the tuna steaks with olive oil and season with pepper. Grill or broil the tuna for 3 to 5 minutes on each side, so that the tuna is still a little rare on the inside. Pour sauce in the center of the plates. Place a steak on top and arrange a few pepper strips to the side.
Yield: 6 servings

Toasted Almond Chicken with Amaretto and Porcini Mushrooms

- ➤ ¼ cup all-purpose flour
- ➤ 6 large chicken breasts, skinned and boned
- ➤ Butter
- ➤ Olive oil
- ➤ 2 garlic cloves, crushed
- ➤ 12 ounces porcini mushrooms, thinly sliced
- ➤ 9 ounces pearl onions, peeled and blanched
- ➤ ¼ cup amaretto
- ➤ 1 cup chicken stock, cooked to reduce by ½
- ➤ ½ cup heavy cream
- ➤ 1 cup slivered almonds, toasted
- ➤ ⅓ cup chopped parsley

1. Preheat the oven to warm. Lightly coat the chicken with flour.
2. In a large skillet heat the butter and oil. Add the chicken and cook over low to medium heat until lightly browned and slightly cooked through. Turn the chicken over and brown the other side. Remove the chicken from the skillet and keep it warm in the oven.
3. In the same skillet add the garlic and mushrooms and sauté them briefly. Add the onions and sauté them until lightly browned. Remove the garlic, mushrooms, and onions. Deglaze the pan with amaretto and reduce it to half. Stir in 6 tablespoons of the reduced chicken stock and the cream. Add the garlic, onion, and mushrooms.
4. Remove the chicken from the oven and arrange it on plates. Drape with the sauce and sprinkle with almonds and parsley.
Yield: 6 servings

Baked Amaretti-Stuffed Pears with Toasted Almonds

Whenever we had a large Italian dinner at home, we always ended it with a round of fresh fruit and nuts followed by a sweet pastry. This recipe combines it all in a one-step dish.

➤ ¼ pound Amaretti cookies (in the Italian foods section of supermarket)

➤ 6 tablespoons brandy

➤ 6 Anjou pears with stems whole and skins peeled

➤ 1½ cups sugar

➤ 5 tablespoons vanilla extract

➤ 2 tablespoons almond extract

➤ 2 cups heavy cream

➤ 4 ounces semisweet or dark chocolate, melted

➤ 1 cup sliced, toasted almonds

1. In a food processor crush the cookies to coarse crumbs. Place the crumbs in a medium bowl and pour brandy over the crumbs.

2. Trim the bottom of the pears just so they can stand upright. With a melon baller hollow out the core from the bottom. Fill each cavity with cookie crumbs.

3. Preheat the oven to 350°. In a 13 x 9 x 2½-inch baking pan evenly spread the sugar to cover the bottom. Sprinkle the extracts over the sugar. Baste the pears very lightly with some of the heavy cream. Place the pears upright in the pan. Bake the pears for 30 minutes or until the pears are tender. Remove the pan from the oven and pour in the cream, allowing more of it to go onto the pears. Stir the cream around the pears and into the sugar. Return the pan to the oven and bake 30 minutes longer or until the pears are slightly browned.

4. Spoon the vanilla sauce onto the bottom of the serving plates. Place a pear on each. Drizzle the melted chocolate over the pears and sprinkle with almonds.

Yield: 6 servings

Biscotti may be dipped in a warm beverage.

Chocolate-Dipped Cherry and Walnut Biscotti

❖

Biscotti are delightfully crisp and traditional Italian dipping cookies.

➤ 6 eggs
➤ 1 cup vegetable oil
➤ 2 cups sugar
➤ 2 teaspoons anise extract
➤ 2 teaspoons lemon extract
➤ 2 tablespoons baking powder
➤ 6 cups all-purpose flour
➤ 1 cup fresh or canned cherries, chopped
➤ 1 cup walnuts, chopped
➤ 1 egg yolk
➤ 1 teaspoon water
➤ ½ cup sweet melted chocolate
➤ ¾ cup or more chopped almonds

1. Preheat the oven to 350°. In a large bowl beat the eggs to a froth. Add the oil while beating. Continue beating, adding the sugar and extracts. Gradually add the baking powder and flour, mixing to incorporate.
2. Fold in the cherries and walnuts with a rubber spatula. Flour a working surface. Roll out logs that are 6 x 2 inches, until the dough is used up. Cut the logs on the diagonal every 2 inches. Place the rolled cookies on waxed paper on baking sheets. Mix the yolk with the water to make an egg wash. Brush the egg wash over the rolls. Bake the biscotti for 12 minutes or until the rolls are set and lightly browned on top.
3. Cool the biscotti and dip each one halfway into the chocolate, then in almonds.
   Yield: 24 biscotti

A Bit of
Bavaria and
Central
Europe

Schumacher's New Prague Hotel
New Prague, Minnesota

INNKEEPER/CHEF JOHN SCHUMACHER

Dinner for Six

✣

Schwarzenwald Sauerkraut Balls

◆

Ruby Beet Borscht

◆

*Cameos of Veal with
Pink Peppercorn Sauce*

◆

*Zucchini with Bacon and
Red Peppers*

◆

Knedlicky (Czech Dumplings)

◆

Viennese Apple Strudel

*J*ohn Schumacher is
a great country inn chef with a wonderful
cookbook all his own. While noteworthy,
that may not seem like a startling accomplishment until you discover that John has
dyslexia. He could have let his difficulties in
reading and spelling hold him back, but he
has built on his success story as a chef with
John Schumacher's New Prague Hotel Cookbook, an impressive innkeeper-produced
cookbook. John wrote his cookbook with
the same sensitivity to good taste that he
exhibits in the kitchen. Every one of the
more than two hundred recipes has a helpful
hint. John took the time, not only to make
his methods clear and consistent, but also to
add a practical cooking idea or observation
at the end of each recipe. John loves cooking
and wants others to be confident enough to

experiment with foreign foods.

Growing up on a farm provided John with a discipline that helped him overcome the trials of dyslexia. Farm chores had him up at five and in bed by ten. "It's not much different today at the inn, which is seven days a week and unlimited hours," he says with a chuckle.

On the farm he delighted in watching his mother cook the family meals. John discovered that working in the kitchen—and not with the alphabet—could produce rewards that were within his grasp. Since learning at school was an unrelenting struggle, he took up a wooden spoon and stirred up a successful career.

He studied at Dunwoody Institute in Minneapolis, earning a baking diploma; then in the Navy he worked as a cook on a submarine. After serving in the armed forces, John attended the Culinary Institute in Hyde Park, New York, graduating with high honors.

In a short time, John worked in a number of prestigious kitchens and at just twenty-five became executive chef at the Key Bridge Marriott Hotel in Rosslyn, Virginia, across the Potomac River from the nation's capital.

John hungered to do his own cooking in a small inn setting. The Hotel Broz, built in 1898, was on sale in Minnesota; so John bought the historic property, located in New Prague, a Czech-American farming community. He and wife Kathleen changed the name to Schumacher's New Prague Hotel and renovated it into eleven attractive guest rooms. Since buying the property in 1974, the Schumachers have created a European haven, complete with Kathleen's gift shop that sells imported Central European china, crystal, jewelry, and artwork.

Since the area has ethnic roots, John decided to create a menu of Czech, Bavarian, and Central European dishes. Basically, he used traditional items to create some dishes that meet heartland expectations and others that have an accent on the gourmet nouvelle. Examples of the latter include his Mandarin Pineapple Soup with Cointreau and his Cabbage Rolls filled with vegetables, mushrooms, apples, and meat in a Hungarian raisin sauce. John's recipe for Quail Helena is a must-try. Named after his mother, who inspired his cooking, the dish is made with plums, bacon, and caraway. These recipes are available in John's book.

The recipes I have given you here are traditional favorites at the New Prague Hotel. The beet borscht is an elegant soup that will take your guests pleasantly by surprise. After making John's veal with pink peppercorn sauce, I realized I needed to use the seasoning more often and began to write a few recipes of my own using pink peppercorns. I think you will be inspired, too, at least to use the peppercorns in place of traditional black pepper. Don't miss making the Schwarzenwald Sauerkraut Balls. The name of these appetizing edibles refers to the Black Forest area of Germany. My guests could not stop eating them. I always say I am a better cook than baker, but I found the apple strudel to be easier than expected. After making it a few times, I feel just as John said I would: "like a pro."

Dining at the New Prague means sitting in Bavarian furniture surrounded by knotty pine woodwork from the Black Forest and folk-art painting. Bedrooms are dainty but comfortable, with handmade lace curtains, plump pillows, and eiderdown comforters.

When John is not at the inn, he may be found at a meeting of the Chaine de Rotisseurs, upholding this international body's pursuit of culinary excellence. John proudly wears his badge of membership whenever he speaks to groups. He loves to give back to society by working with dyslexic boys who see him as a role model. "They look at me and, instead of giving up, feel there's a way to be an important person," notes John, who is most assuredly a role model for any one of us to follow.

Schwarzenwald Sauerkraut Balls

❖

- ➤ 2 tablespoons butter
- ➤ ½ cup minced onions
- ➤ ¼ cup finely shredded carrots
- ➤ ½ cup lean ground beef
- ➤ 1 cup ham, finely diced
- ➤ 4 cups sauerkraut, well-drained, chopped
- ➤ ⅔ cup all-purpose flour
- ➤ ¼ cup heavy cream
- ➤ ¼ cup beef stock or broth
- ➤ ¼ teaspoon each salt and white pepper
- ➤ ½ teaspoon allspice
- ➤ 1 teaspoon caraway seeds (optional)
- ➤ ¼ teaspoon mustard, any style
- ➤ 1 cup all-purpose flour
- ➤ 4 eggs, beaten
- ➤ 2 cups any-style crackers or gingersnap crumbs
- ➤ Oil for frying

1. In a large skillet melt the butter and sauté the onions and carrots until tender. Add the beef and cook until brown. Add the ham and sauerkraut. Cook over low heat for 5 minutes. Stir in the flour and cook until thick. Add the cream, stock, spices, and mustard, and cook over low heat for 5 minutes. Remove the mixture from the pan and place it on a cookie sheet to cool.
2. When cool and firm, form the mixture into 1-inch balls. Roll each ball in the flour, dip it into the eggs, then roll it in the crumbs. Deep-fry the balls in hot oil until golden brown.
Yield: 12 to 16 balls

Ruby Beet Borscht

❖

Borscht is a favorite soup in Russia and Central Europe. You can prepare this cold soup a week ahead.

- ➤ 2¼ pounds raw beets, peeled and ends trimmed
- ➤ 1¼ cups diced onion
- ➤ 1 quart beef stock or broth
- ➤ 2 tablespoons fresh lemon juice
- ➤ 1 teaspoon each salt and black pepper
- ➤ ¼ cup sherry
- ➤ 1 cup sour cream
- ➤ Fresh chives and lemon slices for garnish

1. In a blender purée the beets and onion with 1 cup of the beef stock. Pour the mixture into a soup pot and add the remaining stock, lemon juice, salt, and pepper. Cover the pot and simmer for 45 minutes. Strain the soup. Add the sherry and chill.
2. Pour the soup into chilled bowls. Add a dollop of sour cream and a sprinkling of chives. Place a lemon slice on the rim of each bowl.
Yield: 8 servings

Fresh beets for borscht

Cameos of Veal with Pink Peppercorn Sauce

❖

I've included John Schumacher's recipe for brown sauce here, but you may substitute with packaged brown sauce or gravy.

Brown Sauce

- ➤ 6 tablespoons (¾ stick) butter
- ➤ 1 cup diced onions
- ➤ ½ cup diced celery
- ➤ ½ cup diced carrots
- ➤ ¾ cup all-purpose flour
- ➤ 6 cups double strength beef stock (12 cups reduced by ½)
- ➤ ¼ cup tomato purée
- ➤ 1 bay leaf
- ➤ 1 teaspoon salt
- ➤ ¼ teaspoon black pepper

Veal Preparation

- ➤ 2 pounds veal loin, sliced into 24 pieces, pounded to ⅛-inch thickness
- ➤ 2 cups all-purpose flour seasoned with 2 teaspoons salt and ½ teaspoon black pepper
- ➤ ½ cup clarified butter
- ➤ ⅔ cup minced shallots
- ➤ 2 tablespoons fresh lemon juice
- ➤ 3 cups brown sauce (see step 1)
- ➤ 2 cups dry white wine
- ➤ 4 teaspoons pink peppercorns
- ➤ 1 teaspoon salt
- ➤ ½ teaspoon black pepper
- ➤ 4 teaspoons freshly chopped parsley flakes

Ruby Beet Borscht

1. In a heavy saucepan heat the butter to a fast bubble and sauté the onions and vegetables until the onions are translucent. Add the flour and cook for 2 minutes over low heat, stirring often with a wooden spoon. In another saucepan heat the beef stock and then add it to the sautéed vegetables. Add the tomato purée, bay leaf, salt, and pepper. Cook for 30 minutes. Pour the brown sauce through a fine strainer. Set it aside.

2. Dredge the veal in the seasoned flour. In a large skillet heat the clarified butter to a fast bubble. Add the veal slices and shallots, and sauté for 1 minute. Turn the veal slices over and sauté for 30 seconds, taking care not to brown the shallots. Add the lemon juice, 3 cups of brown sauce, wine, peppercorns, salt, and pepper. Reduce the heat and simmer over low heat for 15 minutes, gently stirring occasionally to keep it from sticking. Add the parsley. Adjust the sauce consistency with white wine if necessary. Bring the sauce to a boil and serve.

Yield: 6 to 8 servings

Zucchini with Bacon and Red Peppers

❖

- ➤ ½ cup diced bacon, uncooked
- ➤ 2 cloves garlic, crushed
- ➤ 1½ cups diced onion
- ➤ 1 cup diced celery
- ➤ 1 cup chicken stock or broth
- ➤ 1 teaspoon coarsely ground pepper
- ➤ 1 teaspoon Worcestershire sauce
- ➤ 1 tablespoon cider vinegar
- ➤ 1 tablespoon chopped fresh basil
- ➤ 6 cups zucchini (between 1½ and 2 pounds) cut into ½-inch-thick slices
- ➤ 2 medium red bell peppers, seeded and cut into 1½-inch strips

1. In a medium saucepan cook the bacon until it browns. Add the garlic, onion, and celery, and cook until just tender.
2. Stir in the chicken stock, pepper, Worcestershire, vinegar, and basil. Add the zucchini and peppers. Cover the pan and simmer over low heat for 15 minutes, or until tender.
3. Arrange the zucchini mixture on a serving platter. Drizzle the vinegar mixture over all.
Yield: 6 servings

Knedliky (Czech Dumplings)

❖

- ➤ 5 medium to large potatoes, peeled, boiled, mashed, and cooled
- ➤ 4 cups bread flour or all-purpose flour
- ➤ 1 tablespoon farina
- ➤ 1 teaspoon salt
- ➤ 1 egg, beaten
- ➤ ¼ cup (½ stick) butter, melted

Veal with Pink Peppercorn Sauce

1. In a large bowl mix all of the ingredients except the butter by hand. Let the dough stand for 5 minutes. Shape it into 4-inch long (3-ounce) cylinder dumplings.
2. In a large saucepan bring salted water to a boil. Add the dumplings and stir them gently to keep them from hugging the bottom of the pan. Return the water to a boil, cooking for 15 minutes or until the dumplings are fluffy and white when slicing one through the middle. Remove the dumplings from the water carefully with a slotted spoon. Make a slit in the center of each and brush with melted butter.
Yield: 10 dumplings

Viennese Apple Strudel

❖

Dough

➤ 2 tablespoons butter, melted
➤ 2 tablespoons warm water
➤ 1 egg, beaten
➤ 1½ teaspoons sugar
➤ ⅛ teaspoon salt
➤ ½ teaspoon vanilla extract
➤ 1½ cups all-purpose flour

Filling

➤ 1 cup crushed corn flakes, moistened with 2 tablespoons butter
➤ ¾ cup fresh bread crumbs
➤ 6 cups Granny Smith apples, cored, peeled, and diced
➤ ¾ cup raisins
➤ ¾ cup coarsely chopped walnuts
➤ 1 cup firmly packed dark brown sugar
➤ ½ teaspoon cinnamon
➤ ½ cup flaked coconut

Assembly

➤ Egg wash or water
➤ 2 tablespoons butter, melted, for brushing

Frosting

➤ ⅓ cup confectioners' sugar
➤ ⅓ cup whipping cream

1. In a large bowl mix together all the dough ingredients except the flour. Add the flour to make a soft but not sticky dough. Turn the dough onto a floured surface and knead for about 150 strokes. Place the dough in a greased bowl. Cover the bowl with a kitchen towel and let the dough rise in a warm place for 1 hour. Roll the dough out on a floured cloth and stretch it very thin, making an 18 x 24-inch rectangle.

2. Preheat the oven to 350°. To make the strudel layer the filling ingredients over the dough in the order listed, making sure the ingredients are evenly distributed. Dampen the edge of the crust with egg wash or water. Roll the strudel up jelly roll-style, beginning at the shorter end. Place the strudel on a greased baking sheet, seam side down, and brush it with melted butter. Bake the strudel for 50 minutes or until golden brown.

3. In a small bowl whip the sugar and cream to a glaze consistency. Frost the hot strudel immediately. Cool well and slice.

Yield: 6 servings

Treasures from a British Port-of-Call

Under Mountain Inn
Salisbury, Connecticut

INNKEEPER/CHEF PETER HIGGINSON

Dinner for Eight

Steak and Kidney Pie

◆

Cream of Leek Soup

◆

Orange Marmalade Bread

◆

*Lamb Curry Stew with Apples
and Raisins*

◆

Turnip Soufflé

◆

*Bread Pudding with
Brandied-Custard Sauce*

I say, ol' chap, how fortunate we are to have a country inn at the foot of the American Berkshire mountains, where we can savor the tastes of traditional English fare and enjoy the atmosphere of a subdued English pub. How doubly lucky to have a British chef willing to share his secrets so we can re-create an English evening at home.

Peter Higginson is the man with the white apron and rolled-up sleeves who often doubles as Under Mountain Inn's host extraordinaire. When he's not in the kitchen rolling out a crust for shepherd's pie, he regales guests with seafaring stories from behind his bar.

The menu is carved in chalk, and there is purposely no traditional dartboard to interfere with the ritual of intimate dining here. The Higginsons keep it country inn classic all the way: no boisterous goings on in this eatery—just tasty foods, good times, and quiet conversations. On any given night, guests may find Scottish salmon, bangers and mash (sausage and potatoes), English trifle, or roasted goose.

Salisbury here in Connecticut—like its namesake cathedral town in Southern England—isn't far from places bearing other English names: Cornwall, Kent, and Sheffield. As a result, the inn draws many English guests who have settled on this side of the Atlantic. In fact, one of the inn's most devoted diners would not buy a house unless it was within walking distance of an English pub, and she moved practically next door to Under Mountain. To please such avid regulars of the inn, Peter designated Sundays in summertime as fish-and-chips days.

The English-born chef's first experience in food service came at fifteen, when he was a waiter at the Adelphi Hotel in Liverpool. He recalls that the first guests he served were Katharine Hepburn and her five bodyguards. Later he joined the merchant marines as a steward aboard luxury cruise ships, always nosing his way into the kitchen and eating in every new port, "Sherlocking" for new cooking ideas.

Peter's attic is lined with steamer trunks full of memories, including a cache of autographs. His most cherished is that of James Beard, obtained after a cooking lecture. Peter handed the revered chef his kitchen-stained copy of the *James Beard Cookbook,* causing the author to react with mock surprise, "You actually use the book!" Before it was signed, yes, but not much anymore. Peter framed the cover for an upstairs hall and stored the book away, relying on Beard's later books, unsigned but nonetheless in the kitchen and well-soiled, too.

A native of Manchester, Peter has been around the world three times (you can spot his destinations on a flagged map in the pub), and also has been to all fifty American

states. Nowadays, he does less traveling, finding the world, instead, at his own doorstep. Visitors seek a vicarious trip to England and go out of their way for a meal and a good night's sleep in the homey Under Mountain.

Overnight rooms are all very different, and the parlor is long and comfortable—filled to the brim with interesting books to thumb through and a piano to play. The breakfast room overlooks the outdoors.

Marged is Peter's wife and a great match for the head matey. While the chef is shy with a droll sense of humor, Marged is outgoing and peppy, so much so that you sometimes wonder, "Who's really the Brit here?" She sends playful barbs her husband's way and loves to remind people that while Peter traveled the world, he ended up falling for her, "just a little, sixteen-year-old teenager." A native of New Jersey, Marged met Peter on a blind date one night when the *Ocean Monarch* docked in New York. "We only had a few hours together, but then he wrote me romantic letters from around the world and sent me classical records," she recalls. "I hated popular music, and no other boy shared my love of the classics until Peter came along."

One night while in port, Peter took Marged to the top of the Statue of Liberty, the first landmark he saw whenever he pulled into American waters. He proposed to her there, "in front of a pack of Cub Scouts, who just weren't leaving," Marged remembers with a grin. They married in 1959. Peter left the high seas a year later and went to work as a cosmetician for Charles of the Ritz. He earned his U.S. citizenship papers in 1968, and they now hang proudly in the pub.

The couple had two girls while Marged attended college full time and then worked as a respiratory therapist. After twenty-five years at the cosmetic company, Peter retired to start Peter of Rumson Traveling Gourmet Catering Service in Rumson, New Jersey. He also worked for the Rumson Hotel as a

Steak and Kidney Pie

Steak and Kidney Pie

Under Mountain offers this as an entrée. It is suggested here as an appetizer. Soak the kidneys in a mixture of 2 cups water and 3 tablespoons red wine vinegar for 2 hours or overnight.

- ➤ ¼ cup bacon fat
- ➤ 1 large onion, finely chopped
- ➤ 2 cups beef stock or broth
- ➤ 12 ounces mushrooms, sliced
- ➤ ½ teaspoon each dried marjoram, thyme, and savory
- ➤ 2 tablespoons Worcestershire sauce
- ➤ 10 ounces puréed Italian tomatoes
- ➤ 1 cup sherry
- ➤ 1 pound pre-soaked beef kidneys, drained, fat trimmed, and cut into 1-inch pieces
- ➤ 1 pound chuck steak, cut into 1-inch pieces
- ➤ Salt and pepper
- ➤ ½ teaspoon dried savory
- ➤ 1 17¼-ounce package puff pastry sheets
- ➤ 1 egg, beaten

1. In a medium saucepan heat the bacon fat and sauté the onions until soft.
2. Add the stock, mushrooms, herbs, and Worcestershire. Stir well. Add the tomato purée and sherry, and simmer for 30 minutes. Add the kidneys and set the mixture aside.
3. In a large saucepan brown the steak in the remaining bacon fat. Sprinkle with salt and pepper to taste. Add the savory, beef, and kidney mixture and simmer for 1 hour, or until the beef is tender and cooked through.
4. Preheat the oven to 400°. Line 4 8-ounce ramekins with the mixture. Cover each with a pastry sheet, and cut steam holes. Brush the pastry with egg. Bake the pies for 30 minutes or until very lightly browned. Offer each guest a sampling.

Yield: 8 appetizer-size servings

chef, but the abnormal hours were getting to them both. "That's when I decided that if we were going to be married to Peter's job, I wanted it to be from our home," says Marged.

So began the hunt for a country inn. Marged had her heart set on Vermont and resisted the suggestion of well-known inn consultant Bill Oates to look at a place in Connecticut. "I was pouting like a brat as they dragged me to Salisbury," she recalls. But one walk through the house, and Marged came out beaming like a Cheshire cat. They all knew they had found their inn, their home, and Peter's most enduring port-of-call.

Orange Marmalade Bread

❖

- ➤ 2 cups all-purpose flour
- ➤ 2 teaspoons baking powder
- ➤ ⅓ cup sugar
- ➤ 2 eggs, beaten
- ➤ ⅔ cup milk
- ➤ ⅓ cup shortening, melted
- ➤ ⅔ cup pecans, chopped
- ➤ ½ cup orange marmalade (or other flavor if desired)

1. Preheat the oven to 350°. In a large bowl mix together the flour, baking powder, and sugar. Gradually stir in the eggs, milk, and shortening. Stir in the pecans and marmalade.
2. Pour the batter into a greased 9 x 5-inch loaf pan. Bake the bread for 1 hour or until a tester comes out clean.
   Yield: 1 loaf

Cream of Leek Soup

❖

The soup is a soothing prelude to the spicy lamb stew.

- ➤ ½ cup (1 stick) butter
- ➤ 6 leeks, diced, including green tops
- ➤ 2 medium onions, diced
- ➤ 7 cups chicken stock or broth
- ➤ 1 tablespoon Worcestershire sauce
- ➤ Salt and pepper to taste
- ➤ 2 cups heavy cream
- ➤ Nutmeg

1. Heat the butter in a medium saucepan and sauté the leeks and onions until tender but not browned.
2. Add the stock, Worcestershire, salt, pepper, and cream. Heat the soup through. Thicken if desired with a cornstarch-and-water mixture. Pour the soup through a strainer. Garnish each bowl with a sprinkling of nutmeg.
   Yield: 8 servings

Lamb Curry Stew with Apples and Raisins

❖

- ➤ ¾ cup (1½ sticks) butter
- ➤ 4 large onions, finely chopped
- ➤ 4 Granny Smith unpeeled apples, cored and finely chopped
- ➤ 4 teaspoons curry powder
- ➤ 2 teaspoons ginger
- ➤ 2 teaspoons chili powder
- ➤ 2 teaspoons ground black pepper
- ➤ ¼ teaspoon cloves
- ➤ 6 tablespoons tomato paste
- ➤ 5 pounds roasted lamb, cut into 1-inch cubes
- ➤ 6 cups chicken broth, or more, to cover meat
- ➤ 2 cups raisins

1. In a skillet melt the butter and gently sauté the onions and apples. Stir in the curry, ginger, chili, pepper, cloves, and tomato paste.
2. Add the cooked lamb, broth, and raisins, and stir well. Simmer uncovered for 1 hour, skimming off any fat that floats to the top during the first half-hour. If necessary, thicken with 3 tablespoons of cornstarch mixed into ½ cup of water 10 minutes before serving time.
   Yield: 8 servings

Turnip Soufflé

➤ 3 pounds turnips, peeled and cubed
➤ 3 pounds white potatoes, peeled and cubed
➤ 6 tablespoons (¾ stick) butter
➤ 1 small onion, finely chopped
➤ ¼ cup diced green bell pepper
➤ 2 eggs
➤ 1 cup mayonnaise
➤ 1 cup grated Parmesan cheese
➤ Freshly ground pepper to taste
➤ ¼ cup or more dry bread crumbs
➤ Paprika
➤ 2 tablespoons butter, melted

1. Cook the turnips and potatoes in separate saucepans until tender. In a large bowl mash them together with 4 tablespoons of the butter. Let the mixture cool.
2. In a small skillet heat the remaining butter and sauté the onion and green pepper. Set aside.
3. Preheat the oven to 350°. In a small bowl whip the eggs with the mayonnaise. Stir in the cheese and pepper.
4. When the turnip-potato mixture has cooled, mix in the sautéed onion, green pepper, and the whipped egg mixture.
5. Pour the mixture into a greased 9-inch square pan. Bake the soufflé 30 minutes or until golden brown on the edges.
   Yield: 8 servings

Bread Pudding with Brandied Custard Sauce

Pudding

➤ 8 to 10 slices quality white bread, cubed
➤ ¼ cup (½ stick) butter, melted
➤ 2 eggs
➤ 2 cups milk
➤ ¾ cup packed brown sugar
➤ 2 tablespoons vanilla extract
➤ 1 teaspoon cinnamon
➤ 1 teaspoon nutmeg
➤ 1 cup chopped pecans
➤ 1 cup chopped raisins

Custard Sauce

➤ 2¼ cups milk
➤ 3 tablespoons cornstarch
➤ 4 drops yellow food coloring (optional)
➤ 2 tablespoons vanilla extract
➤ 5 tablespoons sugar
➤ 1 tablespoon brandy (optional)

1. In a large bowl toss the bread with the melted butter.
2. Preheat the oven to 325°. In a separate bowl beat the eggs with the milk. Add the sugar, vanilla, cinnamon, and nutmeg. Mix well and add the nuts and raisins. Pour the mixture into the bread mixture. Turn the mixture into a 13 x 9 x 2½-inch baking pan. Bake the pudding for 1 hour or until it is golden.
3. While the pudding is baking, prepare the custard sauce. In a small bowl mix ¼ cup of the milk with the cornstarch. Add the food coloring and stir until smooth.
4. In a saucepan heat the remaining milk with the vanilla and sugar until simmering. Add the cornstarch-milk mixture gradually, stirring constantly until thickened. Stir in the brandy. Serve the sauce over the pudding.
   Yield: 8 servings

The French Connection: A Taste of Provence

L'Auberge Provençale
White Post, Virginia

INNKEEPER/CHEF ALAIN BOREL

Dinner for Eight

L'Auberge's Tapenade

◆

Garlic Soup with Lentils

◆

Smoked Rabbit with Chanterelle Mushroom Sauce over Fettucine

◆

Venison with Bourbon and Chutney Sauce

◆

Bohémienne Gypsy Eggplant Provençale

◆

Pumpkin Caramel Flan

When Alain Borel was growing up in Avignon, he thought that everyone cooked. Everyone in the Borel family did cook, and that was the world as Alain knew it. He is the fourth generation of Borel chefs, carrying on a tradition from his great-grandmother, who was the chef at the Hotel du Louvre in Avignon at the height of the Victorian era. So, you see, cooking is second nature to Alain, who opened L'Auberge in 1981.

"The area reminded me of the south of France," recalls Alain, who came to America when he was sixteen. Before opening his own inn, he worked in Florida, Vermont, and Washington. In 1970 he married Celeste, and they opened the Chez Emile restaurant in Key West.

Celeste and Alain were vacationing in the

Virginia area when they spotted eight acres and a stone house for sale—the perfect spot to create a piece of southern France in America. That is just what they did. So much so, that the peacefulness and simple European country style of L'Auberge has been sought out by celebrities, including Robert Duvall and Dan Aykroyd.

Driving out to White Post from the Washington, D.C., area, is certainly a reminder of the European countryside with its rolling hills and farmlands. As you turn into L'Auberge, you might as well be in France. They speak the language here, and menu items are in French as well as English. Inside the château are unusual handicrafts, including a menagerie of hand-carved animals of wood—some done by Alain's father, a well-known wood carver, and some made of cactus flowers. Alain and Celeste bring the latter in from France and have been approached by Bloomingdale's to import thousands of them. "But the crafters won't turn them out factory-style and aren't passing on the cactus-flower art to others," says Celeste. The only place you can buy them here seems to be at the inn, so I felt fortunate to go home with a proud chanticleer for my kitchen.

Provençale fabrics decorate the tables in two of the three small dining rooms. An original Picasso lines one wall, and a dramatic Bernard Buffet crowns another. But Alain's artistry is on the table—classic French with nouvelle cuisine. "My sauces have seasonings distinctive to my homeland," he says. You will see what he means in the menu here. He often determines the bill-of-fare based on how the herbs in his garden are coming along. He shops at local farms for many of his main dishes, including pheasant, rabbit, venison, partridge, quail, and lamb—much the same way chefs and private cooks shop for meats in Provence. Recipes for rabbit and venison are provided in this menu. Choose either for an entrée, or offer a little of both.

Alain's cooking is rich in flavors but not

One of three dining rooms at the inn

in weight. A meal at L'Auberge is satisfyingly abundant but not uncomfortably filling. Dining at L'Auberge is truly one of the most peaceful evenings you may ever spend. If you've read the best-selling book *A Year in Provence,* I assure you that the next best thing to being there is a few days at L'Auberge. (If you haven't read the book, you may get the chance at the inn. There is a copy of the splendid tale in each guest room.) Alain and Celeste have a knack for blending elegant with country, while providing some of the best food anywhere. They greet you warmly, and, although you are treated with respect, they also open their inn as if you are a visitor to their home.

Guest rooms are a mixture of Colonial and country French styles, with sun-dried tiles from Mexico in bathrooms and hand-painted, story-telling tiles from Spain around fireplaces.

Breakfast is also a gourmet affair, which you will need for energy as there is lots to see and do in this area of the Shenandoah— from wineries to historic sites and gorgeous drives through the mountains.

Alain tells us amateur cooks not to be afraid to try any new recipe. "Even if it's a brioche. If you want it, make it. Follow the steps and take your time, and call a chef if you need help." We can't help but rejoice that we have Alain Borel here in America, not Avignon.

Smoked rabbit with chanterelles

It was a meal that we shall never forget; more accurately, it was several meals that we shall never forget, because it went beyond the gastronomic frontiers of anything we had ever experienced, both in quantity and length.

Peter Mayle
A Year in Provence

L'Auberge's Tapenade
✥

A tapenade, sometimes called the black butter of Provence, is a condiment from Provence, usually made with capers as the word is derived from the Provençale *tapeno,* meaning "caper." Serve with toasted bread or crudités.

➤ *⅔ pound pitted Calamata or Niçoise olives*
➤ *6 anchovy fillets, washed and patted dry*
➤ *¼ cup small capers*
➤ *6 tablespoons quality olive oil*
➤ *Juice of 1 lemon*
➤ *Freshly ground pepper*
➤ *½ teaspoon hot mustard*
➤ *1 teaspoon fresh cilantro, chopped*

In food processor whirl together the olives, anchovies, and capers until combined. Add the oil, lemon juice, pepper from 6 full turns of the mill, mustard, and cilantro. Mix well.
Yield: 1 cup

Garlic Soup with Lentils
✥

➤ *2 tablespoons olive oil*
➤ *1 cup chopped garlic*
➤ *¼ cup chopped shallots*
➤ *2 medium carrots, finely chopped*
➤ *½ cup all-purpose flour*
➤ *2 cups Côte du Rhône red wine*
➤ *1 gallon stock (lamb for best flavor)*
➤ *2 bay leaves*
➤ *1 sprig each tarragon, thyme, and rosemary, chopped*
➤ *1½ cups cleaned and picked-over lentils*
➤ *Salt and pepper*

1. In a large stock pot heat the olive oil over medium heat and sauté the garlic, shallots, and carrots until tender but not brown. Add the flour and mix well. Add the red wine and stir to incorporate. Add the lamb stock, bay leaves, herbs, and lentils.
2. Bring the mixture to a boil. Simmer until reduced by ¼ and the lentils are tender. Season with salt and pepper to taste. Serve hot.
Yield: 16 servings

Smoked Rabbit with Chanterelle Mushroom Sauce over Fettucine

❖

Rabbit is a delicious alternative to chicken, lower in cholesterol and higher in protein. A local farmer raises the rabbits for L'Auberge, just as they do in Provence, where rabbit is a staple food. If you do not have a smoker, you can order smoked rabbit from specialty and gourmet food stores.

Rabbit Marinade
➤ *2 (3-pound) rabbits, cleaned*
➤ *1½ cups olive oil*
➤ *½ cup white wine vinegar*
➤ *2 sprigs tarragon, chopped*
➤ *2 sprigs thyme, chopped*
➤ *6 cloves garlic, minced*
➤ *1 large onion, chopped*
➤ *1 teaspoon each salt and freshly ground pepper*

Chanterelle Mushroom Sauce
➤ *1½ cups chanterelle, shiitake, or morel mushrooms*
➤ *3 tablespoons butter*
➤ *1½ cups heavy cream*
➤ *Salt and freshly ground pepper to taste*
➤ *2 pounds fettucine pasta, cooked and drained*

Venison, pumpkin flan and folk art from the south of France

1. In a large baking pan marinate the rabbits in the oil, vinegar, and spices. Refrigerate for 24 hours, turning the rabbits a couple of times while they marinate.
2. Remove the rabbits from the marinade and place them in a hot smoker. Smoke for 45 minutes, turning every 15 minutes. Allow the rabbits to cool after smoking. Debone the rabbits and cut the meat into bite-size pieces.
3. In a large skillet sauté the mushrooms in butter. Add the cream and rabbit. Bring the cream to a boil, and cook it until it thickens and coats a spoon. Sprinkle with salt and pepper.
4. Add the fettucine to the cream mixture and heat it through.
Yield: 8 to 10 servings

Venison with Bourbon and Chutney Sauce

❖

When venison is not in season or is hard to get, you may substitute with beef. The chutney will yield two quarts, so store the extra in a covered container for future recipes.

- ➤ 3 pounds venison loin
- ➤ Olive oil
- ➤ Freshly ground black pepper
  Chutney
- ➤ 1 pound plums or mangoes, diced into ½-inch pieces
- ➤ 1 pound apples, diced
- ➤ 1 pound tomatoes, diced
- ➤ 4 medium onions, diced
- ➤ 2 large cloves garlic, minced
- ➤ 1 pound golden raisins
- ➤ 2½ cups wine vinegar
- ➤ ¼ teaspoon mace
- ➤ ¼ teaspoon apple pie spice
- ➤ 2 tablespoons ginger
- ➤ 2⅔ cups packed light brown sugar
  Bourbon Chutney Sauce
- ➤ ½ cup bourbon
- ➤ 2 cups chutney
- ➤ 2 cups veal demi-glacé or brown sauce (see page 224 for brown sauce recipe, or use a packaged brand)
- ➤ White pepper

1. Preheat the oven to 350°. Rub all sides of the venison in oil. Roll in black pepper. In a large skillet brown the venison. Place the skillet in the oven for 15 to 20 minutes or until the loin is medium rare. Remove it from the oven and set it aside to rest on a warm platter. Prepare the chutney.
2. In a large saucepan mix together all of the chutney ingredients except the sugar. Simmer for 30 minutes. Add the sugar and simmer until thick.
3. Wipe the skillet with a paper towel. Pour in ½ cup of the bourbon, the chutney, and the demi-glacé*, and bring the mixture to a boil. Season with pepper to taste. Set the sauce aside.
4. Slice the venison into ½-inch thick pieces. Serve the venison with a swathing of the bourbon sauce.
   *Demi-glacé is a rich, brown sauce traditionally made from espagnole sauce, Madeira, and brown stock. It's available in gourmet stores.
   Yield: 8 servings

Bohémienne Gypsy Eggplant Provençale

❖

Although this dish originated in Nice, it is indigenous to Avignon and was a recipe named for a count.

- ➤ 6 medium eggplants, peeled and coarsely chopped
- ➤ Salt and pepper
- ➤ 1 cup olive oil
- ➤ 8 ripe tomatoes, peeled, cut, and seeds removed
- ➤ 7 cloves garlic, finely chopped
- ➤ 1 tablespoon chopped fennel
- ➤ 1 tablespoon chopped thyme
- ➤ Salt and pepper
- ➤ ¾ cup seasoned bread crumbs
- ➤ 4 anchovy fillets, unsalted
- ➤ 1 tablespoon all-purpose flour
- ➤ ¾ cup milk

1. Sprinkle the eggplant with salt and pepper. In a large skillet heat ½ cup of the olive oil and sauté the eggplants, tomatoes, garlic, fennel, and thyme. Season with salt and pepper to taste. Stir in the bread crumbs. While cooking, mash the vegetables with a fork when they become tender. Continue to cook slowly.

2. Preheat the oven to 350°. In a small skillet heat the remaining olive oil with the anchovies. When hot, add the flour and mix well. Add the milk, stirring until thickened. Stir the anchovy mixture into the eggplant mixture and transfer the mixture to a casserole dish. Bake for 20 to 30 minutes or until golden. Serve hot.
Yield: 8 to 10 servings

Pumpkin Caramel Flan

❖

Flan
➤ *2 cups heavy cream*
➤ *1 cup sugar*
➤ *1 cup pumpkin purée*
➤ *1 teaspoon vanilla extract*
➤ *¼ teaspoon nutmeg*
➤ *½ teaspoon cinnamon*
➤ *⅛ teaspoon cloves*
➤ *7 large eggs*
Caramel Syrup
➤ *½ cup sugar*
➤ *¼ cup water*
➤ *¼ cup cream of tartar*
➤ *½ teaspoon white vinegar*

1. In a medium saucepan combine the cream, ½ cup of the sugar, pumpkin, vanilla, and spices. Bring the mixture to a boil and set it aside to cool.
2. Whip the eggs with the remaining sugar until frothy. When the cream mixture has cooled, fold it into the eggs. Pour the custard mixture through a strainer.
3. Coat 8 4½-ounce aluminum cups or ramekins with non-stick spray.
4. Preheat the oven to 350°. In a small saucepan combine the syrup ingredients and boil until golden brown and syrupy. Pour the syrup into prepared cups, about ¼ inch per cup. When the syrup begins to set, top it with the custard mixture.
5. Prepare a bain marie by placing the cups in a baking pan and filling the pan about ⅓ of the way up with hot water. Bake the flan for 30 minutes or until the custard is firm when touched. Cool overnight. Serve by inverting onto a dessert plate.
Yield: 8 servings

Asia on the Menu

Madrona Manor
Healdsburg, California

INNKEEPER/CHEF TODD MUIR

Dinner for Eight

Goat Cheese Wonton Soup

◆

Salmon Stuffed with Eggplant and Scallops
in an Asian Sauce

◆

Thai Pheasant with Red Curry
Coconut Milk

◆

Soft-Shelled Crabs and Chinese
Sausages with Sun-dried
Tomato Beurre Blanc

◆

Trio of Crème Brûlée:
Ginger, Orange, and Coconut

I was toasty by the open hearth at Randall's Ordinary in Connecticut, enjoying Cindy Clark's Colonial victuals, when a dinner guest beseeched me to consider the exotic creations of another great chef clear across the country.

"You've got to go to Madrona Manor in California," he urged me. "The inn would be great for your new book. They have a fabulous dining room, too."

Well, few who study small-inn travel haven't heard of Madrona Manor, and I was no different. In fact, I was already one step ahead of the Randall's visitor. "You're right on the mark, and they're already in the book," I assured him.

Todd Muir, I told this avid inn-goer, is a worthy chef, indeed. His fascination with food stretches far beyond the usual, and yet his dishes are done with utmost respect for the palate. Todd introduces diners to a variety of cooking styles, and the West Coast inn has become known for its varied cuisine. The manor has been trumpeted as a country inn with a dining room equal to that of any famous city restaurant.

Todd invites many visiting European chefs to the inn, thus bringing guests not only his own international interpretations but the specialties of those who cook in a foreign land every day as well. Noted chefs from Milan and Paris, for instance, have presented menus at Todd's invitation. Todd knows how to host these chefs from other lands, for he has been asked abroad himself; he once traveled to Bangkok, where he was asked to prepare California cuisine at a food festival. There he prepared—among other coastal creations—apple-leek soup, corn cakes with prawn salsa, duck taquito with mole´ sauce, and veal loin with a potpourri of peppers and corn mustard.

I asked Todd to offer us a taste of the Orient for this book. California is understandably big on Asian cuisine, which—according to the National Restaurant Association—remains the third most common choice among ethnic entrées on American menus, behind Italian and Mexican.

Together, Todd and I selected a number of his dishes that we feel are easy enough for the home cook and yet yield the most interesting flavors and combinations. I think you will enjoy trying, for instance, the wontons. The result is quite rewarding. And the unusual crème brûlées are simply fun to create. The Thai chicken is divine, and don't shy away from the soft-shell crabs or Chinese sausage dish. When I prepared this menu at my house, I invited two couples to take part. The fun of it all was cooking with good friends. You might try that, too. There may not be a Todd Muir among you, but following his methods will yield pleasingly similar results. And cooking with friends takes any burden out of entertaining virtuoso-style.

Todd, a graduate of the California Culinary Academy, is a highly praised chef

whose experience runs the gamut from assistant chef de cuisine at the famous Chez Panisse in Berkeley, to the Cafe Reggio in San Francisco. He has been the executive chef at Madrona Manor, which is owned by his parents, since 1983.

The mansion itself is a majestic, circa 1881, three-story, mansard Victorian with nine bedrooms plus cottages. One cottage is a splendidly renovated carriage house with a hipped roof and gabled dormers; another is the mansion's former kitchen; and the third is a cottage, romantically tucked away in a plush garden.

Madrona Manor is a gentrified Victorian inn, as different as it is distant from the more rustic and quite Colonial Randall's. Both are tops at what they do. What makes my exchange with the Randall's guest so interesting is that it raises a point I have made many times. The country inn cooking story is not just about one type of inn or cuisine. Variety and surprise are the rewards of country inn-going. You can enjoy these rewards at both Randall's Ordinary and Madrona Manor, even though chefs Cindy Clark and Todd Muir are as different as east is from west and night is from day.

Goat Cheese Wonton Soup
❖

It is said that the word *wonton* means "swallowing the pillow."

Wontons
➤ 3 ounces goat cheese, crumbled
➤ 1 tablespoon chopped chives
➤   Salt and pepper
➤ 1 egg, separated
➤ ¼ cup water
➤ 12 wonton wrappers
Broth
➤ 2 tablespoons poached egg white, diced
➤ 2 tablespoons thinly sliced shiitake mushrooms
➤ 1 tablespoon thinly sliced green onion
➤ 8 paper-thin slices garlic
➤ 8 paper-thin slices fresh ginger
➤ 8 fine strands orange zest
Garnish
➤ 8 cilantro leaves
➤   Hot chili pepper oil

Making wontons for the soup

1. In a small bowl mix the goat cheese with the chives. Season with salt and pepper to taste.
2. Make an egg wash by mixing the beaten egg yolk with the water. Place 1½ teaspoons of the goat cheese mixture in the center of each wonton skin. Brush the edges with egg wash. Fold corner to corner to form a triangle. Press the edges together to seal. Fold the 2 opposite corners around a finger. Moisten with the egg wash and press together to seal. (See the photo at left on page 240.)
3. In a saucepan poach the wontons in simmering salted water for 3 minutes. In a separate saucepan heat the broth ingredients. Divide the wontons between 8 small soup bowls and add the broth. Garnish with cilantro and a few drops of hot chili oil.
Yield: 8 sampler servings

Salmon Stuffed with Eggplant and Scallops in an Asian Sauce

✥

- ➤ 1 pound salmon fillet
- ➤ ¼ pound eggplant, finely diced (about 1 cup)
- ➤ 2 tablespoons peanut oil
- ➤ 4 ounces scallops, chopped and sautéed
- ➤ 1 tablespoon thinly sliced green onions
- ➤ 1 teaspoon grated fresh ginger
- ➤ ½ teaspoon sesame oil
- ➤ Salt and pepper to taste
  Sauce
- ➤ ¼ cup peanut oil
- ➤ 1 tablespoon soy sauce
- ➤ 1 teaspoon Szechwan pepper oil

---

1. Slice the salmon into 8 2-ounce slices. Place it between plastic wrap and pound it lightly.
2. In a skillet heat the peanut oil and sauté the eggplant pieces for 5 minutes or until cooked through and lightly browned. Remove the eggplant to a mixing bowl. Add the scallops,

onion, ginger, sesame oil, salt, and pepper.
3. Stuff the salmon by placing a tablespoon or so of the mixture on each slice. Fold the salmon around the filling and roll each up with plastic wrap. Twist the ends of the wrap. Poach the salmon balls in simmering water for 5 to 8 minutes. Remove the salmon from the plastic and place 1 ball on each plate. Surround with a ring of rice and garnish with blanched snow peas and carrots.
4. In a small bowl mix together the peanut oil, soy sauce, and Szechwan oil and sprinkle it over the salmon.
Yield: 8 servings

Salmon Stuffed with Eggplant

Asian dessert of three flavors

Thai Pheasant with Red Curry Coconut Milk

✣

Lemon grass is here to stay. It flavors everything from soups to salads and chicken dishes. It contains citral as does the zest of a lemon.

- ➤ 2 pounds pheasant (or chicken breast), cut into 2-inch pieces
- ➤ ¼ cup peanut oil
- ➤ ½ cup chopped fresh lemon grass
- ➤ 1 medium onion, chopped
- ➤ 2 tablespoons fresh ginger, julienned
- ➤ 2 tablespoons chopped basil
- ➤ 2 tablespoons minced garlic
- ➤ 1 tablespoon lime zest
- ➤ 2 cups chicken stock or broth
- ➤ 2 cups coconut milk
- ➤ 1 tablespoon red curry paste
- ➤ 1 tablespoon fish sauce or salt to taste
- ➤ Sugar to taste
- ➤ 1 cup green beans, sliced and snapped in half
- ➤ 1 cup white potatoes, peeled, quartered, and sliced

1. In a large skillet heat the oil and sauté the pheasant pieces until golden brown on all sides. Add the lemon grass, onion, ginger, basil, garlic, and lime. Sauté the mixture for a few minutes and then add the remaining ingredients except the beans and potatoes. Bring the mixture to a boil. Reduce the heat to a simmer, and cook for 15 minutes.

2. Add the beans and potatoes, and simmer until the potatoes are tender. Serve with steamed rice.
Yield: 8 servings

Soft-Shelled Crabs and Chinese Sausages with Sun-Dried Tomato Beurre Blanc

✣

- ➤ 8 soft-shelled crabs
- ➤ All-purpose flour for dredging
- ➤ 4 cups vegetable oil
- ➤ 2 links Chinese sausage
  Beurre Blanc
- ➤ ½ bottle white wine
- ➤ 2 cups (4 sticks) butter
- ➤ 2 tablespoons sun-dried tomatoes, chopped
- ➤ 1 bunch fresh cilantro leaves for garnish

1. Clean the crabs by removing the underside tail flap and pressing to remove the non-meat contents. Flour the crabs. In a large skillet fry the crabs in oil a few minutes on each side over medium heat. Pat dry with paper towels to remove the excess oil.
2. Cut the sausages into small rounds and sauté until browned. Set aside.
3. In a large skillet over high heat reduce the wine to 1 tablespoon, keeping a close eye on it so it does not burn. Remove the pan from the heat. Allow the sauce to cool. Slowly whisk in the butter over low heat. Add the tomatoes. Place the sauce on serving plates. Top with a crab in the center surrounded by sausage rounds and garnished with cilantro leaves.

Yield: 8 servings

Thai Pheasant with Red Curry Coconut Milk

Trio of Crème Brûlée: Ginger, Orange, and Coconut

Make these unusual crème brûlées in sake cups or very small ramekins, so that each person gets to try all three flavors. You will need twenty-four cups for 8 people.

Ginger Crème Brûlée

➤ ¾ ounce fresh ginger, minced
➤ 2 cups heavy cream
➤ 8 egg yolks
➤ ¼ cup sugar
➤ Superfine sugar

Orange Crème Brûlée

➤ Zest of 4 oranges
➤ 8 egg yolks
➤ 2 cups heavy cream
➤ ¼ cup sugar
➤ Superfine sugar

Coconut Crème Brûlée

➤ 5 ounces unsweetened coconut flakes
➤ 8 egg yolks
➤ 2½ cups heavy cream
➤ ¼ cup sugar

---

1. For the Ginger Crème Brûlée, in a small saucepan bring the ginger and cream to a boil.
2. In the top pan of a double boiler combine the egg yolks and ¼ cup of sugar. After the cream and ginger have come to a boil, strain it over the egg mixture, whisking constantly. Place the mixture over barely simmering water and cook very slowly, whisking occasionally until thickened. This may take from 30 to 60 minutes. If the water gets too hot the mixture will curdle, so keep an eye on it and be patient. The mixture is done when the whisk leaves tracks or ribbons on the surface for at least 30 seconds. The consistency will be like loose pudding. Remove the pan from the water.
3. In a blender or food processor purée the hot mixture. Strain it and cool it in the refrigerator.
4. To serve, spoon or pipe the mixture into cups. Level with a knife. Sprinkle generously with superfine sugar and caramelize under a hot broiler or a small propane torch.
5. For the Orange Crème Brûlée, follow the same directions as for the Ginger Crème Brûlee, using orange zest instead of ginger.
6. For the Coconut Crème Brûlée, in a small saucepan bring the coconut and cream to a boil. Remove the pan from the heat and let the mixture steep for 30 minutes. Strain the mixture through a cheesecloth, twisting tightly to extract as much cream as possible. Measure the cream to yield 2 cups. If there is 1 tablespoon or more than 2 cups, that's fine. If there is less than 2 cups, add enough cream to make 2 cups.
7. In the top pan of a double boiler combine the egg yolks and ¼ cup of sugar. Pour the cream into the egg mixture and place the pan over barely simmering water. Cook very slowly, whisking occasionally until thickened. This may take longer than the others, because the cream is cooler.
8. In a blender or food processor purée the hot mixture. Strain it and cool it in the refrigerator. Serve the crème brûlée the same way as in step 4.

Yield: 8 servings

Inn Directory

ANTRIM 1844
30 Trevanion Road
Taneytown, MD 21787
(301) 756-6812
Rooms: 13
Dining: Overnight guests;
   public by reservation

THE BIRCHWOOD INN
Route 45
Temple, NH 03084
(603) 878-3285
Rooms: 7
Dining: Overnight guests;
   public by reservation

THE BUXTON INN
313 East Broadway
Granville, OH 43023
(614) 587-0001
Dining: Overnight guests;
   public reservations
   recommended

THE CHECKERBERRY INN
62644 County Road 37
Goshen, IN 46526
(219) 642-4445
Rooms: 12
Dining: Overnight guests;
   public by reservation

THE CHESTERFIELD INN
Route 9
West Chesterfield, NH 03466
(603) 256-3211
Rooms: 11
Dining: Overnight guests;
   public reservations
   recommended

GLEN-ELLA SPRINGS INN
Bear Gap Road
Route 3, Box 3304
Clarkesville, GA 30523
(404) 754-7295
Rooms: 16
Dining: Overnight guests;
   public reservations
   recommended

HIGH MEADOWS
Route 4, Box 6
Scottsville, VA 24590
(804) 286-2218
Rooms: 5
Dining: Overnight guests;
   public by special reservation

**THE INN AT BLACKBERRY
FARM**
1471 West Millers Cove
Walland, TN 37886
(615) 984-8166
Rooms: 25
Dining: Overnight guests;
   public by special reservation
   only

THE INN AT BUCKEYSTOWN
Main Street (General
   Delivery)
Buckeystown, MD 21717
(301) 874-5755
Rooms: 10 plus cottage
Dining: Overnight guests;
   public by reservation only

THE INN OF THE ANASAZI
113 Washington Avenue
Santa Fe, NM 87501
(505) 988-3030
Rooms: 59
Dining: Overnight guests and
   public reservations
   recommended

THE INTERLAKEN INN
15 Interlaken Avenue
Lake Placid, NY 12946
(518) 523-3180
Rooms: 12
Dining: Overnight guests;
   public reservations
   recommended

THE JOHN PALMER HOUSE
4314 North Mississippi
   Avenue
Portland, OR 97217
(503) 284-5893
Rooms: 5, main house; 3,
   Grandma's Cottage
Dining: Overnight guests;
   public by reservation only

**THE JOSHUA WILTON
HOUSE**
412 South Main Street
Harrisonburg, VA 22801
(703) 434-4464
Rooms: 5
Dining: Overnight guests;
   public reservations
   recommended

KEDRON VALLEY INN
Route 106, P.O. Box 145
South Woodstock, VT 05071
(802) 457-1473
Rooms: 28
Dining: Overnight guests;
   public reservations
   recommended

KILAUEA LODGE
P.O. Box 116
Volcano Village, HI 96785
(808) 967-7366
Rooms: 4 plus a cottage
Dining: Overnight guests;
   public reservations
   recommended

L'Auberge Provençale
P.O. Box 119
White Post, VA 22663
(703) 837-1375
Rooms: 10
Dining: Overnight guests;
   public by reservation

Madrona Manor
1001 Westside Road
Box 818
Healdsburg, CA 95448
(707) 433-4231
Rooms: 20
Dining: Overnight guests;
   public by reservation

**The Mansion at
   Elfindale**
1701 South Fort
Springfield, MO 65807
(417) 831-5400
Rooms: 13
Tea-Time: 2–4 P.M.
   Wednesday–Saturday by
   reservation

October Country Inn
Route 4, P.O. Box 66
Bridgewater Corners, VT
   05035
(802) 672-3412
Rooms: 10
Dining: Overnight guests;
   public by special reservation
   only

Randall's Ordinary
Route 2, P.O. Box 243
North Stonington, CT 06359
(203) 599-4540
Rooms: 13
Dining: Overnight guests;
   public by reservation

Richmond Hill Inn
87 Richmond Hill Drive
Asheville, NC 28806
(704) 252-7313
Rooms: 12, main house; 9,
   croquet cottages
Dining: Overnight guests;
   public reservations
   recommended

Rowell's 1820 Inn
Route 11
Rural Route 1, Box 269
Simonsville, VT 05143
(802) 875-3658
Rooms: 5
Dining: Overnight guests;
   public by special reservation
   only

**Schumacher's New
   Prague Hotel**
212 West Main Street
New Prague, MN 56071
(612) 758-2133
Rooms: 11
Dining: Overnight guests;
   public reservations
   recommended

The Shelburne Inn
Pacific Highway 103 & 45th
   Street
P.O. Box 250
Seaview, WA 98644
(206) 642-2442
Rooms: 16
Dining: Breakfast for
   overnight guests; public by
   special reservation. Dinner:
   public reservations
   recommended

The Shire Inn
Box 37
Chelsea, VT 05038
(802) 685-3031
Rooms: 6
Dining: Overnight guests;
   public by reservation only

The Inn at Twin Linden
2092 Main Street
Churchtown, PA 17555
(215) 445-7619
Rooms: 6
Dining: Overnight; public by
   reservation

Under Mountain Inn
Route 41
Salisbury, CT 06068
(203) 435-0242
Rooms: 7
Dining: Overnight guests;
   public by reservation

The White Barn Inn
Beach Street
P.O. Box 560 C
Kennebunkport, ME 04046
(207) 967-2321
Rooms: 25
Dining: Overnight guests;
   public reservations
   recommended

The White Hart Inn
The Village Green
P.O. Box 385
Salisbury, CT 06068
(203) 435-0030
Rooms: 26
Dining: Overnight guests;
   public reservations
   recommended

Windflower
684 South Egremont Road
Great Barrington, MA 01230
(413) 528-2720
Rooms: 13
Dining: Overnight guests;
   public by reservation

Windham Hill
Rural Route 1, Box 44
West Townshend, VT 05359
(802) 874-4080
Rooms: 15
Dining: Overnight guests;
   public by special reservation
   only

Index

Cooking Notes